The Tyndale New Testament Commentaries

General Editor:
THE REV. CANON LEON MORRIS, M.Sc., M.Th., Ph.D.

THE PASTORAL EPISTLES

D0632192

THE PASTORAL EPISTLES

AN INTRODUCTION AND COMMENTARY

by

DONALD GUTHRIE, B.D., M.Th., Ph.D.
President of The London Bible College,
formerly Vice-Principal
and Senior New Testament Lecturer

Inter-Varsity Press
Leicester, England

William B. Eerdmans Publishing Company
Grand Rapids, Michigan

Inter-Varsity Press
38 De Montfort Street, Leicester LE1 7GP, England

Wm. B. Eerdmans Publishing Company
255 Jefferson S.E., Grand Rapids, MI 49503

Published and sold only in the USA and Canada by Wm. B. Eerdmans Publishing Co.

British Library Cataloguing in Publication Data

Guthrie, Donald
The Pastoral Epistles. – 2nd ed.
1. Bible. N. T. Pastoral Epistles
I. Title.
227. 83

IVP ISBN 0-85111-883-6

Set in Palatino
Typeset in Great Britain by Parker Typesetting Service, Leicester
Printed in USA by Eerdmans Printing Company, Grand Rapids, Michigan

Inter-Varsity Press is the book-publishing division of the Universities and Colleges Christian Fellowship (formerly the Inter-Varsity Fellowship), a student movement linking Christian Unions in universities and colleges throughout the United Kingdom and the Republic of Ireland, and a member movement of the International Fellowship of Evangelical Students. For information about local and national activities write to UCCF, 38 De Montfort Street, Leicester LE1 7GP.

GENERAL PREFACE

The original *Tyndale Commentaries* aimed at providing help for the general reader of the Bible. They concentrated on the meaning of the text without going into scholarly technicalities. They sought to avoid 'the extremes of being unduly technical or unhelpfully brief'. Most who have used the books agree that there has been a fair measure of success in reaching that aim.

Times, however, change. A series that has served so well for so long is perhaps not quite as relevant as when it was first launched. New knowledge has come to light. The discussion of critical questions has moved on. Bible-reading habits have changed. When the original series was commenced it could be presumed that most readers used the Authorized Version and one could make one's comments accordingly, but this situation no longer obtains.

The decision to revise and up-date the whole series was not reached lightly, but in the end it was thought that this is what is required in the present situation. There are new needs, and they will be better served by new books or by a thorough up-dating of the old books. The aims of the original series remain. The new commentaries are neither minuscule nor unduly long. They are exegetical rather than homiletic. They do not discuss all the critical questions, but none is written without an awareness of the problems that engage the attention of New Testament scholars. Where it is felt that formal consideration should be given to such questions, they are discussed in the Introduction and sometimes in Additional Notes.

But the main thrust of these commentaries is not critical. These books are written to help the non-technical reader to understand the Bible better. They do not presume a knowledge of Greek, and all Greek words discussed are transliterated; but the authors have the Greek text before them and their comments are made on the basis of the originals. The authors are free to choose their own modern translation, but are asked to bear in mind the variety of translations in current use.

The new series of *Tyndale Commentaries* goes forth, as the former series did, in the hope that God will graciously use these books to help the general reader to understand as fully and clearly as possible the meaning of the New Testament.

LEON MORRIS

CONTENTS

AUTHOR'S PREFACE TO THE FIRST EDITION

The Pastoral Epistles have played an important part in the history of the Christian Church and have amply justified their inclusion in the New Testament Canon. Their appeal lies in their blend of sound practical advice and theological statement, which has proved invaluable to Christians both personally and collectively. It is not surprising that the injunctions directed to Timothy and Titus regarding their responsibilities have served as a pattern for the Christian ministry, and have been used so widely in services of ordination.

I have been conscious of many difficulties in approaching my task of commenting upon these letters. Over a considerable period serious doubts have been cast upon their authenticity by many scholars and this has tended to decrease their authority. I have felt obliged to make a thorough investigation of these objections, and the results are given as fully as space will permit in the Introduction. A special examination has been made of the linguistic problem. Because of the technical nature of this study, the conclusions reached are given in an Appendix.

It is impossible to acknowledge indebtedness separately to all those writers who have preceded me in this field and who have contributed to my understanding of these Epistles. There are some, however, who must be singled out for special mention. Among those commentators who have maintained Pauline authorship, Bernard, Lock, Spicq and Simpson have been specially helpful, while Newport White, Horton, Parry and Jeremias have furnished many useful suggestions. On the other hand, Scott and Easton, who do not favour Pauline authorship, have been constantly consulted, and Dibelius has proved valuable for literary parallels. Harrison's book on *The Problem of the Pastorals* has been indispensable in dealing with the linguistic problem and forms the basis of the investigations given in the Appendix.

It is my sincere hope that this short commentary will stimulate greater interest in and understanding of these concluding Epistles of the great apostle.

DONALD GUTHRIE

AUTHOR'S PREFACE TO
THE SECOND EDITION

The main reason for the revision of this commentary has been the need to base it on a modern English version of the text of the Pastorals. I have chosen to adjust the text of the commentary to conform to the text of the New International Version, although in several cases reference is made to other modern versions.

The opportunity has also been taken to make minor changes in the commentary itself in the interests of greater clarity. Reference has also been made to more recent commentators and these are reflected at various points in the commentary.

I have seen no reason to depart from my conviction that the view which sees Paul himself as the author of these letters is the most probable, although I am aware that several recent writers on these Epistles have adopted the view that they are fictional and pseudonymous. In my opinion no further evidence has been brought to bear on the issue since my first edition which calls for any change of stance. No doubt the authenticity of these Epistles will continue to be a bone of contention among scholars.

It is my sincere hope that this revised edition will prove a continuing help to those who wish to explore the teaching of the Epistles.

DONALD GUTHRIE

CHIEF ABBREVIATIONS

Abbott-Smith	G. Abbott-Smith, *A Manual Greek Lexicon of the New Testament*, 3rd ed. (1937).
AV	Authorized (King James's) Version, 1611.
CBQ	*Catholic Biblical Quarterly.*
ExpT	*Expository Times.*
Gk.	Greek.
HDB	J. Hastings (ed.), *A Dictionary of the Bible* (Edinburgh, 1898–1904).
JBL	*Journal of Biblical Literature.*
JTS	*Journal of Theological Studies.*
LXX	The Septuagint (pre-Christian Greek version of the Old Testament).
M & M	J. H. Moulton and G. Milligan, *The Vocabulary of the Greek Testament* (1914–29).
mg.	margin.
Moffatt	J. Moffatt, *A New Translation of the Bible*, 1913.
MS(S)	manuscript(s).
NCB	New Century Bible.
NIV	New International Version, 1973, 1978, 1984.
NTS	*New Testament Studies.*
RSV	Revised Standard Version: Old Testament, 1952; New Testament, ²1971.
RV	Revised Version, 1884.
SJT	*Scottish Journal of Theology.*
ZNTW	*Zeitschrift für die neutestamentliche Wissenschaft.*

SELECT BIBLIOGRAPHY

COMMENTARIES

Barrett, C. K., *The Pastoral Epistles*, New Clarendon Bible (Oxford, 1963).

Bengel, J. A., *Gnomen of the New Testament*, vol. iv, translated by James Bryce (Edinburgh, 1866).

Bernard, J. H., *The Pastoral Epistles*, Cambridge Greek Testament (Cambridge, 1899).

Brox, N., *Die Pastoralbriefe*, Regensburger Neues Testament (Regensburg, 1969).

Bürki, H., *Der erste Brief des Paulus an Timotheus* (Wuppertal, 1974).

Dibelius, M., *Die Pastoralbriefe*, Handbuch zum Neuen Testament, 3rd ed. revised by H. Conzelmann (Tübingen, 1955).

Dornier, P., *Les Epîtres Pastorales*, Sources Bibliques (Paris, 1969).

Easton, B. S., *The Pastoral Epistles* (London, 1948).

Falconer, R., *The Pastoral Epistles* (Oxford, 1937).

Fee, G. D., *1 and 2 Timothy and Titus*, New International Biblical Commentary (Peabody, Mass., 1988).

Gealy, F. D., *The Pastoral Epistles*, Interpreter's Bible 11 (New York, 1955).

Hanson, A. T., *The Pastoral Epistles*, Cambridge Bible Commentary (Cambridge, 1966).

Hanson, A. T., *The Pastoral Epistles*, New Century Bible (London, 1982).

Hasler, V., *Die Briefe an Timotheus und Titus* (Zurich, 1978).

Higgins, A. J. B., 'The Pastoral Epistles' in *Peake's Commentary on the Bible* (London, 1962).

Holtz, G., *Die Pastoralbriefe*, Theologischer Handkommentar zum Zeuen Testament 13, 2nd ed. (Berlin, 1972).

Horton, R. F., *The Pastoral Epistles*, The Century Bible (1911).

Houldon, J. L., *The Pastoral Epistles*, Pelican New Testament Commentaries (Penguin, 1976).

Jeremias, J., *Die Briefe an Timotheus und Titus*, Das Neue Testament Deutsch 9 (Gottingen, 1963).

Kelly, J. N. D., *The Pastoral Epistles*, Black's New Testament Commentaries (London, 1963).

Leaney, A. R. C., *The Epistles to Timothy, Titus and Philemon*, Torch Commentary (London, 1960).

Lock, W., *The Pastoral Epistles*, International Critical Commentary (Edinburgh, 1924).

Parry, J., *The Pastoral Epistles* (Cambridge, 1920).

Plummer, A., *The Pastoral Epistles*, Expositor's Bible (London, 1888).

Scott, E. F., *The Pastoral Epistles*, Moffat's New Testament Commentary (1936).

Simpson, E. K., *The Pastoral Epistles* (London, 1954).

Spicq, C., *Les Epîtres Pastorales*, Etudes Bibliques, 4th ed. (Paris, 1969).

Ward, R. A., *Commentary on 1 and 2 Timothy and Titus* (Waco, 1974).

White, N., *The Pastoral Epistles*, Expositor's Greek Testament (London, 1910).

OTHER WORKS

Guthrie, D., *New Testament Introduction*, 4th ed. (Leicester, 1990).

Guthrie, D., *The Pastoral Epistles and the Mind of Paul* (London, 1956).

Hanson, A. T., *Studies in the Pastoral Epistles* (London, 1968).

Harrison, P. N., *The Problem of the Pastorals* (Oxford, 1921).

James, J. D., *The Genuineness and Authorship of the Pastoral Epistles* (London, 1906).

Knight, G. W., *The Faithful Sayings in the Pastoral Epistles* (Kampen, 1968).

Lestapis, S. de, *L'Enigme des Pastorales de Saint Paul* (Paris, 1976).

Rigaux, B., *Saint Paul et ses Lettres* (Paris, 1962).

Trummer, P., *Die Paulustradition der Pastorbriefe* (Frankfurt, 1978).

Verner, D. C., *The Household of God: The Social World of the Pastoral Epistles* (Scholar's Press, Chico, 1983).

Wilson, S. G., *Luke and the Pastoral Epistles* (London, 1979).

INTRODUCTION

I. THE DESIGNATION AND CHARACTER OF THE EPISTLES

These three Epistles have so much in common in type, doctrine and historical situation that they have always been treated as a single group in the same way as the great 'evangelical' and 'captivity' Epistles. It was not until 1703 that D. N. Berdot, followed later by Paul Anton in 1726, who popularized it, used the term 'Pastoral' to describe them. While this title is not technically quite correct in that the Epistles do not deal with pastoral duties in the sense of the cure of souls, yet it is popularly appropriate as denoting the essentially practical nature of the subject matter as distinguished from the other Epistles attributed to Paul. The Epistles certainly do not contain a manual of pastoral theology, but their usefulness in the ordering of ecclesiastical discipline was recognized at an early date.[1]

In contrast with the other Pauline letters which are addressed to churches, all three Epistles are directed to individuals, and many of the injunctions are clearly personal. Yet much of the material appears to be designed for the communities to which Timothy and Titus were ministering. Thus they are generally thought to be quasi-public Epistles, although their character as

[1] e.g. The Muratorian Canon mentions that one epistle to Titus and two to Timothy are 'still hallowed in the respect of the Catholic Church, in the arrangement of ecclesiastical discipline'. Tertullian and Augustine bear witness to the same fact (see C. Spicq, *Les Epîtres Pastorales*, 1948, p. xxi).

true letters must not be overlooked.[1] The apostle must have written many such letters in the course of his missionary journeys, maintaining in this way not only an interchange of news but an active direction of the many Christian projects he had commenced. That these three Epistles have survived (together with Philemon) to be included in the canon enhances their value as documents throwing light upon the practical problem of early Christianity.

When the literary characteristics of these Epistles are examined, certain features are at once apparent. There is a lack of studied order, some subjects being treated more than once in the same letter without apparent premeditation. The various brief doctrinal statements are intermixed with personal requests or ecclesiastical advice. These letters are, therefore, far removed from literary exercises. They are the natural and human expressions of the apostle's own reflections about the future of the work he is obliged to delegate to others. They reveal, therefore, as much about their author's reactions to the situations he faced as contemporary conditions in the church.

II. THE EPISTLES IN THE ANCIENT CHURCH

There is a modern tendency to play down the significance of the external evidence. But it is only against the background of early Christian views about the Epistles that a fair assessment can be made of modern theories unfavourable to Pauline authorship. Indeed, as the following evidence will show, there are no grounds for holding that the early church had any doubts about the authenticity of these Epistles. In fact it was not until the nineteenth century that critical opinions began to be entertained adverse to the Pauline authorship.

Although there are many parallels to the language of these Epistles in the early Apostolic Fathers, Clement of Rome and Ignatius, these are generally not considered sufficient to amount to proof that these authors were genuinely using the Epistles.

[1] Cf. Spicq, op. cit., pp. xxi–xxxi. Cf. also J. D. James, The Genuineness and Authorship of the Pastoral Epistles (1906), p. 109, and Sir W. Ramsay, HDB, Extra Vol., p. 401.

Even where these parallels have been admitted the evidence has been interpreted in different ways. It has even been proposed that the author of the Pastorals used the writings of Clement and Ignatius. Some consider that this evidence at least shows that the Pastorals belong to the same period as Clement and Ignatius. But this cannot be maintained in view of the more primitive character of the contents of the Pastorals compared with the Apostolic Fathers. This will become more evident in our further discussion. In view of the insubstantial nature of the parallels little significance can be attached to them, although if on other grounds the early provenance of the Pastorals can be established, parallels of language may have more force than otherwise. What cannot be established with any certainty from this evidence is that the Pastorals were definitely not in existence when Clement or Ignatius wrote.

The evidence from Polycarp is of a different kind, for he shows much closer acquaintance with these Epistles. It is generally agreed that Polycarp knew and used them, although some have disputed this. The view, for instance, that the author of the Pastorals is citing only current popular maxims is an attempt to minimize the value of this evidence. But the similarities are too strong for such a view, and Polycarp must remain the earliest certain user of our Epistles (at least of 1 and 2 Timothy). There are allusions to these letters in Justin Martyr, Heracleon, Hegesippus, Athenagoras, Theophilus and Irenaeus, which show that they were widely known, while Theophilus definitely believed them to be inspired.[1]

In addition to this second-century evidence, the witness of the Muratorian Canon must be mentioned for in this list these three Epistles are placed after the church epistles of Paul, together with Philemon. We have noted that the compiler mentions that the two letters to Timothy and the letter to Titus are valuable in matters of ecclesiastical discipline. There is no mention of any doubts about their Pauline origin. Subsequent to the period of the publication of this ancient canon, the Pastorals were widely used by Christian writers.

The preceding attestation is as strong as most of the Pauline

---

[1] *Ad Autolycum*, 3.

Epistles, with the exception of Romans and 1 Corinthians. Yet there are two other lines of evidence which are sometimes claimed to make the external attestation as a whole unfavourable to the authenticity of the Epistles. All of them were rejected by Marcion, and are lacking from the Chester Beatty Papyrus (P^{46}). It is Tertullian[1] who tells us that Marcion cut them out of his collection of Paul's letters, which shows that he considered Marcion to have known them but not accepted them. Some scholars, however, think that Marcion was not even acquainted with them and therefore do not take Tertullian at his face value. But there are good grounds for maintaining that some parts of the Pastorals would not have been conducive to Marcion's viewpoint and for this reason he is likely to have rejected them. Their anti-heretical stance and their use of the Old Testament would have run counter to Marcion's opinions. In view of this it is precarious to maintain that by Marcion's time the Pastorals were not included in the Pauline Canon. It might on the contrary be argued that the orthodox church began more specifically to regard the Pastorals as canonical as a counter-blast to Marcion's restricted Pauline Canon. It has been asserted that if Marcion had known them he could have deleted passages unconducive to him, as he did with other books, but it is more satisfactory to take Tertullian's word for it and to accept his deliberate rejection of these Epistles.

The second line of evidence, the Chester Beatty papyri, is considered by many scholars to be of more significance in discussions of authenticity. The fact is that P^{46} is not complete, with both its beginning and ending missing. But because it was in codex form it is possible to calculate that the missing ending would not have contained enough sheets to contain the Pastoral Epistles. It is not, however, self-evident from such a calculation that the Epistles must have been missing, for there is evidence that the scribe has crowded more lines into the latter part than the former. Moreover, it was not unknown for scribes, when short of space, to add additional sheets at the end of a codex, but there is no means of knowing whether this happened in this case. Another possibility is that the Pastorals were included in

[1] *Adversus Marcionem*, v.21.

another codex, but we have no knowledge whether this was so. There is no reason to suppose that the lack of any evidence of the inclusion of the Epistles in P^{46} means that at the time of its production (mid-third-century) these Epistles were unknown in Egypt.

Our conclusion must be that the external evidence raises no serious doubts about the acceptance and canonical status of these letters. When credence is given to the strength of the external evidence, the onus of proof in discussions of authenticity must rest with those who regard these Epistles as non-Pauline.

III. THE EPISTLES IN THE MODERN CHURCH

The unbroken tradition of the church until the nineteenth century was to regard the Pastorals as the work of Paul and therefore authentic. The first determined attack against apostolic authorship was made when Schleiermacher (1807) disputed the Pauline authorship of 1 Timothy on stylistic and linguistic grounds, thus becoming the father of that school of modern criticism which decides questions of authenticity on philological evidence. The main advocates of the non-apostolic authorship of all the Epistles have been Eichhorn (1812), Baur (1835), de Wette (1844), Holtzmann (1880), Moffatt (1901), Bultmann (1930), Dibelius (1931, revised by Conzelmann in 1955), Gealy (1955), Higgins (1962), Brox (1969), Houlden (1976), Hasler (1978) and A. T. Hanson (1982). Many have denied the Pauline authorship, but have sought to retain a few genuine fragments. Among these the leading exponents have been Von Soden (1893), Harrison (1921), Scott (1936), Falconer (1937), Easton (1948), Barrett (1963), Strobel (1969) and Dornier (1961). Hanson in his first commentary (1966) adopted this view, but later abandoned it.

On the other hand, throughout this period of criticism, many careful scholars have maintained the authenticity of these Epistles, among whom the most notable have been Ellicott (1864), Bertrand (1887), Plummer (1888), Godet (1893), Hort (1894), Bernard (1902), B. Weiss (1902), Zahn (1906), James (1906),

Ramsay (1909–11), White (1910), Bartlet (1913), Parry (1920), Wohlenberg (1923), Lock (1924), Meinertz (1931), Schlatter (1936), Spicq (1947), Jeremias (1953), Simpson (1954), Kelly (1963), Knight (1968), de Lestapis (1976) and Fee (1984). The fact that so impressive a list of scholars can be cited in favour of Pauline authorship serves as a warning against the tacit assumption of some scholars that no grounds remain for the traditional position, and that all who maintain it are obliged to resort to special pleading.[1]

It should be noted that there is general agreement on the existence of differences between the Pastorals and the other Pauline Epistles. These differences concern the ecclesiastical situation, the doctrinal point of view and the linguistic evidence. There are also problems relating to the historical allusions. Scholarly opinion diverges widely, however, over how these differences may be explained. We shall begin by noting the historical difficulties, followed by an examination of the ecclesiastical, doctrinal and linguistic difficulties.

IV. THE PROBLEM OF THE HISTORICAL ALLUSIONS

Since there are many allusions to historical events in these Epistles it is important to enquire where these can be placed within the framework of the life of Paul as we know it. This means in effect a comparison of these Pastoral allusions with the events in Paul's life recorded in the book of Acts, in conjunction with the remaining Pauline Epistles. Many scholars rule out the possibility of any reconciliation between these two lines of evidence and therefore conclude that the Pastorals' allusions cannot be authentic. In order to assess the objection to Pauline authorship based on evidence of this kind, we must bear in mind that our knowledge of the events in the life of Paul is necessarily fragmentary and this must temper our judgment concerning the evidence. Our first task must be to set out the historical allusions as they occur in the separate Epistles.

[1]*Cf.* A. M. Hunter's comment in *Interpreting the New Testament* (1951), p. 64.

A. A STATEMENT OF THE EVIDENCE

1. 1 Timothy 1:3 states, 'As I urged you when I went into Macedonia, stay there in Ephesus', which specifically mentions a visit of Paul to Macedonia, but does not necessarily mean that he had himself just been to Ephesus. If Paul is now in Macedonia, he is writing to instruct Timothy, whom he has left in charge of the Ephesian church, concerning certain ecclesiastical procedures. No other historical allusion occurs in 1 Timothy.

2. In the opening section of the Epistle to Titus, the apostle states, 'The reason I left you in Crete was that you might straighten out what was left unfinished' (1:5). These words appear at first sight to require that Paul has himself paid a personal visit to Crete. There would be no necessity to suppose that the visit was lengthy for there is no implication that Paul himself established the churches in the island. Nevertheless he is clearly well acquainted with the situation with which Titus has to deal. On the other hand, it has been cogently argued that the verb (*I left*) need not imply a recent visit. It may simply mean that Paul left Titus in Crete while he went elsewhere.[1]

In closing this Epistle the apostle mentions his determination to spend the winter in Nicopolis where he hopes Titus will be able to join him (Tit. 3:12). While it is not certain where this Nicopolis was situated, it is generally assumed to have been the city of that name in Epirus. If this is correct it is the only evidence that Paul ever went into this district.

3. It is 2 Timothy that supplies the greatest number of historical details. From the reference to Onesiphorus in 1:17, 'when he was in Rome, he searched hard for me until he found me', it is a reasonable deduction that Paul is at the time of writing in Rome. It is at least certain that he has already been in Rome and equally certain that he is now a prisoner. He mentions that Onesiphorus 'was not ashamed of my chains' (1:16), and he calls himself a 'prisoner' (1:8), while chapter 4 contains a clear reference to his trial (4:16).

There is a curious request for a cloak left at the house of

---

[1]*Cf.* S. de Lestapis, *L'Enigme des Pastorales de Saint Paul* (1976), pp. 52–54. *Cf.* also J. van Bruggen, *Die geschichtliche Einordnung der Pastoralbriefe* (1981), and J. A. T. Robinson, *Redating the New Testament* (1976), pp. 67–85.

Carpus at Troas (4:13), which would seem to demand a relatively recent visit to make such a request intelligible. The apostle also gives the news, 'Erastus stayed at Corinth, and I left Trophimus sick in Miletus' (4:20), which is again only intelligible as a piece of information unknown to Timothy, suggesting that the events related occurred in the recent past.

Various attempts have been made to fit events into the life of Paul in the book of Acts. The method adopted depends on whether the three Epistles can be slotted in independently and at different periods, or whether they must be regarded as having been written within a short time of each other. Since Paul is a prisoner, there are only two practical possibilities. He must have been either at Caesarea or at Rome, unless of course the hypothesis of an Ephesian imprisonment is regarded as a possibility.

i. *The view that Paul was at Caesarea when he wrote the Pastorals*

It is clearly impossible to assign 2 Timothy to any other imprisonment than Rome if the text of 2 Timothy 1:17 is authentic. Those who have treated the reference to Rome as an emendation have done so without any textual support, and this must be regarded as unsatisfactory. The attempt to link the Pastorals as a whole to Caesarea must be abandoned. Quite apart from the reference to Rome, the allusion to Trophimus' illness at Miletus (2 Tim. 4:20) seems impossible from a Caesarean location, since Trophimus was with Paul in Jerusalem and was the indirect cause of his arrest (Acts 21:29). Furthermore, Timothy also accompanied Paul to Jerusalem (Acts 20:4) and was not, therefore, left behind at Ephesus.

ii. *The view that Paul was at Ephesus when he wrote the Pastorals*

The proposal to assign the Pastorals to an Ephesian imprisonment is beset with many difficulties.[1] (a) While there may be good grounds for postulating an Ephesian imprisonment, the

---

[1]For support for an Ephesian imprisonment, *cf.* G. Duncan, *St. Paul's Ephesian Ministry* (1929), pp. 184–216. Earlier T. C. Laughlin had attempted to assign the defence mentioned in 2 Tim. 4:16–17 to an Ephesian trial.

evidence can never be conclusive and the suggestion must therefore remain speculative. (b) The theory depends on treating the reference to Rome in 2 Timothy 1:17 as a textual emendation, and this must raise suspicions against it. (c) If the Pastorals are treated as a whole the ecclesiastical directions affecting Ephesus would not readily fit into the period immediately following Paul's own ministry there, while room would presumably need to be found for a mission to Crete which appears to be excluded by Acts 20:31,[1] unless of course someone other than Paul had instigated this. Timothy would hardly have needed such specific instructions had he been working with the apostle so shortly before. (d) Paul's mention of a journey from Ephesus to Macedonia (1 Tim. 1:3) could conceivably relate to Acts 20:1; but if so it must have taken place after the suggested Ephesian imprisonment. Moreover, according to 1 Timothy 1:3, Timothy was left at Ephesus, although Acts 20 makes it clear that he soon afterwards accompanied Paul to Jerusalem to deliver the collection for the poverty-stricken Christians there. It is a fair conclusion that, as far as the Pastorals are concerned, the Ephesian hypothesis raises more problems than it solves.

iii. The Roman imprisonment

Some have attempted to fit 2 Timothy into the imprisonment mentioned at the end of Acts and the other two Epistles into earlier periods in the Acts history. Such theories go against the widely held view that the three Epistles belong together. It is certainly clear that all three Epistles cannot belong to the Roman confinement of Acts 28. But are there grounds for dating 1 Timothy and Titus earlier than the Roman imprisonment? One recent theory is that 1 Timothy belongs to the same period as the

[1]These difficulties would, of course, vanish if part only of the Pastorals are accepted as genuine notes. Duncan admitted his approach to these Epistles is 'wholly tentative' ('St Paul's ministry in Asia – the Last Phase', *NTS*, 1957, pp. 217–218).

Harrison criticized Duncan's proposals mainly on the grounds of the 'inherent contradictions' of 2 Tim. 4. But even if these 'contradictions' are not admitted, the evidence of 1 Tim. 4:6–8 and 16–18 certainly appears to support a Roman rather than Ephesian imprisonment, as Harrison observed (*cf.* 'The Pastoral Epistles and Duncan's Ephesian Theory', *NTS*, 1956, pp. 250–261).

Corinthian correspondence and Titus to the same period as Philippians, assuming a Caesarean origin for this letter.[1] It would then be possible to place 2 Timothy within the period of the Roman imprisonment and this would dispense with the necessity to postulate a release.

Another theory which has been proposed is that 1 Timothy and Titus should be placed within the Ephesian ministry of Paul, assuming a journey which is not mentioned in Acts.[2] This would necessitate a longer interval between these two Epistles and 2 Timothy which would be placed at the end of the Roman imprisonment. Such references as those to the cloak left with Carpus and to Trophimus being left ill at Miletus become more difficult if these events relate to an earlier period. But there is nothing intrinsically against the idea of some unrecorded journey from Ephesus, although the statement of Acts 20:31 is difficult to reconcile with it. At least it cannot be said quite as confidently as used to be the case that there is no possibility of fitting the historical allusions into the Acts story. The matter must remain open.

B. VARIOUS ALTERNATIVE EXPLANATIONS

In addition to the attempt to fit the historical allusions into the Acts record, there have been three other solutions proposed.

i. The second Roman imprisonment theory

Acts 28:30, 31 states that Paul spent two whole years in his own rented house, but since nothing is said beyond this, there is at least the possibility that he was released. Those who dispute the Pauline authorship of the Pastorals make much of the fact that the Acts narrative is silent about such a release. If of course the Acts contains a complete history of Paul it would be more reasonable to suppose that Paul met his death at the end of this imprisonment than to posit a release theory. But in no way can

[1]Cf. J. A. T. Robinson, *Redating the New Testament* (1976), pp. 67ff.
[2]Cf. J. van Bruggen, *Die geschichtliche Einordnung der Pastoralbriefe* (1981).

Acts be considered a complete history since there are historical allusions in the other Pauline Epistles which are not mentioned in Acts. Arguments from silence in this case are bound to be open to question. It cannot be supposed that the imprisonment mentioned in Acts 28 must have ended in martyrdom, for some explanation would be needed for the writer's omission to mention it. Indeed, the leniency of the detention, which seems to have allowed Paul unrestricted visiting, is more suggestive of release than martyrdom.

Another consideration pointing to the probability of release is the terms of Agrippa's declaration, with which the proconsul Festus apparently concurred (Acts 26:32). In his report to the imperial authorities the proconsul could not, in view of this, have been unfavourable to Paul, and this would, in the normal course of Roman justice, have disposed towards a successful trial in the period before Christianity became illicit. The captivity Epistles bear witness to Paul's expectation of release (Phil. 1:25; 2:23–24; Phm. 22).[1]

Certain external evidence may be cited in support of a period of further activity, although opinions differ regarding the value of this evidence. Clement of Rome's vague reference to Paul having reached the boundary (*to terma*) of the West can either mean that he had reached his western goal when in Rome, or that he had reached the western boundary of the Empire (*i.e.* Spain). Some scholars go to great lengths to disprove the Spanish visit, maintaining that later patristic citations quoted in support of it are explicable as deductions from Romans 15:24, 28.[2] But the second imprisonment theory is independent of the Spanish mission, and indeed is almost exclusive of it for it involves considerable further activity in the East. It is reasonable to suppose that Paul had already abandoned his proposed Spanish mission by the time he wrote the captivity Epistles.[3]

Eusebius records a report that Paul was sent on a further

---

[1] *Cf.* Schlatter's admirably balanced examination of the probability of Paul's release, *The Church in the New Testament Period* (1926, Eng. trans. 1955), pp. 232–239. *Cf.* also Spitta, *Zur Geschichte und Litteratur des Urchristentum* (1893), i, pp. 106f. If Philippians and Philemon were written from Ephesus, as Duncan suggested, they would of course furnish no data for the Roman imprisonment.

[2] *Cf.* Harrison, *The Problem of the Pastorals* (1921), pp. 102ff.

[3] *Cf.* Schlatter, *op. cit.*, p. 236.

ministry of preaching after his first defence before ending his life in martyrdom in Rome.[1] But this report could easily be a piece of popular exegesis based on the pastoralia of 2 Timothy, and is unlikely to have much value as an independent witness. It is nevertheless a valuable indication of fourth-century interpretation of the historical allusions in the Pastorals. Subsequent to Eusebius' time the release theory became the accepted explanation, and although many modern scholars dispose of this evidence on the grounds that later writers have perpetrated an early error,[2] traditional opinion may preserve more truth than is often allowed. The absence of any specific early attestation cannot of itself render the hypothesis untenable, while the absence of any contrary evidence leaves the possibility of a release. These historical allusions cannot, therefore, weigh against the authenticity while such a possibility remains.

ii. The fiction hypothesis

All the more radical critics of Pauline authorship have adopted the view that the pseudonymous author of the Pastorals has made up the historical allusions to give the Epistles some semblance of authenticity. According to this theory any discrepancies of detail would then be attributed to the author's lack of historical perspective. But there are grave difficulties about this view. It does not adequately account for the realism of some of these allusions. The request for the cloak left with Carpus requires some explanation. It is not satisfactory to suggest that it was a fictional element after the analogy of the cloak passed from Elijah to Elisha as some have maintained.[3] This together with other sections of a similar realistic character give the impression of being genuine pieces of Pauline information. Even some who maintain the fictional composition of the Pastorals cannot avoid this sense of reality and accordingly suggest that the author did not confine himself to fictional materials,[4] but this still does not avoid the problem of distinguishing the fictional from the genuine.

---

[1] *Ecclesiastical History*, ii. 22.   [2] So, for instance, Harrison, *op. cit.*, p. 104.

[3] *Cf.* V. Hasler, *ad loc.* Trummer also regards all the historical allusions as fictional.

[4] *Cf.* A. T. Hanson, NCB, p. 23, He speaks of the fictional elements as a series of anachronisms rather than a carefully constructed piece of deliberate forgery.

iii. The fragment theory

Because of the unsatisfactory treatment of the historical allusions by the fiction theory, some scholars have suggested that although the Epistles as they stand are the work of a non-Pauline author, that author has included in his compositions certain genuine fragments. This type of theory was popularized by Harrison, who criticized the traditional view on the grounds that history would have repeated itself. Paul would again visit Troas with Timothy and Trophimus, again go to Miletus, be troubled once more by Asiatic Jews, be pursued by the same Alexander even as far as Rome, and have the same recent prison-companions, Luke, Mark, Timothy, Demas and Tychicus, the latter on both occasions being sent to Ephesus.

But it is not surprising, if Paul made a second visit to the East after his release, that he again visited Troas and Miletus and was again in touch with many of his former associates. It would be more surprising if it were otherwise. And as for Alexander, there are no grounds for identifying the Alexander of 2 Timothy 4 with the would-be spokesman for the Jews in the Ephesian riot, nor is there any suggestion in 2 Timothy 4 that the coppersmith's subversive activities were taking place at that time in Rome. These data therefore form a precarious basis for claiming a repetition of history.

Yet it is mainly on the basis of the unlikelihood of such historical repetition that Harrison justifies his fragment theory, together with the alleged internal contradictions in the personalia of 2 Timothy 4. We shall briefly outline Harrison's theory and then note other suggestions of a similar kind, although we shall note that no two theories agree in detail. Harrison asks whether it is probable that Paul would have given Timothy careful instructions for the preservation of apostolic teaching and then urged him to come as soon as possible because of the imminence of the apostle's departure. He suggests it is impossible to reconcile the noble farewell with the detailed commissions because of the lack of sufficient time for the latter to be fulfilled and for Timothy to reach Paul before it would be too late. But this misunderstands the purpose of 2 Timothy. As compared with 1 Timothy and Titus there is surprisingly little ecclesiastical instruction. The Epistle mostly comprises personal advice and encouragement to Timothy, and any references to ecclesiastical discipline are so general that it is not at all inconceivable that Paul would touch upon them, aware as he seems to be that this might well be his last communication to Timothy. If there was a considerable delay between the initial examination and the legal trial Paul might well have hoped that Timothy would be able to reach him in time. But if not, Timothy would have in his possession this last precious document from his beloved master. Even if such a solution were to rob the farewell of some of its pathos, is the case to be judged on a preconceived notion of impressiveness? Might not that notion itself be misconceived?

Harrison suggested that all the 'genuine' personalia in the Pastorals can be fitted into the Acts record at different times and places. Originally he proposed five fragments, but later reduced these to three: (i) Titus 3:12–15, written from Macedonia to Titus, who is at Corinth, just after Paul's severe letter to the church there. Titus is told to proceed to Epirus. (ii) 2 Timothy 4:9–15, 20–21a and 22b, written when Paul was at Nicopolis. (iii) 2 Timothy 1:16–18; 3:10–11; 4:1, 2a, 5b–8, 16–19, 21b–22a, written from Rome at the close of the imprisonment mentioned in Acts 28. There is no general agreement between this scheme and others which have been proposed, for instance by McGiffert, Falconer, Easton, Holtz and Dornier. A. T. Hanson wrote one commentary based on a fragment theory, but abandoned this position in his second commentary.

All fragment theories are improbable for the following reasons.

1. The disintegrated character of the so-called fragments belies them, especially the theory of Harrison detailed above. It is difficult to see what process of composition the editor of 2 Timothy used in preserving these genuine fragments for posterity. He could hardly have mixed them up more than he apparently did in chapter 4 had he been completely indiscriminate and lacking not only in historical discernment but also in common sense. Yet the fact remains that chapter 4 does not read like a haphazard hotch-potch, and it would be necessary to assume, therefore, on this theory that the editor must have done

his work superhumanly well to have belied all suspicion of disjointedness until nineteenth- and twentieth-century criticism tracked down the muddle.[1]

2. The preservation of these disjointed fragments constitutes another problem, for they are not, for the most part, the type of fragments which would normally have had much appeal. Even if an early Christian with antiquarian interests had accidently discovered and highly prized these genuine Pauline relics there would still be need to give an adequate motive for their incorporation so unevenly in Titus and 2 Timothy. No satisfactory explanation of this procedure has so far been given. It is not enough to state that the Pauline editor composed the Epistles as a means of preserving the fragments or else added the fragments to existing drafts of the Epistles to enhance their authority and to ensure their reception, unless adequate contemporary parallels can be cited as supporting evidence that such a process was normal in early Christian literary practice. But no such parallels are forthcoming.

3. As a process of historical investigation fragment theories are open to criticism on the grounds that they suppose that the Acts history contains the complete history of Paul. To propose fragments to fit into the existing Acts structure effectively changes the nature of the historical data, but this cannot be said to be sound historical method.

There can be little doubt that the traditional explanation is least open to objection on historical grounds. Both the fiction and fragment theories raise as many problems as they claim to solve.

V. THE ECCLESIASTICAL SITUATION

It has usually been maintained by disputants of the Pauline authorship that the ecclesiastical situation reflected in the Pastorals is akin to that of the early second century, and therefore is

[1] *Cf.* Harrison's unconvincing explanation of the editor's procedure of intercalating the

much too developed to belong to the age of Paul. If the evidence supports this claim it would, of course, be impossible to maintain the authenticity of the letters, but an examination of the data shows an entirely different position. Before dealing with the Pastorals' data it should be noted that it is quite erroneous to regard these Epistles as manuals of church order in the sense in which later manuals were used, for there is an almost complete absence of instruction on administration, civil relationships or conduct of worship. The entire ecclesiastical teaching (1 Tim. 3:1–13; 5:3–22 and Tit. 1:5–9) comprises no more than about a tenth of the subject matter of the Pastorals, and even this is much more concerned with personnel than office. The position may be conveniently summarized as follows:

1. The offices mentioned are those of overseer (*episkopos*), elder (*presbyteros*) and deacon. In both 1 Timothy and Titus certain qualities of a wholly personal character are demanded of overseers, but it is noteworthy that these qualities are generally unexceptional. In fact it is surprising that some of the requirements needed to be specified at all. It is significant that in both Epistles the bishops are required to have the ability to teach, but this is no more than would be expected from the more responsible members of the church. 1 Timothy alone contains instructions for the choice of deacons, but nothing is said about their duties.

2. In both Epistles the terms 'elder' and 'overseer' appear to be used interchangeably. Titus 1:5–7 is conclusive for the view that these two terms could describe the same people, and this fact is now generally accepted among New Testament scholars. In this case the term 'overseer' or 'bishop' could not have been used in the Pastorals in the later sense of a monarchical episcopate. There is nothing in these letters, in fact, to suggest that a bishop was in sole charge of any one community, nor that each community was restricted to one bishop. It is true that, whereas elders are spoken of in the plural, the overseer is mentioned

---

various notes in 'The Pastoral Epistles and Duncan's Ephesian Theory', *NTS* (1956), p. 251. For further discussion of the difficulties of the fragment theory, *cf.* my *New Testament Introduction* (1990), pp. 636ff.

only in the singular. These singular references are, however, to be interpreted in a generic sense, *i.e.* of the class of overseers, and no deduction with regard to dating can be made from this detail.[1]

3. A group known as 'widows' is specifically mentioned in 1 Timothy 5:3–16, but no other references to these occur in the New Testament. All that this passage states is that a list was to be kept on which the names of widows were enrolled if they were eligible for the church's support. The evidence is not sufficient to conclude that a distinct order was envisaged.

From this data two opposing deductions have been made. The traditional view is that there is nothing in the Pastorals' ecclesiastical situation which necessitates a date later than the time of Paul. At the other extreme is the view, both of those who regard the Pastorals as wholly fictional and of those who maintain genuine fragments, that the ecclesiastical situation is much too advanced for the mid-first-century church. It is claimed that the stage of development is beyond what we have any evidence of from the life of Paul, but in line with the early second century. In dealing with this ecclesiastical line of approach the reasons which have led some scholars to deny an early date for the Pastorals on the grounds of the late organization reflected will be examined.

A. IT IS MAINTAINED THAT PAUL HAD NO INTEREST IN CHURCH GOVERNMENT

This idea, current in New Testament criticism since the time of Baur, is based on the assumption that the great evangelical Epistles are the primary criteria for Paul's approach. Since in none of these does he signify any concern about the organization within the church it must follow that he gave it no thought. Indeed, on the contrary, he envisages a charismatic ministry to be operating in the Corinthian community. There is, however, strong evidence that Paul was not unmindful of church

---

[1]*Cf.* J. N. D. Kelly, *The Pastoral Epistles* (1963), p. 74.

organization where circumstances demanded it. Unless Acts 14:23, where Paul and Barnabas are said to have appointed elders in all the south Galatian churches which had been established on the first missionary journey, is an anachronism, the apostles must have recognized the need for the elder system at the very beginning of the Gentile mission, at least in some communities. It would appear that the only reason for regarding the reference as an anachronism is that it fails to support the theory that the elder-system was a later development to supply the need among other things of tradition-bearers. But a method which has to rely on such modification of evidence in the interest of a preconceived theory cannot but arouse some suspicion.

A further support for Pauline acknowledgement of established orders within the church is the address to the Philippian bishops (overseers) and deacons (Phil. 1:1), who are incidently mentioned after the rank and file of Christian believers.[1] Whether Paul had anything to do with the appointment of these it is impossible to say, but it is, at least, not inconceivable, as this church was founded by the apostle and had had intimate communications with him as the Epistle to the Philippians shows. Yet some scholars seek to lessen the force of this evidence by maintaining that the overseers (*episkopoi*) are not to be identified as rule-elders, but more generally as officials of whatever office or rank. But this is much less convincing than to suppose that some kind of leaders are in mind, which is certainly the most natural understanding of the term. Since one of the motives which Paul had in writing his letter to the Philippians was to express gratitude for a gift which the people had sent to Paul, he would naturally include in his opening address a mention of the officials who had no doubt been responsible for the collection. In no other of Paul's Epistles does such a situation arise and this may possibly account for the lack of allusion to church officials in the salutations to the other churches. But we should not forget the veiled allusion to

---

[1] Hanson, NCB, p. 31, admits the difficulty of this reference, but follows Rohde's suggestion that they were not church officers in the later sense (for Rohde, *cf. Urchristliche und frühkatholische Ämter*, 1976, pp. 54–55).

'those over you' in 1 Thessalonians 5:12.[1]

Another line of evidence comes from Ephesians 4:11 where among the offices mentioned are 'pastors and teachers', which appears to describe one office and not two. Evidently variety of function was fully recognized when this Epistle was written, although this would carry little weight with those who regard Ephesians as a late non-Pauline work.

There is, therefore, considerable evidence to show that Paul was not unmindful of church organization. The absence of uniformity of government in Pauline churches is capable of other explanations than that Paul was completely disinterested. He appears to have been sufficiently flexible in his approach to allow any system which suited local conditions and was dictated by the Holy Spirit. Perhaps the strongest refutation of the notion of Paul's disinterestedness in church organization is to be found in his words to the Ephesian elders (Acts 20:28). 'Keep watch over yourselves and all the flock of which the Holy Spirit has made you overseers. Be shepherds of the church of God.' Here is an acknowledgement that the Ephesian elder-system was the Holy Spirit's appointment and an indirect confirmation that such a system was fully operative some time before Timothy arrived to take up his duties. It is further significant that Paul addresses these elders as overseers (*episkopoi*).

B. IT IS MAINTAINED THAT THE PASTORALS ASSUME A RULE-SYSTEM WHICH COULD NOT FUNCTION IN THE APOSTOLIC AGE

Since there is much in the Pastorals about the passing on of the tradition, of 'the faith' and the 'deposit', it is supposed that these conditions could not have existed until the traditions had become standardized which, it is claimed, did not happen in the apostolic age. It is suggested that the elder-system was not needed until the time when there was a fixed tradition to pass on. But such a view is unjustified in view of the fact that the developing tradition equally needed some authorized means of

[1]Hort considered that elders must here be meant (*Christian Ecclesia*, 1897, p. 126). But Hanson thinks 'those over you' do not belong to the same category as the ordained clergy encountered in the Pastorals, *op. cit.*, p. 31.

preservation. Granted, there is evidence in the Pastorals that local leaders were to be tradition-bearers (2 Tim. 2:2; Tit. 1:9), and Timothy himself is more than once exhorted to guard the 'truth' committed to him as a trust or deposit. Yet this seems so elementary a requirement for any church which was to survive that it cannot be thought surprising that Paul should mention it as a requisite for the future. Moreover, in 1 Corinthians 15:3–4, Paul states that certain basic facts about the gospel were passed on to him and by him to the Corinthians. The position in the Pastorals seems to be a natural development from this.

C. IT IS MAINTAINED THAT THE CHURCH ORGANIZATION IN THE PASTORALS REQUIRES A CONSIDERABLE TIME TO HAVE ELAPSED SINCE THE APOSTOLIC AGE

The main evidence brought to support this criticism is 1 Timothy 3:6 where it is specifically stated that an overseer must not be a new convert (*neophytos*). It may appear at first sight that such a stipulation rules out a church established only a few years earlier by the apostle Paul, but this does not necessarily follow. The church at Ephesus was probably one of the largest churches established by Paul for he spent three years in that city, and consequently after a few years there would be many Christians who had only just come to a knowledge of the faith and many others who had been Christians almost from the start. It would be a policy of natural prudence to exclude the former from eligibility to the overseer's office, but there is no need to visualize the eligible candidates as venerable greybeards who had served a long apprenticeship. As in all primitive communities measures had to be taken at the inception of the church to select some members for special responsibility, and as the membership increased more rigid selection was later possible because of a wider choice. In 1 Timothy 3:6, therefore, the apostle warns only against too rapid promotion.

It is perhaps not without significance that no mention is made of 'neophytes' in the directions given to Titus, and this may well be because the Cretan church was of much more recent establishment than that of Ephesus, in which case such a prohibition would therefore be inapplicable. Another point that should not be overlooked is that the elder-system which, according to Acts 20 was in operation in Ephesus and which may even have been suggested by the apostle himself, was presumably instituted immediately after his departure. There must have been 'neophytes' among these.

The existence of a so-called order of widows is also cited as an evidence of a more fully developed church. But even if 1 Timothy 5 is understood of a distinct 'order' of widows, which is extremely doubtful, there is no evidence to show when such an order began,[1] and only if such evidence were forthcoming could this passage be used to prove a late date for the Pastorals. Admittedly no other New Testament evidence supports such a women's order, but the balance of probability supports the early use of women for official duties. The reference to Phoebe as a 'deacon' (Rom. 16:1) may be a possible parallel, although the word used there probably denotes service in general and does not refer to a specialized order.[2]

D. IT IS ALSO MAINTAINED THAT THE FUNCTIONS OF TIMOTHY AND TITUS ARE AKIN TO THOSE OF AN IGNATIAN TYPE OF BISHOP

Some scholars are adamant that the Pastorals reflect a situation in which monarchical episcopacy as seen in the Ignatian letters is already established. But because the internal evidence of the Pastoral Epistles is not strong in support of this, the fictional Timothy and Titus are claimed to exercise a monarchical or even archiepiscopal function. This view was held by Easton[3] and has since been maintained by Käsemann.[4] Hanson[5] disputes that there were any actual characters corresponding to the historical Timothy and Titus, and considers that the latter are called on to exercise the same kind of functions as the Ignatian-type bishops.

---

[1]The earliest unambiguous use of 'deaconess' as a distinctive office appears in the *Didascalia* iii.12–13, but a wide gap separates this office from the reference in the Pastorals to widows.

[2]*Cf.* Easton, *The Pastoral Epistles* (1948), p. 185.   [3]Easton, *op. cit.*, pp. 177ff.

[4]Käsemann, *Essays on New Testament Themes* (1964), p. 87.

[5]NCB, p. 33.

But when the functions of the fictitious Timothy and Titus are examined the demands do not exceed those which were expected of apostolic delegates.[1] They ordain clergy and are to deal with any charges against elders. Moreover they are thought to be free to make their own choice when appointing elders. It is also maintained on the basis of 1 Timothy 2:1 that they needed to know how to conduct public worship. They were to be custodians of the teaching, with authority to appoint others to carry on the same tradition. Although it is true that these functions were performed by Ignatius-type bishops, it is a *non sequitur* to maintain that to perform them the persons concerned had to be Ignatius-type bishops. Indeed, not all of those who dispute Pauline authorship are equally convinced about such an identification. Some will concede only that the Pastorals' ecclesiastical evidence is moving towards but not yet arrived at an Ignatian style of bishop.[2] Kelly is surely right when he confirms that there is nothing in these Pastoral Epistles which requires us to place them outside the life-time of Paul.[3] It is significant that Kelly the church historian should be more favourable to this view than the New Testament scholars who oppose it.

A criticism of the Ignatian-type theory is the absence from the Pastorals of any suggestion that only one man should hold the office of bishop. After all if the writer of the Pastorals really wanted to claim Pauline support for a monarchical system, it is surprising that he did not make the matter more obvious. Had he done so his purpose would surely have been more effectively served. It is also surprising that he left the distinction between elders and bishops so ambiguous, if by the time of writing there was no possibility of the terms being used for the same office, as they are in the Pastorals.

There will no doubt continue to be differences of opinion regarding the part played by Timothy and Titus, but it will not do for the opponents of Pauline authorship to ignore the weighty opinions of those who consider the ecclesiastical situation to be much earlier than the second century. If the evidence

[1] Lock called them 'Vicars Apostolic' (*The Pastoral Epistles*, 1924, p. xix).
[2] *Cf.* Brox, *Die Pastoralbriefe* (1969), pp. 148ff.
[3] Kelly, *op. cit.*, p. 15.

need not go beyond the time of the apostolic age, the ecclesiastical argument cannot be used to exclude the possibility of Pauline authorship. So many approaches to the Pastorals adapt the church situation to a second-century type because of conclusions reached on other grounds against the authenticity. It would be a fairer assessment of the evidence to suppose that it would not naturally point to a later situation unless on other grounds a late date is unavoidable.

We may therefore sum up the evidence for the ecclesiastical situation in the Pastorals as follows. At the time of writing there was already a definite system of teaching, apostolically authenticated, committed particularly to apostolical delegates and generally to the church elders. Ordinations were probably held for church officials, at which the laying on of hands was used to symbolize the transference of a special gift to carry out the office. A variety of ministry existed within the churches and great emphasis was laid on the moral qualities of all aspirants for office. Thus the Pastorals' ecclesiastical data not only provide a picture of an orderly developing church, but show the apostle in a significant light as an ecclesiastical architect. It is not that orthodoxy and organization have become the absorbing passion in his last days, but rather that sagacious provisions have been made for a time when no apostolic witness will remain, and the Spirit of God will use other means to direct his people.

VI. THE HERESIES REFLECTED IN THE EPISTLES

The treatment of the false teaching current at the time when the Pastorals were written is of first importance to the study of the Epistles, since it was undoubtedly one of the reasons why they were written. Many scholars have maintained that the heresies reflected are akin to those current in the early second century, and therefore the Pastorals must be of similar dating and consequently non-Pauline.

In all three letters there is advice about repelling false teaching which shows that it was an urgent matter. Yet there have been a variety of suggestions regarding the identity of this false teaching. Easton[1] maintained that 'a coherent and powerful heresy'

[1] *Op. cit.*, pp. 2–3.

was in mind. But as the following evidence will show, this is an exaggeration and by no means supported by the Epistles themselves. Many have argued for a gnostic alignment, or else a pre-gnostic state of affairs. Yet others have stressed the Jewish elements, including Qumran. To make any reasonable assessment it will be necessary to detail the evidence from each of the Pastorals.

In 1 Timothy 1:3–7 Timothy is told to 'command certain men not to teach false doctrines any longer nor to devote themselves to myths and endless genealogies'. These persons were apparently desirous of being teachers of the law without understanding it. Much discussion has surrounded the meaning of the word 'genealogies' in this passage, but Hort's conclusion[1] that the Pastorals' heresies are more closely connected with Jewish legend than Greek speculation seems a reasonable explanation of the scant data available.[2] The interest in the law in this passage would serve to confirm this conclusion.[3]

The next evidence from 1 Timothy is the obscure reference to those who have made shipwreck of their faith, of whom Hymenaeus and Alexander are specially mentioned (1:19–20). This must presumably be linked with the reference in 2 Timothy 2:17ff. to a man named Hymenaeus who had swerved from the truth in declaring that the resurrection was already past, but in this latter instance his name is coupled with Philetus and not Alexander. In the former passage it is clear that those mentioned must have caused the apostle considerable and dangerous trouble for such drastic action to be taken as 'delivery to Satan'

---

[1] *Judaistic Christianity* (1894), pp. 135ff.

[2] Bernard says, 'In the curious production called the *Book of Jubilees* we have a conspicuous proof of the stress laid upon the genealogies as the bases upon which legends might be reared' (*Pastoral Epistles*, 1899, p. li). *Jubilees* is thought by some to have originated in the Qumran community (*cf.* C. T. Fritsch, *The Qumran Community*, 1956, pp. 70, 106–107). Spicq (I.2), makes much of the parallels between the literature of the Qumran community and the Pastoral Epistles.

[3] Lock considered that both Jewish and Hellenistic tendencies co-existed in Ephesus and Crete (*op. cit.*, p. xvii), and Scott remarked that while gnosticism in its developed state was strongly anti-Jewish, yet at its outset 'it seems to have welcomed Jewish ideas and never ceased to employ Jewish material in the construction of its myths' (*The Pastoral Epistles*, 1936, p. xxix). More recent writers have tended to place more emphasis on the gnostic use of genealogies. *Cf.* Hanson (NCB, p. 25). Dibelius-Conzelmann (*Die Pastoralbriefe*, 1955, pp. 53ff.) speak of Jewish proto-gnosticism.

(see note on 1 Tim. 1:20). Easton[1] assumed that 2 Timothy must precede 1 Timothy and therefore regarded the 1 Timothy treatment of Hymenaeus as evidence of a progressively less tolerant spirit in the church. But it is probable that Paul in 2 Timothy is merely citing these people as examples of godless chatter, in which case no chronological deduction may be made from their incidental mention. On Easton's hypothesis a considerable interval would be required to separate the two Epistles, but this is most unlikely.

There are important data found in 1 Timothy 4:1–5 which speaks of 'doctrines of demons', specially mentioning such ascetic practices as celibacy and abstinence from food. The latter feature occurs elsewhere in Paul's allusions to false teaching, for in the Colossian heresy there were apparently definite regulations about food (Col. 2:16, 20–22), while even in the church at Rome there were some who had a lack of balance over food procedure (Rom. 14). No allusion to celibacy, however, occurs in the Colossian letter. Since Paul's words are here prophetic rather than historic, we may reasonably assume, as Bernard suggested,[2] that this practice had not yet affected the Christian church. In that case Paul is merely warning Timothy against tendencies which he clearly foresaw, and which in fact were already observable outside the Christian community. It is known for instance that the strictest sect of the Essenes practised celibacy.[3] It is interesting to note that Paul gives the Christian answer to abstinence from food, but not to celibacy, in 1 Timothy 4:3–5. This may have been because he was himself attracted to the celibate life, but would not have endorsed the enforcement of it on all Christians.[4]

The only other clear allusions to false teaching are in 6:3–5, which repeats the warning against controversy and wrangling, and 6:20 which is closely allied, but which links 'godless chatter'

[1]*Op. cit.*, p. 18. Hanson regards both references to Hymenaeus as a reference to a genuine opponent of Paul who may have had followers in the writer's day (*cf.* NCB, pp. 65, 135).
[2]*Op. cit.*, p. 66.
[3]*Cf.* Pliny's *Natural History*, V.xv. Josephus speaks of an Essenic group which allowed a kind of marriage by trial. N.B. Celibacy does not appear to have been enforced in the Qumran community.
[4]Spicq (*ad loc.*) makes comparisons with the Qumran sect, but Hanson (*ad loc.*) claims the reference to celibacy points to early gnosticism.

to the much discussed *antitheseis*. This latter word occurs frequently in second-century gnosticism, but any specific reference to Marcion's 'Antitheses' is more than doubtful. It has been suggested that every orator was equipped with a stock of 'antitheses' as part of his stock in trade and no more than this need be implied in this Pastorals' occurrence.

In 2 Timothy, apart from the reference to Hymenaeus already mentioned, the main emphasis is again on irrelevant controversies (2:14, 16, 23). The apostle proceeds to describe the last days which would be characterized by those 'having a form of godliness but denying its power' (3:5). A similar foresight envisages a time when people will have itching ears and will desire teachers to suit themselves (4:3). These apocalyptic pre-visions cannot, however, supply specific data for determining the nature of the contemporary errors about which Paul is particularly concerned. The added emphasis on controversies in this more personal second Epistle to Timothy suggests that the apostle is fearful lest his lieutenant should devote too much attention to these futilities, whereas he feels the best policy is to ignore them.

In Titus 1:10 a significant reference to empty talkers of the circumcision party clearly shows that the heresy in this case had a Jewish origin. This is further substantiated by the specific reference to Jewish myths (Tit. 1:14), as compared with the similar but vaguer allusion in 1 Timothy 1:4. A further mention of futile and unprofitable controversies occurs in Titus 3:9, linked with genealogies and quarrels over the law (*cf.* 1 Tim. 1:7–8). From this data it is evident that in Crete some form of Jewish controversies of an entirely speculative and irrelevant nature had arisen.

While there were undoubtedly minor differences between the false teaching in Ephesus and in Crete, the major features seem to be common, and there is strong justification for regarding them as separate manifestations of a general contemporary tendency. From the data considered above the following facts may be adduced in summary form. (1) The teaching was dangerous, more because of its irrelevance than because of its falseness. (2) It led to two opposite tendencies; asceticism on the one hand (1 Tim. 4:1–4) and probably licentiousness on the other hand (as 1 Tim. 5:22 seems to suggest). (3) There were many Jewish characteristics as Titus 1:10, 14, 1 Timothy 1:7 and Titus 3:9 show. (4) There was also some kind of all-absorbing interest in genealogies.

Two problems arising from this evidence require discussion. First, what is the relationship of this false teaching to second-century gnosticism? Second, is the manner of dealing with the false teachers consistent with Paul's approach to the Colossian heresy? If the answer to the first question were to show an undeniable connection with developed gnosticism, it would be conclusive against Pauline authorship, as also would a negative answer to the second question. For this reason the importance of these enquiries cannot be overrated.

A. THE RELATIONSHIP OF THE FALSE TEACHING TO SECOND-CENTURY GNOSTICISM

To illustrate this relationship the following features which gnosticism has in common with the Pastorals heresy have been brought forward to show a contemporary setting:

1. Gnosticism was fundamentally dualistic, various systems being proposed to bridge the gap between God and the evil world. The fruit of such dualism was seen in rigid asceticism, as for instance prohibition of marriage and severe restrictions on certain foods.

2. There was a general tendency to allegorize the Old Testament, although Marcion, who was not really a gnostic in the fullest sense, rejected the Old Testament altogether.

3. The Christology of gnosticism was generally Docetic, denying the possibility of the incarnation because of a belief in the inherent evil of matter. For the same reason the reality of the resurrection was denied.

Undoubtedly a good case can be made out for the supposition that the Pastorals would answer such erroneous tendencies as these. The presentation of Christ as the 'one mediator between God and men' (1 Tim. 2:5), for instance, could well be the Christian answer to the theory of endless emanations in the more developed gnostic systems. But such a statement would equally well fit any other situation in which the unique mediatorial position of Christ was being challenged, and there is no need to go to gnosticism to find the earliest examples of this. It must have been one of the most primitive crises for Christian apologetics.

Again it might be maintained that 2 Timothy 3:15–17 may reprove the rejection of the Old Testament Scriptures and Titus 1:14 and 1 Timothy 1:7 the allegorizing of Scripture. But this latter tendency was widely found in first-century Jewish speculation, while the former statement need have no reference at all to a tendency to reject Scripture (see note on 2 Tim. 3:15–17). The Christology of the Pastorals would certainly be useful in combating Docetism, but no more directly so than that of any of Paul's Epistles, or for that matter, any of the other New Testament books with enough data to set forth a doctrine of Christ's person. The denial of the resurrection, however, is a much closer point of contact.

Gnostic insincerity and bestial practices show a striking similarity with the evil propagated by the Pastorals' false teachers; but the key question is whether similar errors do not always produce similar effects, for if they do (and there are strong reasons for believing they do) similarity of effects cannot be regarded as proof of unity of origin.

It will be seen, then, that all that can satisfactorily be claimed is that these false teachers in the Pastorals have a remote kinship with gnosticism; but the evidence is far from conclusive that the writer is, in fact, combating developed gnosticism. It might be maintained, with some reason, that the evidence shows an incipient form of such gnosticism but no more than this can be claimed. This is being increasingly recognized by many who nevertheless dispute the Pauline authorship.[1] Although the view that the Pastorals deal with Marcionism has found advocates in the past, there are now few who would support this idea.

---

[1] Cf. Spicq, op. cit., p. lxxi, for details. Kelly, op. cit., p. 12, concludes that the Pastorals are concerned with something much more elementary than developed gnosticism. He suggests some gnosticizing form of Jewish Christianity. As already noted, Dibelius-Conzelmann (op. cit., pp. 53f.) speak of proto-gnosticism.

B. THE WRITER'S ATTITUDE TOWARDS FALSE TEACHING

The manner in which the writer advises his lieutenants to deal
with the false teachers has been strongly urged as evidence
against Pauline authorship, for it is alleged that, whereas in the
case of Colossians, Paul refutes the heresy, here the writer
denounces it. Such a change of attitude is then considered to be
evidence of a lesser mind than the apostle's. Both Timothy and
Titus are urged to deal strongly with the trouble-makers (1 Tim.
1:3; 2 Tim. 2:14; Tit. 1:13). But would Paul have refuted such
action? The apostle's attitude in this situation can hardly be
assessed from his Colossian letter since there he directs his
remarks to the church as a whole, a church which, incidentally,
he had never visited, and for that reason careful positive teaching is given to counteract the error. But in the Pastorals the
instructions are directed to Paul's special representatives
advising what line of action they themselves must take. Is it
likely that they would need an exposition of Paul's method of
refutation? It can scarcely be assumed that the apostle had never
had to deal with any false teachers while Timothy and Titus
were in his company.

It has been claimed that the writer shows no real acquaintance
with the heresy which he condemns.[1] He is content to ridicule it
as vain babbling, old wive's tales, a spreading cancer, make-
believe knowledge. But the irrelevance of the teaching was
apparent enough to lead the apostle to advise denunciation,
while the fruits were of sufficient unworthiness to condemn the
system from which they had sprung.

VII. THE DOCTRINAL PROBLEM

Opponents of authenticity have always pointed out with
varying degrees of emphasis the theological differences between
these Epistles and the other Epistles of Paul. This is certainly
one of the strongest contributory factors in the cumulative

---

[1]So Scott, *op. cit.*, p. xxx. C. K. Barrett's view is that the writer lumped together all the
heresies he had met (*NTS* 20, 1973–74, pp. 240–241).

evidence against Pauline authorship and merits the closest attention.

Not even the strongest critics of authenticity have been able to deny the Pauline basis of the Pastorals' theology. Even the radical Tübingen school used this fact in its attempts to create a polemical situation between Peter and Paul as the background of the New Testament literature. It is advisable, therefore, to begin by citing the Pauline parallels of thought. Scott[1] summed it up succinctly as follows. The writer 'declares that Christ gave Himself for our redemption, that we are justified not by our own righteousness but by faith in Christ, that God called us by His grace before the world was, and that we are destined to an eternal life on which we can enter even now. These are no mere perfunctory echoes of Pauline thought.' In view of this any attempt to assess the allegedly non-Pauline elements of doctrine must be examined against this Pauline background. A common theological background cannot, of course, be conclusive for Pauline authorship, for a secondary work might proceed from the same school of thought bearing upon it the marks of its doctrinal origin. Thus those who deny authenticity postulate as an alternative solution an earnest devotee of the great apostle, who wrote to represent his master's teaching to his own later age. But the important question is whether such a hypothesis is demanded by the data. To answer this question a survey of the difference between the other Pauline Epistles and the Pastorals is necessary.

One view of the writer's religious attitude is that his thought centres on *eusebeia*,[2] and his interest therefore lies more in religion than in theology, more with orthodoxy than with formative Christian thought. According to this view the age of speculative thinking is over. It has been said that whereas Paul was inspired, the writer of these Epistles is sometimes only orthodox.[3] But the question arises whether right belief or sound doctrine, which so dominates the Pastorals, is completely out of the range of the inspired apostle's thought. Is it entirely certain that the apostle Paul would never have descended from his

---

[1] *Op. cit.*, p. xxx.   [2] *Cf.* Scott, *op. cit.*, pp. xxx, xxxi.
[3] *Cf.* J. Denney, *The Death of Christ* (1911), p. 147.

formative thinking to consider the need for conservation of doctrine? The key to the problem may lie in a true understanding of Paul's theological vision rather than in a bare comparison between two sets of Epistles. The alleged non-Pauline features, which must, however, be examined, may be enumerated as follows:

1. The conception of God is said to be partially Jewish and partially Hellenistic.[1] Such terms as 'immortal' and 'invisible' are Hellenistic, but most of the other terms used for God are Judaistic (*e.g.* 'Ruler' or 'Potentate', *cf.* 2 Macc. 12:15, 'King of kings and Lord of lords', *cf.* Ex. 26:7; 2 Macc. 13:4, 'unapproachable light', *cf.* Enoch 12:15ff.). The problem is not so much the use of terms not found in the other Pauline Epistles, but the absence of what is claimed to be Paul's most characteristic conception of God, *i.e.* his Fatherhood. Such passages as 1 Timothy 1:17 and 6:15–16 certainly impress the reader with a great sense of the unapproachable majesty of God, but it cannot be maintained that such remoteness obtains in every case. The two passages cited are dominated by a desire to magnify God and a sense of holy awe is most becoming; but these must be balanced by those setting forth God as Saviour (1 Tim. 1:1; 2:3; 4:10; Tit. 1:3; 2:10; 3:4), who desires the salvation of all (1 Tim. 2:4), whose saving work is motivated by goodness and loving-kindness (Tit. 3:4), whose purpose is described as proceeding from grace (2 Tim. 1:9; *cf.* Tit. 2:11), who commissioned Paul to preach the gospel (1 Tim. 1:1; 2 Tim. 1:1; Tit. 1:3), and who in Christ 'gave himself for us to redeem us from all wickedness and to purify for himself a people that are his very own, eager to do what is good'. No-one can reasonably charge a writer of words such as these with being overawed by God's remoteness. If the absence of the title 'Father' from the body of each Epistle be deemed a difficulty, it should be remembered that it occurs twice only in the body of 1 Corinthians (see 8:6; 15:24) and of Romans (6:4; 15:6; but *cf.* 8:15).

2. There are various opinions regarding the Christology of the Pastorals. Some find an epiphany Christology,[2] others a

---

[1] *Cf.* Easton, *op. cit.*, p. 166. [2] *Cf.* Dibelius-Conzelmann, on 1 Tim. 3:16.

'title' Christology,[1] yet others a subordination Christology.[2] These differences of opinion, held by those who dispute Pauline authorship, arise through emphasizing certain statements in the Pastorals to the exclusion of the rest. Whereas there are not the same clear Christological statements in the Pastorals as in some of the other Pauline Epistles, there is insufficient evidence that the Christology of the Pastorals excludes Pauline authorship.

Another issue of a Christological kind is the absence of the Pauline teaching of the believer's mystical union with Christ. The phrase 'in Christ', so characteristic of Paul, occurs seven times in 2 Timothy (1:1, 9, 13; 2:1, 10; 3:12, 15) and twice in 1 Timothy (1:14; 3:13), but in none of these cases in a mystical sense.[3] Yet a detailed study of these instances does not bear out the claim that the phrase means no more than 'Christian', for where qualities are said to be 'in Christ' the phrase must surely imply more than that. It is difficult to see any difference of approach between 2 Timothy 1:13 'with faith and love in Christ Jesus', and Colossians 1:4 'your faith in Christ Jesus'. Moreover if 'in Christ' is generally a synonym for 'Christian' in the Pastorals, it must also be considered in the same way in certain Pauline usages (e.g. the saints in Christ at Colossae, Col. 1:2). Admittedly the most frequent Pauline usage is to describe persons rather than qualities, but where applied to qualities it is most probable that some mystical element is intended.

Consider for instance 2 Timothy 1:9, 'this grace was given us in Christ Jesus before the beginning of time', where the meaning appears to be that grace was given before the world began to those who are in Christ, i.e. in a mystical union with him (see comment ad loc.).[4] Opponents of Pauline authorship do not give full weight to this meaning. Hanson,[5] for example, although admitting some parallels in the other Pauline Epistles (Rom. 16:25–26; Eph. 1:11; 2:5–10; 3:11) nevertheless treats these as deutero-Pauline and thus discounts them. He even goes as

---

[1] Cf. P. Trummer, Die Paulustradition der Pastorbriefe (1978), pp. 193ff.
[2] Cf. Dibelius-Conzelmann on 1 Tim. 2:5–6.
[3] Cf. Easton, op. cit., p. 2
[4] Easton, op. cit., pp. 210–211, rendered this 'assured to us from eternity by the act of Christ's existence', which considerably weakened the force of the Greek text here. Cf. my monograph, The Pastoral Epistles and the Mind of Paul (1956), p. 25.
[5] NCB, pp. 122–123.

far as to question whether the writer, although using these 'Paul-ine' sources, always understood their theological implications. But such a method of disposing of the Pauline parallels is uncon-vincing.

3. A more serious difficulty is the infrequency of mention of the Holy Spirit. This doctrine is therefore thought to have meant little to the writer. Three times the Holy Spirit is clearly men-tioned distinct from the human spirit (1 Tim. 4:1; 2 Tim. 1:14 and Tit. 3:5). The reference in Titus 3:5 is disposed of by being treated as a liturgical passage where the writer is therefore regarded as not using his own language.[1] If, however, the statement is given its full weight, not only must it be regarded as a Trinitarian statement but its view of the Spirit is in line with the Pauline doctrine of the Spirit.[2] 1 Timothy 4:1 refers to the prophetic function of the Spirit and cannot explicitly be regarded as non-Pauline since Paul recognized just such a func-tion of the Spirit. 2 Timothy 1:14 is similarly a thoroughly Paul-ine concept, which even those who dismiss Pauline authorship admit,[3] although they treat it as a case of the writer adapting Paul's language for his own use.

It will be seen that there is nothing in any of these statements which Paul himself could not have written. If the absence of further reference to the Spirit's activities be considered non-Pauline, it should be remembered that such references are not evenly spread over all Paul's earlier Epistles, for in the case of Colossians the Spirit is mentioned once only (1:8), in 2 Thessa-lonians once only (2:13) and in Philemon not at all.

4. The Pastorals' use of the word 'faith' (*pistis*) is said to be non-Pauline, while the characteristic Pauline usage is con-spicuously absent. For Paul *pistis* generally denotes the quality of abiding trust in Christ and has passed beyond the root mean-ing of 'fidelity'. But in the Pastorals the latter meaning is most frequent, together with an objective sense when used with the article representing 'the totality of truths to be believed'.[4] In the

---

[1] *Cf.* Hanson, NCB, p. 40.

[2] *Cf.* G. W. Knight, *The Faithful Sayings of the Pastoral Epistles* (1968), p. 91.

[3] *Cf.* Hanson, *ad loc.*

[4] Easton, *op. cit.*, p. 203. Jeremias (*Die Briefe an Timotheus und Titus*, 1963, p. 4) considered that the stress on faith-teaching as a fixed norm is explained by the writer's preoccupation with the heresy conflict.

Pastorals the objective use with the article accounts for nine out of the thirty-three occurrences of the word (1 Tim. 1:19; 3:9; 4:1, 6; 5:8; 6:10, 12, 21 and 2 Tim. 3:8), but this in itself presents no great difficulty when Pauline parallels such as Philippians 1:27; Colossians 2:7; Ephesians 4:5 are borne in mind. In many other cases 'faith' is linked with 'love' (2 Tim. 1:13; 2:22; 3:10; 1 Tim. 1:5, 14; 2:15; 4:12; 6:11), and 'hope' (Tit. 1:1–2). But if it be urged that in these cases faith is treated as a fruit of salvation rather than as a root from which other virtues spring,[1] comparison with 1 Corinthians 12:9; 2 Corinthians 8:7; Galatians 5:22; Ephesians 6:23; 1 Thessalonians 1:3; 3:6; 2 Thessalonians 1:3–4; Philemon 5 will supply ample justification from Paul's earlier writings for such treatment of *pistis*, while the great Pauline hymn of 1 Corinthians 13 sets love as superior to faith among the three major virtues. A few occurrences such as 1 Timothy 5:12, where *pistis* means 'pledge' (some commentators would also add Tit. 2:10, where it clearly means 'fidelity', and 2 Tim. 4:7), are not readily paralleled in other Pauline writings, but are quite incidental to the main uses in the Pastorals.

It is still necessary, however, to examine the claim that the most conspicuous Pauline use is absent, *i.e.* as the justifying principle. It is true that faith is not mentioned in the key passage on justification (Tit. 3:5–7), but we cannot assume that such faith is excluded. 1 Corinthians 6:11, in fact, furnishes a close parallel in which the same verb is used without mention of faith (*cf.* note on Tit. 3:5). It is not unimportant in this connection to observe that the apostle uses this verb *dikaioō* in the theological sense of 'justify' or declare righteous only in Romans and Galatians, the two Epistles specifically devoted to the theme. If the absence of the idea in the Pastorals is a problem, it would apply equally to many of the Pauline Epistles, although the idea of salvation by faith does occur. Admittedly there is an absence of the Pauline antithesis between faith and works, although Titus 3:5 can hardly be understood in any other way, a fact which critics of Pauline authorship are prepared to admit.[2] Taking the evidence as a

---

[1]Scott, *op. cit.*, p. xxxi, says, 'In the Pastorals faith is not so much a root as a foundation (*cf.* 1 Tim. 3:15; 6:19) – the necessary basis of all right living, though it does not of itself produce it.'

[2]Easton, *op. cit.*, p. 102, treats this as a slightly forced attempt to introduce Pauline

whole the Pastorals' use of *pistis* cannot be considered an insuperable obstacle to their authenticity, even though some aspects of Paul's earlier use are missing.

5. A similar objection has been raised over the Pastorals' use of 'grace' (*charis*). Scott expressed the difficulty in the following way: 'While the writer thinks of salvation as the free gift of God he allows for a co-operation on the part of men. He describes grace as acting by a process of education (Tit. 2:11-12). Through the grace bestowed on us in the gift of Christ we are enabled to master all lower desires and follow the way of godliness'.[1] But nothing could be more Pauline than the expression 'justified by his grace' in Titus 3:7, which is exactly paralleled in Romans 3:24. The expression in Titus is clearly antithetical to verse 5 'not because of righteous things we have done', in which case the meaning of 'grace' is the usual Pauline one of favour.

These are the main doctrinal problems advanced against the Pauline authorship of the Pastorals. But certain other considerations need mentioning.

1. The advocates of the fragment theory are placed in rather a dilemma over their Paulinist editor for they are bound to maintain *ex hypothesi* that he was well acquainted with the authentic Pauline Epistles, to such a degree, in fact, that his mind must have been soaked in Pauline thought.[2] Yet the differences between the theology of the Pastorals and Pauline theology force these advocates to admit that 'this disciple of Paul has failed, in not a few respects, to understand him'.[3] In other words, where Pauline parallels can be provided it is evidence of echoes of Pauline thought lodged in another mind, but where variations are discernible the Paulinist's own thoughts are expressed. Now such a theory is certainly feasible and indeed necessary if the

---

language. Hanson, NCB, p. 191, regards it as an attempt to reproduce Pauline thought, but not in a very Pauline way of putting it. Houlden, *The Pastoral Epistles* (1976), p. 28, quite unjustifiably calls it a parody of Paul's doctrine.

[1]Scott, *op. cit.*, p. xxxi. Hanson, NCB, p. 183, does not regard these verses as Pauline. But Spicq is nearer the heart of the matter when he claims that these verses are among the most Pauline passages in the Pastorals (*ad loc.*).

[2]*Cf.* Harrison, *op. cit.*, pp. 87ff.

[3]Scott, *op. cit.*, p. xxv. Those who adopt the through-going fiction theory are obliged to regard all the Pauline parallels as attempts, not always successful, to reproduce Pauline thought. Writers like Hanson, Brox and Houlden, however, consider that the writer did not understand Paul.

non-Pauline elements are substantiated. But if these elements can reasonably be interpreted in a way consistent with Pauline usage, it is a much more credible hypothesis to regard them as variations from one fertile mind rather than as a mixture of two.

2. A second important consideration is whether Paul can be conceived of as using stereotyped doctrine. Is not the emphasis on 'sound doctrine', 'the truth', 'the deposit', so frequently met with in the Pastorals, alien to the creative mind of the great apostle? It may seem as if the man from whom the early church inherited some of its noblest doctrinal thinking has descended to a most uncharacteristic concern for maintaining the tradition; but to conclude that this could not have happened is to beg the question. The only information we have is that the apostle shows little concern for such tradition in his other Epistles, and much concern for it in the Pastorals. Yet it does not follow from this that different circumstances, particularly the realization that his own work was almost finished, could not have led to a different approach. In addition, the use of stereotyped phraseology would have been much more probable in letters directed to close personal associates than to mixed communities.

Another aspect of the same problem is the citation in these Epistles of such liturgical formulae as the five faithful sayings and the Christian hymn in 1 Timothy 3:16. Not only is this type of citation entirely unknown in the other Pauline writings, but the use of such formal statements is said to be proof of a later development in the church, relating to a period when Christian doctrine was reduced to formal statements for catechetical purposes. But the problem is really whether the creative Paul would have cited current formulae, since there is no reason to suppose that such formulae were not used at a very early stage in the history of the church.

If it be maintained that the apostle had no interest in conservation of doctrine, it will, of course, be impossible to conceive that he would have cited current formulae. But is it conceivable that Paul had no interest in conservation? Satabier's frequently quoted statement supplies the answer, 'Paul was an apostle before he was a theologian. To him the need of conservation was more urgent than that of innovation.'[1] It would have been

[1]Sabatier, *Paul* (1903), p. 270.

extreme short-sightedness on the part of the apostle if he had neglected to endorse, if not to create, some effective means for the propagation of the truths he had himself helped to formulate.[1] Nor should it be thought strange that the main evidence for such conservative tendencies on the apostle's part should come to us in writings to his closest associates, for their main task seems to have been to ensure the continuity of apostolic teaching. If the latter point be considered as evidence of sub-apostolic dating, it requires only a detailed comparison between the Pastorals and the sub-apostolic Fathers to demonstrate conclusively that the latter failed, if they ever attempted, to preserve intact the apostolic tradition. No-one can deny the gulf which separates the most 'formalized' doctrinal statements in the Pastorals from the most 'inspired' extant utterances of the second-century Apostolic Fathers.

VIII. THE LINGUISTIC PROBLEM

It remains to consider what is often regarded as the most pressing criticism against Pauline authorship and the one which undoubtedly weighs the balance in favour of rejecting the Epistles as authentic in the minds of many scholars. This is the marked difference in language between the Pauline Epistles and the Pastorals. This was first brought into the open as the spearhead of criticism by Schleiermacher (1807) in his work on 1 Timothy. During the nineteenth century this criticism gained momentum, being particularly embraced and enlarged upon by F. C. Baur (1835) and H. J. Holtzmann (1880). But it was following P. N. Harrison's treatment of the linguistic data in 1921[2] that many who had hitherto leaned to the traditional Pauline authorship found the position no longer tenable. Even as ardent an advocate of authenticity as Lock showed signs of vacillation in his commentary issued three years later than Harrison's book. In more recent times the linguistic data has been submitted to statistical examination of a more sophisticated type than Harrison used, but his basic approach has remained the

[1] For a full discussion of this problem and of the use of the faithful sayings, cf. my The Pastoral Epistles and the Mind of Paul (1956), pp. 17–29.
[2] The Problem of the Pastorals.

standard treatment and demands examination.

Harrison's presentation of the problem is fourfold: (1) The problem of the large number of words unique to the Pastorals in the New Testament (*i.e.* 175 Hapaxes, that is, words that occur once only in the New Testament). (2) The problem of the large number of words common to the Pastorals and other New Testament writings but unknown in the other ten Pauline letters. (3) The problem of characteristic Pauline words and groups of words missing from the Pastorals. (4) The problem of grammatical and stylistic differences. He brings a mass of statistics to support his double contention that the Pastorals cannot be attributed to Paul and that they belong to the current speech of the second century. A detailed examination of Harrison's evidence is given in the Appendix and it will consequently be necessary to give here only the conclusions of this linguistic study.

There are certainly many differences between these Epistles and the other ten Paulines, but these differences are not uniform and cannot be held as conclusive evidence of non-Pauline authorship. Such an approach would imply the impossibility of any change in an author's style or language, and this position cannot be decided on numerical data without reference to psychological probability, but Harrison has given no consideration to this latter point. If full allowance is made for dissimilarity of subject matter, variations due to advancing age, enlargement of vocabulary due to changing environment and the difference in the recipients as compared with the earlier letters, the linguistic peculiarities of the Pastorals can in large measure be satisfactorily explained.

The further claim that the language of the Pastorals is the current language of the second century would, if proved, greatly weigh against Pauline authenticity. Harrison appeals to certain similarities with the Apostolic Fathers and Apologists, but on examination his evidence is not as striking as he supposes, and in any case seems to be vitiated by the fact that greater similarities can be shown when the language of the Pastorals is compared with the language of the LXX. Harrison finds it necessary to appeal also to the secular writers of the second century to support his thesis and claims that this evidence proves that words peculiar to the Pastorals in the Greek

Testament were in very frequent use in this second-century period. But in view of the fact that all but a small group of these words were known in Greek literature before AD 50, Harrison's evidence proves nothing. Only if it could be shown that the language of the Pastorals could not have been used in the first century would there be definite grounds for assigning them to the second century. But none of the linguistic arguments are able, in fact, to establish this position.

Since Harrison's time there have been various criticisms of the basis of his approach. It has been pointed out that the Pastoral Epistles do not provide sufficient material for an adequate sample.[1] It has also been questioned whether the assumption that there is consistency of language in the other ten Pauline Epistles is valid.[2] There has been a lessening of emphasis on the Hapaxes in assessing the Pastorals' language, but it still continues to exercise a subtle influence. Some scholars have challenged the statistical approach from the point of view that Paul may not himself have been responsible for the wording of his letters, *i.e.* on the hypothesis that a secretary was responsible for the compilation.[3]

IX. THE PROBLEM OF AUTHORSHIP

All the major objections to authenticity having been examined, it is now possible to assess the problem of authorship and to mention the various solutions proposed.

---

[1] *Cf.* W. Metzger, *ExpT* 70, 3 (1958), pp. 91–94, who appeals to the work of G. U. Yule, *The Statistical Study of Literary Vocabulary* (1944). For other criticisms of the linguistic argument, *cf.* my *New Testament Introduction*, pp. 632ff.

[2] *Cf.* W. Michaelis, *ZNTW* 28 (1929), pp. 70ff.

[3] J. N. D. Kelly, *The Pastoral Epistles* (1963), pp. 25f., considers a secretary hypothesis would nullify much of the statistical evidence. Since the appearance of Harrison's book many studies have been produced which challenge his statistical methods. The most recent study is that of A. Kenny, *A Stylometric Study of the New Testament* (1986) which concludes on statistical grounds that the only one of the Pastorals which may perhaps be challenged is Titus, and it is doubtful whether even this is of sufficient length to allow any dependable conclusions. *Cf.* also J. J. O'Rourke, *CBQ* 35 (1973), pp. 483–490.

A. Q. Morton and J. McLeman, *Christianity and the Computer* (1964) and *Paul, The Man and the Myth* (1966), have also attempted to apply statistical methods to the Pauline Epistles and concluded that not only the Pastorals but all but four of the other Pauline Epistles must be pronounced non-Pauline. But their methods have been strongly criticized. *Cf.* C.

A. PAUL

That Paul himself was the author is supported by the salutation in each of the Pastorals and by the undisputed testimony of the church. While there are undoubted difficulties in such a view, there are none which make it impossible.

Some scholars, while convinced of the Pauline character of the Pastorals, nevertheless consider that some other hand produced the letters. The linguistic and other differences are due to greater freedom allowed to the amanuensis. Because of the close linguistic affinity of the Pastorals with Luke–Acts, it has been suggested that Luke may have been responsible for the stylistic peculiarities.[1] But it is open to question whether Paul would have allowed such freedom.

B. TIMOTHY AND TITUS

A theory has been suggested that the two close associates of Paul edited the Pauline material in their possession and published it in the form in which we now possess it after Paul's death.[2] But there seems no adequate motive for such a procedure unless Paul had left the material substantially in its present form, and if he had there seems little gain in this hypothesis.

Dinwoodie, *SJT* 18 (1965), pp. 204–218, G. B. Caird, *ExpT* 76 (1965), p. 176, H. K. McArthur, *ExpT* 76, pp. 367–370, *idem, NTS* 15 (1969), pp. 339–349, J. J. O'Rourke, *JBL* 86 (1967), pp. 110–112.

[1] H. J. Holtzmann, *Die Pastoralbriefe* (1880), pp. 92ff., drew attention to the remarkable affinities between the Pastorals and the Lucan writings. Another who favoured Luke as writer of the Pastorals was R. Scott, *The Pauline Epistles* (1909), pp. 329–371, on the grounds of general vocabulary, parallels which suggest interdependence, medical terminology, Greek religious ideas and similar favourite words and idioms. A more recent writer, S. G. Wilson, *Luke and the Pastoral Epistles* (1979), has made much of the parallels between these writings in supporting a Lucan connection in the Pastorals. *Cf.* also A. Strobel (*NTS* 15, 1969, pp. 191–220) who argued from language and theology, but whose views were criticized by N. Brox (*Jahrbuch für Antike und Christentum* 13, 1970, pp. 62–77) because he thought the Pastorals to have been too late for Lucan authorship.

[2] *Cf.* A. C. Deane, *St Paul and His Letters* (1942), pp. 208–220.

C. AN EDITOR

A modification of the last view is that some other person edited the Pauline material which came into his possession and arranged the notes in their present form shortly after Paul's death,[1] but the problems which are generally claimed to weigh against Pauline authorship are not accounted for by mere arrangement. The editor must in this case have rewritten the material if the objections are to be fully met, although the theory does not suppose this. If the editor did rewrite the material there would seem to be an insufficient motive.

D. A LATER PAULINIST

It is not enough for any disputant of Pauline authorship to provide an alternative theory. He must be prepared to prove that his own hypothesis is relatively free from the objections on the grounds of which he had denied authenticity. We shall begin with a brief summary of the problems of the fragment theory.

i. The problem of compilation

1. It is difficult to see why two Epistles were addressed to Timothy and one to Titus if the writer planned to present the Pauline approach to the contemporary situation. Since two of the supposed 'genuine' sections are in 2 Timothy and the third and less extensive one in Titus, it raises the question why the Paulinist made such an uneven distribution. No satisfactory explanation has yet been provided.

2. There is lack of agreement on the order in which the Epistles were compiled. Some maintain that 1 Timothy and Titus preceded 2 Timothy, which was a more direct appeal to Paul, while others place 2 Timothy first, the success of which spurred the writer to produce the other less obviously Pauline

[1] *Cf.* F. J. Badcock, *The Pauline Epistles and the Epistle to the Hebrews in their Historical Setting* (1937), pp. 115–133.

Epistles. Apart from their mutual contradictions, both these suggestions fail completely to account for the Paulinist's inconsistency. Were not all the letters purporting to be direct appeals to Paul?

3. There are personal allusions scattered about in all three Epistles which are not included in the generally proposed 'genuine' material (*cf.* 1 Tim. 1:3; 3:14; 5:23; 2 Tim. 1:5, 15; Tit. 1:5), and on the fragment theory it is possible to ascribe these only to the Paulinist's imagination. But is it psychologically probable that any devout disciples of Paul would have thought to invent Paul's concern for Timothy's stomach, or his mention of Timothy's mother and grandmother by name? If the genuine fragments themselves were enough to secure the Pauline imprimatur, why invent others?

4. Another problem is the difficulty of conceiving how the genuine fragments were preserved, for they appear to have been incorporated in a particularly disintegrated manner.[1] Evidently the Paulinist did not notice the historical problems he would create by his reconstruction of these fragments.[2]

5. The Paulinist must either have been an old man himself or else have possessed remarkable insight to portray so precisely the psychological traits of advancing age.[3] But he has also given many indications of the characters of Timothy and Titus, which may reasonably be claimed to accord with what we know of them from elsewhere in the New Testament. It is, of course, open to the defenders of the fragment theory to maintain that this reflects the author's antiquarian interests, but they cannot at the same time charge him with an absence of historical perspective.[4] It seems more reasonable to see in the lifelike portrayals a true record of actual events.

6. There is moreover a real linguistic problem in the fragment theory for it supposes that the Paulinist, thoroughly well versed as he was in the genuine Paulines, must have had frequent lapses when he forgot to give a Pauline flavour to what he was

[1]See p. 30 for details.　　[2]*Cf.* the comments on 2 Tim. 4:16–17.
[3]*Cf.* Spicq's excellent discussion of this point, *op. cit.*, pp. lxxxixff.
[4]For a discussion of Easton's opinion that the author has misrepresented the relationship between Paul and Timothy, see my *The Pastoral Epistles and the Mind of Paul*, pp. 31ff.

writing.[1] It is difficult to believe that the Paulinist would write long sections (*e.g.* 1 Tim. 3:1–13; 5:14–25) without attempting, according to Harrison's theory, to give as much as an echo of Pauline phraseology. It should be noted, of course, that some scholars maintain that although acquainted with Paul's Epistles, the author never really understood Paul, but that does not explain the relative absence of Pauline vocabulary in the passages mentioned.

7. Arising from the use of Pauline phraseology, the fragment theory, at least as it was expounded by Harrison[2] appears to use conflicting canons of criticism. Where passages are thick with Pauline phrases it is evidence of an imitator, for Paul would not cite himself so closely, but where such phrases are lacking it is evidence of genuine Pauline fragments. But this distinction is too fine to be psychologically feasible. It is a purely subjective process to determine when a passage is too much or too little Pauline to be genuine.

8. The fragment theory further presupposes that, in spite of his close acquaintance with Paul's Epistles, the Paulinist often failed to understand Paul's doctrinal point of view,[3] and has in fact missed the major factors in Paul's theology. It has already been demonstrated that no essential contradiction exists between Pauline doctrine and that of the Pastorals, but it would certainly have been more incumbent for an imitator to approximate as much as possible to previous patterns than for Paul himself. A kindred difficulty for this theory is adequately to account for the acknowledged superiority of the Pastorals over all the writer's second-century contemporaries.

ii. *The problem of motive*

It is generally agreed by advocates of the fragment theory that the Paulinist had a genuine desire to represent what Paul would have said had he addressed himself to the contemporary situation. His motives, therefore, were of the highest order, and his use of pseudonymity was an evidence of modesty since he had

---

[1] *Cf.* Harrison's argument in *JTS* 49 (1948), p. 209, in reviewing Spicq's *Les Epîtres Pastorales*.

[2] *Cf. op. cit.*, pp. 87–93.   [3] *Cf.* Scott, *op. cit.*, pp. xxi, xxv.

no wish to represent as his own what was in reality his master's thought.[1] But Paul had not given any indication of his approach to a situation in which monarchical episcopacy was either already established, or was, at least, rapidly arising. The Paulinist's difficulties in avoiding anachronisms must have been almost insuperable.

Even if it is possible to conceive of such a purpose, it would still be necessary to conciliate the author's high-minded purpose with his use of genuine fragments. It is not clear whether the possession, accidental or otherwise, of these fragments prompted him to produce his apostolically-backed ecclesiastical directives, or whether he first conceived the desirability of applying his master's principles to his own generation and the acquisition of the fragments provided the immediate opportunity. But neither of these alternatives seems psychologically probable, for the Pastorals would not have been particularly useful in promoting monarchical episcopacy where the system was not already in existence, and would not have been necessary where it was already an accomplished fact.

E. A WRITER OF FICTION

It is because of the many problems associated with the fragment theory that many scholars have concluded for a pure fiction theory. But these are still faced with the necessity to account for the fiction. The three-fold character of the Pastorals is as great a problem as with the fragment theory. Why three letters, and why were Timothy and Titus chosen? Moreover, this type of theory implies that whatever influence the Pauline Epistle had had over the author, he had failed to grasp the impact of Paul's message. If we suppose that such a theory is soundly based, we need then to ask what the original recipients would have made of the attempt. Would they have welcomed the Epistles as sincere efforts to present Paul to them? Had they known the Pauline Epistles, or at least some of them, why did they not suspect that the Pastorals were not in the same league? On the

[1] *Cf.* Easton, *op. cit.*, p. 19.

other hand if they were ignorant of Paul's Epistles, this would place them at a very early date to be credible.

A further question which needs to be asked is whether the reasons for writing which the adherents of the fiction theory advance have the ring of truth about them. Is it valid to claim, as Hanson does, that the author of the Pastorals aimed to make Paul more intelligible to his own generation? This seems to mean that a full presentation of Paul in the manner of the accepted Epistles would not have been intelligible, whereas the considerable watering down of Pauline theology or even the failure to grasp it contributed to a clarification of Paul. Such a theory could have credibility only if the readers had a greater misconception of Pauline theology than the writer. There is an inbuilt contradiction between the assertion that the author wished to make Paul real for his own day, and the view that he failed to understand the apostle. The contention would be more credible if the author had kept more closely to the known Paul.

All theories of non-Pauline authorship are also faced with the problem of pseudonymity, although many modern scholars do not accept it as a problem. Hanson, for instance, can claim that the writer's contemporaries would not have been condemned for writing in Paul's name. The fact is there is no conclusive evidence to support this. To appeal to other New Testament examples of pseudonymity like Ephesians and Colossians as justification for the acceptance of this mode of literature is to beg the question.[1] The pressing demand must be for indisputable evidence that the Christian church would have happily gone along with contemporary practice for its authoritative books. There is no evidence that this happened, but certainly some evidence that such practice was condemned at a later date. Nor will it do to accept the practice and then search for support for it along the lines of parallels in Jewish thinking as has recently been suggested.[2] However confidently many scholars pronounce on the acceptability of pseudonymity, it must be recognized that approaches to the Pastoral Epistles which depend on the validity of pseudonymity are at a discount compared with solutions which do not. Even if it might be conceded that an

---

[1] A. T. Hanson, NCB, p. 49. [2] *Cf.* D. G. Meade, *Pseudonymity and Canon* (1986).

admirer of Paul could genuinely be convinced that it was a valid and helpful thing to do to publish something in Paul's name, the deliberate attempt to give that exercise the appearance of verisimilitude fits in most uneasily with that theory.[1] There has yet to be a satisfactory explanation of the composition of the Pastorals from the point of view of pseudonymous authorship.

X. THE MESSAGE OF THE EPISTLES

These Epistles addressed by the apostle to his close associates reveal much about the author, about the recipients and about the general church situation reflected in them. They provide valuable insights into some of the problems faced by the early church and give pointers to the best way to deal with them. They suggest great care in the ordering of church affairs at least with regard to the appointment of suitable officials. They have for that reason been a constant source of valuable guidance in pastoral matters during the ensuing history of the church.

Especially in 2 Timothy we learn much about the apostle as he faces the prospect of death. It is not without some justification that this Epistle has been called Paul's swan song. The concluding chapter is both courageous and touching. Paul's faith shines through and yet there is also some sadness in the fact that only Luke is with him. It is a fitting climax to the life of the great apostle and has been an inspiration to generations of Christians ever since.

These Epistles are still relevant to our modern age. The need for wise dealing with questions of church arrangements and Christian discipline is ever present, and these Epistles have constantly supplied Christian leaders with sober practical advice in these matters. They may lack the profound theological grasp of some of the other New Testament Epistles, but they are not without their theological gems. The diligent student will not only find himself grappling with the practical problems of a developing church, but will find his soul enriched by many flashes of doctrinal insight.

[1]*Cf.* J. N. D. Kelly, *op. cit.*, p. 33.

1 TIMOTHY: ANALYSIS

I. THE APOSTLE AND TIMOTHY (1:1–20)
A. SALUTATION (1:1–2)
B. THE CONTRAST BETWEEN THE GOSPEL AND ITS COUNTERFEITS (1:3–11)
C. THE APOSTLE'S PERSONAL EXPERIENCE OF THE GOSPEL (1:12–17)
D. THE APOSTLE'S CHARGE TO TIMOTHY (1:18–20)

II. WORSHIP AND ORDER IN THE CHURCH (2:1–4:16)
A. THE IMPORTANCE AND SCOPE OF PUBLIC PRAYER (2:1–8)
B. THE STATUS AND DEMEANOUR OF CHRISTIAN WOMEN (2:9–15)
C. THE QUALIFICATIONS OF CHURCH OFFICIALS (3:1–13)
   i. *Overseers* (3:1–7)
   ii. *Deacons* (3:8–13)
D. THE CHARACTER OF THE CHURCH (3:14–16)
E. THREATS TO THE SAFETY OF THE CHURCH (4:1–16)
   i. *The approaching apostasy* (4:1–5)
   ii. *Methods of dealing with false teaching* (4:6–16)

III. DISCIPLINE AND RESPONSIBILITY (5:1–6:2)
A. VARIOUS AGE GROUPS (5:1–2)
B. WIDOWS (5:3–16)
   i. *Widows in need* (5:3–8)
   ii. *Widows as Christian workers* (5:9–10)
   iii. *Younger widows* (5:11–16)
C. ELDERS (5:17–20)
D. TIMOTHY'S OWN BEHAVIOUR (5:21–25)
E. SERVANTS AND MASTERS (6:1–2)

IV. MISCELLANEOUS INJUNCTIONS (6:3–21)

1 TIMOTHY: COMMENTARY

I. THE APOSTLE AND TIMOTHY (1:1–20)

A. SALUTATION (1:1–2)

1. Following his general usage, Paul commences with a declaration of his own authority in order to make unmistakable the authority of the message he teaches. His design is semi-official as well as personal, for Timothy himself would need no such reminder of the apostle's authority.

The word *apostle* must be given its narrower meaning of 'membership of the apostolic circle'. It may well be that some at Ephesus had questioned Paul's authority, and his claim to this title would therefore immediately correct any misconceptions about his official position in the church. The order of the title *Christ Jesus* may be preferred because for Paul the revelation of the heavenly Messiah was of primary importance. Yet the apostle's use is far from consistent (*cf.* Rom. 1:1; 1 Cor. 1:1).

This idea of authority is intensified by the use of the expression *by the command of God*. Paul is more fond of saying 'by the will of God' (as in 2 Tim. 1:1), but he uses the present expression (*kat' epitagēn*) in Romans 16:26 to bring out the compulsion of the divine commission (see also 1 Cor. 7:6 and 2 Cor. 8:8). He can never, in fact, forget that he is a man under orders.

It is unusual for Paul to speak of *God our Saviour*, since, apart from the Pastorals, he always attributes the title to Christ. But here his mind dwells on the ultimate source of Christian salvation. The title is fashioned on a familiar Old Testament conception, which would spring naturally from the apostle's theological background. It would also have a contemporary significance in that the term *Saviour* (*sōtēr*) was used in the cult of emperor worship and was being applied to the infamous Nero. Perhaps an implied contrast may be found in the apostle's use of the possessive *our*. The omission of the article in the Greek may mean the word had by this time become an accepted Christian title.

The linking of *Christ Jesus our hope* to the former statement adds weight to the apostle's introduction and throws light on his theological position. The co-ordination of Father and Son as sources of the apostle's authority points to his conviction about the deity of Christ (*cf.* Simpson). The Greek word translated *hope* (*elpis*), used in a Christian sense, conveys an element of absolute certainty which is generally lacking in the modern use of the English word.

2. The apostle's description of Timothy as *my true son in the faith* (*gnēsios* means 'genuine, sincere') is striking evidence of the intimate Christian relationship between the two men. There was nothing spurious about Timothy's standing *in the faith*. While there is no article in the Greek phrase, which could therefore be translated 'in faith', it is preferable to interpret the phrase as referring to the gospel. Timothy stood in the same tradition as Paul himself. The father-son terminology to express the master-disciple relationship was widespread in contemporary society, especially in the mysteries (*cf.* Dibelius-Conzelmann). It took on new meaning, however, when related to the Christian faith.

It is interesting to note that Paul uses his fullest formula of salutation, adding to his usual *grace* and *peace* the idea of *mercy*. The same triad is found in Paul elsewhere only in 2 Timothy 1:2. As Bernard well expressed it, 'Even *grace* will not give *peace* to man, unless *mercy* accompany it; for man needs pardon for the past no less than strength for the future'. As in the opening verse, so here, the source of this triad of blessings is given as God and Christ (*from God the Father and Christ Jesus our Lord*). Christ is the mediator of all the blessings which the Father bestows.

B. THE CONTRAST BETWEEN THE GOSPEL AND ITS
COUNTERFEITS (1:3–11)

3. Paul's thoughts flow so rapidly that he forgets to reach the grammatical end of the sentence begun in this verse. NIV renders it *As I urged you . . . stay there in Ephesus*, which at least captures the sense if not the precise grammatical construction. It is not certain what force the Greek verb *parakaleō* should have here. Both NIV and RSV prefer the stronger meaning (*i.e. urged*), but it is not impossible that the gentler 'encouraged' might not fit the context better. The apostle recalls the commission already given to Timothy for the younger man's encouragement.

The reference to *Ephesus* need not imply that Paul had himself recently been there, since the Greek participle *poreuomenos* (present tense) may indicate that he left Timothy en route for Ephesus and charged him to *stay there*. It seems most likely that this occasion belongs to the period subsequent of the Acts history (see Introduction, pp. 22ff.), although there have been persuasive arguments put forward for allotting the incident within the Acts framework. The apostle's words suggest that there was some reluctance on Timothy's part to remain at Ephesus, which was one of the most important of the Asiatic churches, both strategically and culturally. His somewhat timid nature may well have shrunk from so onerous a task.

Timothy is now reminded that he is himself a man of authority. He has a definite commission to hold the false teachers in check, and it is evident that Paul expects him to take a strong line with them, as is shown by the verb translated *command (parangellō)*, a military term which means literally to pass commands from one to the other. *Not to teach false doctrines any longer* suggests that there was already in existence a recognized standard of Christian doctrine (see Introduction, pp. 45ff.). These words give a timely warning to our modern age against the quest for novelties in Christian teaching.

4. The false teaching is next characterized as *myths* and *endless genealogies*. Nothing could be farther removed from the serious content of the gospel. The irrelevance of the spurious doctrine is in direct contrast to the edification which should result from true Christian teaching.

Many scholars see in *genealogies* a clear reference to second-century gnostic emanations. But there seem stronger reasons to suppose that the anonymous false teachers were members of a sect attracted by the more speculative aspects of Judaism. In Titus 1:14, where the same word *myths* (*mythoi*) occurs, they are described as Jewish, and there is a strong presumption that Paul has the same kind of people in mind here. An example of the way in which Jewish delight in such speculation led to the compilation of mythical histories based on the Old Testament is found in the Jewish book of Jubilees.[1] It was inevitable that methods so unrestrained (*endless, aperantos,* may be understood in this sense) would lead to further *controversies,* and the whole unprofitable business impressed the apostle with its utter futility. No wonder he contrasts it with *God's work – which is by faith.* The Greek word translated *work* (*oikonomia*) properly means 'the office of stewardship' (*e.g.* the position held by the manager of an estate) but came to be used in the more general sense of 'administration', which is the general Pauline use (*cf.* 1 Cor. 9:17; Eph. 3:2, 9). There is a contrast here between two activities, not two world views. Paul has just stressed the pointlessness of the false teaching and now contrasts this with the discipline which belongs to faith. RSV renders the phrase 'the divine training', which captures some idea of the discipline needed for God's work.

5. The *command* or injunction (again a military term *parangelia* is used) could possibly indicate the Mosaic Law, in which case the implication would be that these false teachers had misconceived its true purpose; but it is more likely that the Christian's moral obligations are in mind. By *the goal of this command* is meant its purpose (RSV has 'the aim of our charge'). Certainly for the Christian the goal of all exhortations in practical affairs is *love,* which was in all probability conspicuously lacking in these speculative reasoners, whose main purpose was their own intellectual satisfaction.

---

[1] *Cf.* Dibelius-Conzelmann and Jeremias *ad loc.*

The apostle then makes clear the source of this love. The preposition *ek*, which is translated *from*, forcibly draws attention to its origin in a threefold aspect.

1. *A pure heart.* This is a fundamental requisite. Taken over from the Old Testament, the word *heart* stands for the totality of man's moral affections, and without purity there, nobility of character is clearly impossible. Jesus reserved a special promise for the pure in heart (Mt. 5:8) and spoke of the pruning of the vine as an illustration of the cleansing of believers through the word (Jn. 15:3).

2. *A good conscience.* The Greek word for *conscience* (*syneidēsis*) indicates literally 'joint knowledge', and came to be used of the facility to distinguish between right and wrong. The right operation of this facility was given special prominence in Paul's theology. By way of contrast, Timothy is later reminded that apostasizers are those whose consciences are branded (1 Tim. 4:2). This conscience-concept was well known in Hellenistic culture, but acquired under Christian usage a broader application (*cf.* Simpson).

3. *A sincere faith.* Faith which is merely a pretence without solid foundation may well have been evident in the false teachers. What was important was the genuineness of what was professed.

This triad of sources for love has caused some scholars to question the authenticity of the passage, on the grounds that for Paul faith was sufficient of itself. While it may be true that no exact parallel to this use of faith is extant in Paul's writings, there is no reason to doubt that Paul would have endorsed the statement that love proceeds from faith. In his great hymn of love, he links love with faith and hope, although subordinating the latter two to the former (1 Cor. 13:13). In any case, his use of faith there is closely allied to the use here.

6. This Christian triad has clearly been neglected by certain people. They *have wandered away* and *turned*. The two vivid verbs imply that having missed the mark (*astocheō*), they inevitably turned off course (*ektrepō*). By losing their Christian bearings they drifted into trackless waste, for life without this triad of virtues not only lacks love, but produces no more than meaningless chatter. The word translated *meaningless talk* (*mataiologia*) sums up the irrelevance which formed one of the main features of the false teaching.

7. The desire to be *teachers of the law* is a mark of the Jewish character of these men, whose main interest seems to have been to rival contemporary Rabbinical exegesis, rather than to expound the gospel. Paul brings a scathing indictment against instructors so unfitted for their task; they are both unintelligent and ignorant. They have no grasp of the sacred content of the text, and when they speak, their words are as meaningless to themselves as to others. The profundities of Christian truth must never become muffled in meaningless subtleties, a fault which those who indulge in allegorical interpretations do not always succeed in avoiding.

8. The mention of the law in verse 7 leads the apostle to discuss the law and its purpose. He grants that it possesses certain useful functions when used *properly* (*nomimōs*, a word which strictly means 'lawfully'). This adverb, found only here and in 1 Timothy 2:5 in the New Testament, furnished the key to the statement concerning the law. The law must be restricted to its primary purpose – the restraint of evil-doing. In this sense it may be described as *good*, and it is significant that the Greek word used is *kalos* rather than *agathos*, since the former draws attention, not only to excellence of intrinsic quality, but also to beauty of outward form. The apostle is far from decrying the noble precepts of the Mosaic law, but is emphatically opposing the futilities of much Pentateuchal speculation. He goes on, in fact, to describe the various classes for whom the law is especially designed.

A question arises whether this approach to the law is irreconcilable with Paul's doctrine. It has been maintained that the statement is at variance with 2 Timothy 3:16–17. But a comparison with Romans 7:12, 16 would suggest that the approach here does not differ from Paul, as Jeremias has pointed out. Indeed, some scholars opposed to Pauline authorship see the addition of the words *if a man uses it properly* as showing an imperfect grasp of Pauline thought (*cf.* Hanson). The word translated *properly* (*nomimōs*) is the normal word for Jewish observance of the law (Spicq), and this is thought to conflict with Paul's view that such observance of the law is impossible. But Jeremias' opinion seems more valid.

9–10. The NIV in verse 9 follows the Greek in omitting the article before *law*, which makes it more general, but in view of the use of the article in verse 8, it seems right to suppose the Mosaic law is in mind. Paul's proposition is stated both negatively and positively. Negatively, law has little relevance for law-abiding people. When Paul outlines the positive function of the law he appears, at first sight, to restrict himself to gross evil-doers. Yet in enumerating extreme examples, the apostle indicates the limit of the law's restraining and condemnatory purposes. Lesser crimes are naturally included within these limits. There is significance in the order: first offences against God, then crimes against fellow-men as listed in the ten commandments.

It is further significant that nothing in this list corresponds with the law's condemnation of covetousness; this has seemed a difficulty to some since Paul appealed to it in Romans 7:7 when referring to his own experience of the law. But his purpose here is very different for he is obviously concerned with the external function of the law in the restraint of evil-doers. There is no necessity to suppose that this statement excludes every other function of the law. Since its supersession by the gospel, the Decalogue still retains its value as an external instrument of justice, but for 'good men' it can no longer apply as a positive standard of conduct. RSV has 'just' rather than good and this is the more literal meaning of *dikaios*. The law is designed for *lawbreakers* who ignore the law; for *rebels*, who are not amenable to discipline; for the *ungodly* who have no reverence for God; for the *sinful* who oppose him; and for the *unholy and irreligious* who deny sacred things.

The reference to *those who kill their fathers or mothers* should perhaps be understood as describing smiters of parents, an extreme violation of the fifth commandment. The separate reference to *murderers* is to general manslayers. *Adulterers and perverts* are similarly intended as extreme violations of the command not to commit adultery. The latter word could well refer to homosexuals, since certainly a century later there are known to have been many in Ephesus.

It may sound strange to find *slave traders* linked with *liars and perjurers* at the end of this list. The first word could be understood as 'kidnappers' (as RSV), in which case it would have a more modern ring about it. But the reference to those whose word cannot be trusted is a reminder that the law has to do with words as well as deeds. The list of offences is finally rounded off with a proviso for *whatever else is contrary to the sound doctrine*, which suggests the writer regards the offences mentioned as a particular but not exhaustive selection. But why conclude with this reference to *sound doctrine* when the preceding list is concerned with law. Right doctrine is important in the Pastorals and is more frequent there than elsewhere in the New Testament. The switch to doctrine suggests a transference of thought from teaching designed for criminals to teaching intended as the normal rule of life. Hence the description of the doctrine as *sound (hygiainousa)*, a word which frequently occurs in the Pastorals but nowhere else. It denotes the wholesomeness or healthiness of true Christian teaching. The difference between law and doctrine here may be summed up as the difference between medicine and health-giving food. However unexpected, the conclusion of the list shows the ascendancy of the gospel and leads the apostle to make a further statement about it.

11. This verse sums up the section from verse 8 onwards. Paul has not been speaking about the law according to his own opinion but about what *conforms to the glorious gospel*. The Greek here literally means 'the gospel of the glory of the blessed God', which is more expressive than the NIV translation (with AV and RSV), because it connects the glory with the central figure of the drama rather than to the drama itself. The same word is found as a genitive of content in 2 Corinthians 4:4–6, where it describes the gospel as a manifestation of the glory of God in the face of Jesus Christ.

The word *blessed* is applied to God only here and in 6:15, but the usage is frequent in Philo. It describes God not as the object of blessing, but as experiencing within himself the perfection of bliss. Such a thought accords well with the splendour which he radiates through the gospel.

The phrase *which he entrusted to me* applied to the gospel is characteristically Pauline (*cf.* 1 Cor. 9:17; Gal. 2:7). The agent, though unexpressed, must clearly be God.

C. THE APOSTLE'S PERSONAL EXPERIENCE OF THE GOSPEL (1:12–17)

This section appears to be a digression, but is nevertheless necessary to the argument. Paul is appealing to his own experience as evidence of the transforming power of God. If God can call and equip a man like Paul who at one time was so violently opposed to the gospel, is there any limit to that power? By a natural association of ideas, the thought of the magnitude of the gospel committed to him (verse 11) leads the apostle to marvel at his own experience of God's enabling power.

12. The sudden outburst of thanksgiving which now follows is thoroughly typical of Paul, who never ceased to marvel at the gospel. The enabling power of God is a constant theme of his. The aorist tense of the participle (*endynamōsanti*) translated *who has given me strength* indicates a past reality. In an alternative but less well attested reading the present participle (*endynamounti*) is used and this would lay emphasis on Christ as the constant enabler (*cf.* Phil. 4:13). Both readings express a profound truth, but since Paul is here in reminiscent mood, the past tense, in addition to being the better attested, accords better with the context.

The apostle next expresses the reason for his thankfulness, *i.e.* that he was accounted *faithful*, which should here be understood in the sense of 'trustworthy'. That he is making this statement without boasting is evident from the words *appointing me to his service* (*diakonia*) and from the self-revelations which follow. The Greek term used here, which is a favourite Pauline expression, lends support for an early date for the Pastorals, since in second-century times the risk of confusion with the established order of deacons would make the term inapplicable to an apostle.

The expression *appointing me to his service* shows how deeply impressed Paul is with the fact that he had in no way appointed himself. He is stressing the divine initiative, which provided him with the ground of assurance throughout his varied service (*cf.* 1 Cor. 12:28).

13. It is not surprising that Paul's reminiscences lead him to consider his pre-Christian state, for his reflections on Christ's enabling power only magnified his own sense of unworthiness. His self-condemnatory description of himself as *blasphemer* and *persecutor* must, therefore, be given full force. When he adds that he was *a violent man* he is no doubt thinking of the times he hounded the Christians out of their homes in a thoroughly objectionable way. Yet such a man as this *was shown mercy!* The use here of the passive form of the verb is characteristic of Paul (Rom. 11:30–31; 1 Cor. 7:25; 2 Cor. 4:1), whose previous state of wretchedness compelled him to acknowledge the sovereign character of God's merciful provision. But the apostle perceives a reason for the mercy. It was, he says, *because I acted in ignorance.* Unlike the wilful ignorance which increases the guilt (*cf.* Rom. 10:3), Paul's ignorance was linked with a *pure conscience* (2 Tim. 1:3), marred only by *unbelief*. His misguided pre-Christian career had been the object of pity rather than judgment in the sight of God, who recognized in Saul of Tarsus a servant of mighty potential when once he was enlightened.

14. Paul could never write for long without bringing in *The grace of our Lord*. For him it was no mere abstract concept, but an operative and formative force dominating both thought and action. His words here recall those of Romans 5:20, for in both cases the verbs used are compounded with the preposition *hyper* in an attempt to express the super-abundance of divine grace. A difficulty is felt by some scholars over the way the Christian qualities are combined in this verse. It has been suggested that Paul would not have described faith and love as separate from grace and in addition to it or have regarded faith as no more than one of the results of conversion. Many scholars think the use of Pauline language is vague. But there is no need to suppose that any un-Pauline distinction between *grace* and *faith* and *love* finds expression in this verse. In fact, the preposition *meta* (*with*) indicates the closest connection between the grace of God and the two co-ordinate Christian virtues. Paul would readily agree that apart from the operation of divine grace, love and faith would be impossible, yet without the latter there would be no evidence of the former. Nor is there substance in the opinion that grace is here used as 'power' as distinct from 'pure favour' (*cf.* Rom. 5:20), since the word is clearly an enlargement of the mercy mentioned in verse 13. The same virtues, faith and love, qualified by the words in *Christ Jesus* are found in 2 Timothy 1:13. (See note there.)

15. The striking formula, *Here is a trustworthy saying*, meets us nowhere else in the New Testament apart from four other occurrences in the Pastorals. This is alleged to present a problem for Pauline authenticity, but there is no reason to suppose that Paul could not, or would not, have appealed to such sayings.[1] In the present context he seems to be citing, in rhythmical form, a statement current in the churches and acknowledged as *trustworthy*. It may seem strange that he should use the formula when writing to Timothy, but he probably wishes to remind his younger associate of the fundamental character of the statement to which he is about to appeal.

The additional words *that deserves full acceptance* are found only here and in 4:9 in the New Testament, but became a regular formula in the Greek vernacular (see M & M on *apodochē*).

Christ Jesus came into the world to save sinners epitomizes the cardinal fact of Christian truth. It points to the heart of the gospel. The emphasis on the incarnation and its purpose is more Johannine than Pauline, and this adds further weight to the view that Paul is here quoting a current statement of the gospel. Because of its content the words may perhaps be directly traceable to the words of Jesus, contained in the source which formed the basis of the fourth gospel.

Paul never got away from the fact that Christian salvation

[1]See my Tyndale monograph, *The Pastoral Epistles and the Mind of Paul*, pp. 18–21.

was intended for *sinners*, and the more he increased his grasp of the magnitude of God's grace, the more he deepened the consciousness of his own naturally sinful state, until he could write *of whom I am the worst* (the Greek word *prōtos* is used, meaning 'chief'). Some have seen this as over-dramatic, but there is no reason why it cannot be regarded as a mark of sincerest humility. Paul sees himself in the vanguard of those whose sins have called forth the resources of God's mercy. It is Paul's custom to use superlatives of himself, whether ranking himself the least of the apostles (1 Cor. 15:9) or less than the least of all saints (Eph. 3:8) or chief of sinners. Paul's self-abasement is not morbid, any more than John Bunyan was morbid when writing his *Grace Abounding to the Chief of Sinners*.

16. The thought of having received mercy is repeated from verse 13, but here the specific purpose is given. Paul conceives of his own striking case as a special example of what Christ could do with other human lives. Mercy shown to what Paul conceives as the worst of sinners must provide a superlative example for subsequent centuries, especially as Paul's case had shown what he calls Christ's *unlimited patience*. That patience has never ceased towards sinners.

The Greek word rendered *example* (*hypotypōsis*) may be understood either as an outline sketch of an artist, or as a word-illustration expressing an author's burning purpose (*cf.* Simpson). In a sublime sense Paul's experience was to serve as a compelling example to countless numbers *who would believe on him* (*i.e.* Christ). The construction (*epi* with the dative) after the verb translated *believe* indicates that Christ is the firm basis of faith. Such unshakeable assurance serves not only in this life but in eternity.

17. A typical Pauline doxology results from these moving reflections on the mercies of God. New features not found in earlier examples admittedly appear, but there is the same all-absorbing adoration of God and the same sense of the majesty of God. Nowhere else does Paul use the phrase *King eternal* (RSV, 'King of the ages'), which occurs in fact only in Tobit 13:6, 10 and Revelation 15:3 in the Greek Bible. It was probably current in Jewish circles and springs out of the Jewish view of the two ages, the age that is and the age to come. God was King in both spheres, and indeed of the 'ages of the ages' as the phrase *for ever and ever* suggests.

The ascription *immortal* appears to be more Hellenistic than Jewish, yet Romans 1:23 supplies a Pauline parallel. Similarly the adjective *invisible* applied to God finds a Pauline parallel in Colossians 1:15. There seems little doubt that the reading *the only God* is correct, rather than 'the only wise God' as in AV; the adjective 'wise' has been borrowed from Romans 16:27. The omission of the adjective here provides a more emphatic expression of Jewish monotheism.

D. THE APOSTLE'S CHARGE TO TIMOTHY (1:18–20)

These verses are a resumption of verses 3–5, and state precisely the purpose of the apostle's writing.

18. Paul uses the same word *parangelia* to indicate the *instruction* (RSV, 'charge') given to Timothy as he used in verse 5 to denote the Christian injunction to love. As often in military contexts (*e.g.* in Xenophon and Polybius) it conveys a sense of urgent obligation. Timothy is solemnly reminded that the ministry is not a matter to be trifled with, but an order from the commander-in-chief. It is significant that the word *give* (which translates the verb *paratithēmi*), which describes the entrusting of the charge to Timothy, is also used in 2 Timothy 2:2 of Timothy passing it on to others.

In keeping with the prophecies once made about you must be understood in the sense of predictions in some way granted to Paul concerning Timothy before his call to the ministry. It may be parallel to those given to the Antiochene church regarding the missionary vocation of Paul and Barnabas. In any case the words testify not only to the complete confidence of Paul that Timothy was God's choice as his successor, but to the endorsement of that choice by the Christian communities with which Timothy was associated.

Paul continues the military language, in the words *fight the good fight*, as he urges his young lieutenant to follow the several prophecies confirming his calling. The RSV interpretation, 'inspired by them', draws attention to the inspirational effect of the prophetic words concerning Timothy. Timothy would be able to gain strength from the fact that his calling was of God.

19. Whereas in Ephesians 6:10–17 Paul describes in detail the Christian's armour, he confines himself here to two items of equipment which embrace the fundamental aspects of doctrine and practice. *Faith and a good conscience* are three times joined together in this Epistle (*cf.* 1:5 and 3:9), showing the inseparable connection between faith and morals. We need not restrict *faith* here to 'right belief' as some scholars suggest, although this aspect is undoubtedly included. It appears to epitomize the spiritual side of the Christian warrior's armour.

In the next clause, NIV has *rejected these*, but the Greek relative is singular and refers directly to conscience and RSV 'rejecting conscience' is therefore to be preferred. The verb is a strong one (*apōtheō*), implying a violent and deliberate rejection. Since a nautical image is introduced it is possible that Paul is thinking of conscience as a stabilizing factor which when rejected renders the ship unstable. Those who ignore conscience will continue to make shipwreck of *their faith*, as some of these early Christians did.

20. *Hymenaeus* (mentioned again in 2 Tim. 2:17) and *Alexander* are cited as examples of shipwrecked believers. As to the identity of Alexander, the details available are insufficient to conclude that he is the same Alexander mentioned in Acts 19:33 and 2 Timothy 4:14. Whoever these men were their case called for strong disciplinary action, described in the figurative words *handed over to Satan*. The same expression is used in 1 Corinthians 5:5 and both cases must be understood in the same way. If the 1 Corinthians passage is interpreted as implying excommunication, Paul means no more than that they are put out of the church into Satan's province (*i.e.* the non-Christian world). This solution is rejected by some who feel that excommunication would heighten blasphemy rather than deter it and that the words must therefore imply some kind of physical disaster. The instances in Acts 5:1–11 and 13:11 of discipline having physical results and the more obscure allusion in 1 Corinthians 11:30 support the latter idea, but a combination of both may be the correct view. Probably Hymenaeus and Alexander should be regarded as exceptional cases.

The concluding clause *to be taught not to blaspheme* shows clearly that the purpose was remedial and not merely punitive. However stringent the process the motive was mercy, and whenever ecclesiastical discipline has departed from this purpose of restoration, its harshness has proved a barrier to progress. But this is no reason for dispensing with discipline entirely, a failing which frequently characterizes our modern churches.

II. WORSHIP AND ORDER IN THE CHURCH (2:1–4:16)

The main business of the Epistle now begins, and in the opening words of this section Paul appears to continue the theme of 1:3. He deals with several subjects directly concerned with the organization of the church.

A. THE IMPORTANCE AND SCOPE OF PUBLIC PRAYER (2:1–8)

1. The words *first of all* relate not to primacy of time but primacy of importance. It is essential, at the outset, to ensure the noblest approach to public worship. While the verb translated *urge* (*parakaleō*) can bear the sense 'entreat' or 'encourage', the former meaning is probably intended in view of its association with the strong verb *parangellō* (command) in 1:3.

It is not possible to distinguish precisely the meanings covered by the four words here used for prayer. The first three have so much in common that little useful purpose is served in defining their respective meanings; yet there may be significance in the fact that *requests* (*deēseis*) brings out a clearer sense of need than *prayers* (*proseuchai*), which represents the more general word for prayer (in the New Testament used only of prayers to God), while intercession (*enteuxeis*) is a regular term for petition to a superior. The very variety of terms serves to emphasize the richness of this spiritual exercise. *Thanksgiving*, as in Paul's earlier Epistles, is regarded as an integral part of prayer, yet it is an element which has been too often in the background in modern Christian devotions. The reminder that prayer is *for everyone* is timely in view of the temptation to confine our prayers to our own narrow interests. The wider the subjects for prayer the larger becomes the vision of the soul that prays.

2. Examples of the universal scope of prayer are limited to prayer for the ruling classes, perhaps because of the tendency for Christians to leave these out of their devotions, especially when rulers are openly hostile. The plural *kings* need not imply a time when co-emperors shared the imperial throne, for a general principle is being stated, applicable at all times. The Christian attitude towards the State is of utmost importance. Whether the civil authorities are perverted or not they must be made the subjects for prayer, for Christian citizens may in this way influence the course of national affairs, a fact often forgotten except in times of special crisis.

The purpose, rather than the content, of such prayer is now stated. *That we may live peaceful and quiet lives* presupposes that the government can achieve conditions of peace and security, enabling the Christian and his fellow-men to pursue their own lives. Under some governments this could not be guaranteed. The twin synonyms *ēremos* (*peaceful*) and *hēsychios* (*quiet*) are virtually interchangeable (RSV has translated in the reverse order). They are linked here to emphasize the importance of calmness and serenity in social affairs.

The next two words denote the type of character that can best be developed in an atmosphere of calm. The first, *godliness* (*eusebeia*), is a general description of religious devotion, while the second, *holiness* (*semnotēs*), denotes the Christian's dignity of demeanour, or seriousness of purpose. The second word is rendered 'respectful' by RSV and this brings out somewhat better the real meaning. Barrett suggests 'high standards of morality'. For their fullest expression, both these qualities require conditions of external peace, although they may often be intensified in circumstances of stress.

3. *This is good* would appear to connect with verse 1, and to refer to the idea of universal prayer. The two parts of this verse should be taken separately: (a) universal prayer is *good*; (b) it *pleases God*. It is the latter proposition that presents the ultimate standard for all Christian worship.

The title *God our Saviour*, which has already been used in 1:1, has special significance here, as it relates prayer for all men to the saving character of God. There is point in praying on behalf of all men to One whose nature it is to save, a thought developed in the next verse.

4. The statement *who wants all men to be saved* became a centre of controversy between the Calvinists and the Arminians of the seventeenth century, owing to the implied universalism of the words. It has been suggested that the verb used (*thelō*, 'desire') represents the general purpose of God as distinct from a single volition (Bernard). If so it would speak of God's mercy towards all types of people, without distinction of race, colour, condition or status. But many scholars, especially those who reject Pauline authorship (*cf.* Hanson), argue that the words imply salvation (*i.e.* that every single person will be saved). There may have been a tendency towards exclusiveness on the part of some, who were influenced perhaps by the same urge that dróve the later Gnostics into their own exclusive circles of initiates, and Paul, to provide an antidote, may here be stressing God's universal compassion. These words fairly represent the magnanimity of the divine benevolence. The words *all men* must be linked with the 'all' of verse 1. Intercession for all men could be justified only on the ground of God's willingness to save all (*cf.* Jeremias).

Another line of interpretation is to understand the verb 'save' in its weaker sense of 'preserve' or 'protect'. It is possible to understand the prayer as being a request that all should be preserved from lawless misrule (*cf.* Simpson). But the passage as a whole seems too theological to be taken in this sense, and the concluding part of the verse, *to come to a knowledge of the truth*, accords better with spiritual salvation than natural preservation, unless it means that peaceful conditions assist the propagation of the gospel.

The phrase *knowledge of the truth* is reminiscent of John and is not found in Paul outside the Pastorals. It should be understood as the whole revelation of God in Christ, to know which must be the climax of Christian salvation.

5. There are different opinions over whether this verse is a quotation from another source or whether it is the writer's own statement. Because the idea of a mediator is prominent in the Epistle to the Hebrews, it has been suggested that this statement has been influenced by that Epistle. But Paul himself would certainly have agreed with both statements in this verse. He reasoned from the unity of God to the universalism of his mission in answering Jewish exclusivism in Romans 3:29-30. Here the appeal to the doctrine of the unity of God, common to both Judaism and Christianity, links up with the divine desire that all should come to a knowledge of the truth. The second part of the verse adds an exclusively Christian element. The doctrine of Christ as *mediator* is more fully expounded in the Epistle to the Hebrews in connection with the covenant. That no bond between God and man was possible apart from Christ Jesus is also fundamental to Paul's thought. It is because a mediator must be representative that the humanity of Christ (*the man Christ Jesus*) is also brought into prominence.

6. Thinking of Christ as mediator leads Paul to make a more precise declaration regarding the atonement. The mention of *ransom* (*antilytron*) echoes the words of Jesus, 'the Son of Man did not come to be served, but to serve, and to give his life as a ransom (*lytron*) for many' (Mk. 10:45). Here there is a combination of two prepositions which both bring out the fact that Christ was doing something for others. The *anti* in the noun means 'instead of', and the *hyper* following the verb means 'on behalf of' (although it should be noted that *hyper* can in some contexts sustain the meaning 'instead of'). Christ is pictured as an 'exchange price' on behalf of and in the place of *all*, on the grounds of which freedom may be granted. Yet not all enjoy that freedom. The ransom, it is true, has infinite value, but the benefits require appropriation. The apostle is implying here that since the ransom is adequate for all, God must desire the salvation of all.

The precise meaning of the last phrase, *the testimony given in its proper time*, is obscure owing to its compressed character. Since the words follow immediately the profound statement about Christ's saving work, it is best to assume that 'the testimony' intended is God's act in sending his Son at the appointed time (*cf.* Gal. 4:4).

7. The opening words may be paraphrased, 'To spread the testimony I was appointed *a herald* and *an apostle*'. Paul had not appointed himself to so great and hazardous a task; it was laid upon him by God (*cf.* 2 Tim. 1:11). The emphatic *I* expresses the sense of personal wonder. But why need Timothy be reminded of the divine character of Paul's vocation? Surely of all people he should have been well aware of it? And why the strong asseveration, *I am telling the truth, I am not lying*? Many scholars find genuine difficulty in believing that Paul would ever have expressed himself in this manner to the real Timothy, but strong asseverations of this nature may be paralleled elsewhere in Paul's writings (Rom. 9:1; 2 Cor. 11:31; Gal. 1:20). Admittedly these parallels were written in circumstances where Paul's authority had been disputed by some, and this is not the case with Timothy. But if the Pastorals are regarded as semi-public it may well have been necessary for Timothy to possess the strongest possible assertion of Paul's true apostleship to combat some at Ephesus who denied it (*cf.* Jeremias). Timothy's own commission would clearly be implicated in the authenticity of his predecessor's call. Moreover, some strong assertion is not here out of place since the veracity of the Gentile mission was at stake.

A question arises whether this assertion would not be better linked with the following rather than the preceding words. If so, veracity would be given to Paul's claim to be especially appointed *a teacher to the Gentiles* rather than to his claim to apostleship. But the two claims are inseparable. The words *the true faith* represent two words in the Greek, *pistis* (*faith*) and *alētheia* (*truth*), which show the sphere of the teaching. They embrace both the spirit of the teacher and the content of the message, although the latter seems the more prominent.

8. Paul now resumes the subject of prayer. The authority which he has just vindicated shines out in the opening verb *I want* (*boulomai*), which may be regarded almost as a command. Paul is expressing more than a passing desire. For him prayer was a matter of great importance.

Presumably the singling out here of *men* as those who should pray must be taken in conjunction with what is afterwards said about women (verse 9). In using the phrase *everywhere* (lit. 'in every place'), Paul may be echoing Malachi 1:10–11 (*cf.* Brox), but the phrase is typically Pauline (*cf.* 1 Cor. 1:2; 2 Cor. 2:14; 1 Thes. 1:8), while the practice of lifting up *hands* was common among Jews and pagans as well as Christians when in the attitude of prayer (*cf.* Lock). Although constant prayer is here regarded as a matter of Christian obligation, the gesture mentioned is incidental to the qualifying adjective *holy*. Worshippers with hands stained by unworthy deeds must first be cleansed before approaching God in prayer (*cf.* Ps. 26:6). The closing words of this verse *without anger or disputing* show that wrong attitudes of mind are as alien to the holy place of prayer as sullied hands. Not merely pure actions but pure motives are essential in Christian worship.

B. THE STATUS AND DEMEANOUR OF CHRISTIAN WOMEN (2:9–15)

9. Grammatically this section continues the injunction in verse 8, *i.e.* it gives observations on women's conduct in public prayer. But it seems most unlikely that Paul intends to restrict himself in this way, for no clear distinction can be drawn between what is fitting for public worship and what is fitting at other times. The advice given seems to be general and we must therefore suppose that Paul turned from his immediate purpose in order to make wider observations about women's demeanour.

The word translated *dress* (*katastolē*) probably refers to demeanour as well as attire. The emphasis falls on the modesty accompanying the dress. Only orderly or decent conduct accords with the spirit of Christian worship. This reflects a right attitude of mind, for Paul was shrewd enough to know that a woman's dress is a mirror of her mind. He seems to be ruling out any outward ostentation as not being in keeping with a prayerful and devout approach.

The words *with decency and propriety* are added as an explanation of acceptable dress. Again it is a question of dignity and seriousness of purpose, as opposed to levity and frivolity. Paul leaves no doubt as to what he means by adding a list of prohibitions relating to outward adornments.

The plaiting of the hair was a usual feature of Jewish women's hairstyle, and in the more elaborate types the plaits were fastened with ribbons and bows (*cf.* Strack-Billerbeck). Paul is not of course speaking against a reasonable style of hairdressing, but against that which is designed for ostentatious adornment and which would be inappropriate in Christian women. A similar principle applies to the use of costly jewellery or clothing. Any form of ostentation would tend to detract from the main purpose of worship.

10. Paul hastens to add that women are not denied all adornment, but the greatest asset a woman possesses is a devout and godly life. He makes it clear that he speaks only for Christian women, those *who profess to worship God* and whose standards must always be higher than those making no such profession. There is particular stress here, as so often elsewhere in the Pastorals on the necessity of *good deeds*, probably because current speculations tended to divorce doctrine and practice. The idea of good works as an adornment is suggestive, for a life of selfless devotion to others is regarded as an enhancement of the person. A woman's adornment, in short, lies not in what she herself puts on, but in the loving service she gives out.

11. That women should *learn in quietness* is in full accord with 1 Corinthians 14:34–35, although in the latter case the reference is specifically to public worship. It may be that Paul's present stricture is to be taken with the same proviso, and was designed to curb the tendencies of newly emancipated Christian women to abuse their new-found freedom by indecorously lording it over men. Such excesses would bring disrepute on the whole community, as had probably happened at Corinth, and called for firm handling. When taking part in public worship the woman's share is to *learn*, or at least to 'listen quietly' (Moffatt). The equality of the sexes, so much in the forefront of modern thought, received little recognition in ancient times. Not only was the prevailing Greek attitude against it, but Hebrew thought was equally unsympathetic.[1] The *full submission* (*en pasēi hypotagēi*) mentioned by Paul relates primarily to public worship as it was then enacted, and reserve must be exercised in deducing universal principles from particular cases. The idea, however, of woman's subjection is not only engrained in the conviction of the mass of mankind (which would not in itself, of course, be a justification for it), but also appears to be inherent in the divine constitution of the human race. Paul mentions this latter aspect in verse 13.

12. A woman is apparently encouraged to learn yet not allowed *to teach*. There may have been local reasons for this prohibition of which we know nothing. It is noteworthy that no such specific injunction is found in 1 Corinthians, although 1 Corinthians 14:34–35 forbids a woman to be heard in church. If the present prohibition is restricted to public teaching (as seems most probable) it accords perfectly with the 1 Corinthians passage. Paul cannot be accused of being a woman-hater, as is sometimes alleged, on the strength of this evidence, since he acknowledges some women among his own fellow-workers, such as Priscilla (Rom. 16:3–5) and Euodias and Syntyche (Phil. 4:2–3). The prohibition may have been due to the greater facility with which contemporary women were falling under the influence of imposters (*cf.* Falconer). A similar idea is that the tendency among later Gnostics to ignore the differences between men and women is being combated (*cf.* Brox), but this tendency may have had much earlier roots in the first century.

Rabbinic prohibitions were much more severe than the Christian prohibitions, since a woman, although theoretically permitted to read the Torah in public, was in practice not allowed to teach even small children.[2] The teaching of Christian doctrine seems to be confined by Paul to the male sex, and this has been

---

[1] *Cf.* Strack–Billerbeck, *Kommentar zum Neuen Testament aus Talmud und Midrasch* (1922–61), vol. 3, pp. 428ff.

[2] *Cf.* Strack-Billerbeck, *op. cit.*, vol. 3, p. 467.

the almost invariable practice in the subsequent history of the church. But it must not be overlooked that Paul acknowledged that Timothy had been taught the Scriptures from infancy and this would most naturally have been from his mother since his father was a Greek (*cf.* 2 Tim. 1:5; 3:15). Moreover in the modern missionary movement women have all too often had to take on the role of teacher in the absence of male colleagues. It may be possible to regard verse 12 as a relative rather than absolute prohibition if it is interpreted in the light of verse 14. Eve had sought to instruct Adam with insufficient grasp of the issues. Was Paul, in fact, saying that no woman should teach without first taking time to learn, in view of the fact that women had had no opportunity to be taught?

The word rendered *to have authority* (*authenteō*) means 'to have the mastery of' or more colloquially 'lord it over'. In public meetings Christian women must refrain from laying down the law to men and hence are enjoined to silence. It may be that Paul has mainly in mind married women and that *man* should be here understood as 'husband', although this would not be so relevant if church meetings are mainly in view. Indeed, the concluding injunction to silence could not apply to the Christian home and the whole verse must therefore relate to the assembly.

13. In 1 Corinthians 11:9, Paul had already made use of the argument that the priority of man's creation places him in a position of advantage over woman. The assumption seems to be that the original creation, with the Creator's own imprimatur upon it, must set a precedent for determining the true order of the sexes. Yet chronological order alone cannot in this case be regarded as significant since Adam was created after the animals and was nevertheless given dominion over them. The point here is that mankind consisted of a pair (Adam and Eve). Eve was intended as a companion to Adam. Their relationship is not to be considered as competitive but as complementary.

14. Another reason why woman must not teach man is now added. *Adam was not the one deceived; it was the woman.* Whereas Eve was deceived or beguiled, Adam sinned with his eyes open.

As Bengel says, 'The serpent deceived the woman; the woman did not deceive the man, but persuaded him' (Gn. 3:17). Logically this should make Adam more culpable, but Paul is concerned here primarily with the inadvisability of women teachers. Is it possible that since Eve is here specifically in mind, the point being made is that she misled Adam because she was not fully acquainted with the nature of the prohibited tree and was not therefore in a position to instruct Adam? If this view were tenable, it would suggest that Paul's prohibition of women teaching was conditioned by the background of the basic lack of education of women in the contemporary world. This would explain the emphasis on learning rather than teaching in verses 11 and 12. Such a suggestion has its appeal, although its interpretation of the Genesis passage is somewhat forced. Nevertheless, the question of women teachers cannot be divorced from the first-century disparity between men and women in the matter of education.

The concluding words about Eve that she became a sinner are a rendering of the Greek perfect tense which describes an abiding state. That Paul did not absolve Adam from responsibility in the entry of sin into the world is evident from Romans 5:12ff., where Eve is not even mentioned. Nevertheless Paul does mention the serpent's beguiling of Eve in a different context in 2 Corinthians 11:3, and therefore the present reference cannot be considered non-Pauline.[1]

15. From the particular allusion to Eve, Paul seems to pass to women in general, by declaring that *women will be kept safe through childbirth*, but the precise meaning of this is difficult to determine.

1. One interpretation is to understand the words as simply an encouragement to women in their natural sphere. This certainly accords well with the Genesis story which pronounces on Eve the doom that in sorrow she shall conceive, adding the assurance of safe delivery if the conditions are observed. It is probable

---

[1] Hanson, *Studies in the Pastoral Epistles*, pp. 65–77, claims that the Pastoral Epistles reflect the view that Eve's transgression was sexual sin. He thinks that 2 Cor. 11:1–3 suggests that Paul knew of but rejected the tradition that the serpent seduced Eve. But his claim that the

that the duty of child-bearing is emphasized to offset the unnatural abstinence advocated by the false teachers (cf. Jeremias).

2. An early church father, Chrysostom, took the verb in its spiritual sense, but to avoid the manifest absurdity of making the statement suggest that child-bearing is a woman's means of salvation, as if unmarried or childless women are *ipso facto* excluded, he understood the word 'child-bearing' as equivalent to child-nurture, and supplied 'children' as the subject of the verb 'continue'. But this would make women's salvation a matter of good works of a particular kind, and it is inconceivable that Paul meant this.

3. Another suggestion is that the words should read as in the RV 'she shall be saved by means of the child-bearing' (*i.e.* the Messiah, see also RSV mg.). For if that were the writer's intention he could hardly have chosen a more obscure or ambiguous way of saying it. If the birth of the Messiah was intended by the words 'child-bearing' it is strange that Paul did not add some further explanation. The Greek article could be generic, referring to child-birth in general, rather than definitive, referring to one particular instance. Nevertheless, if the whole passage is concentrating on Eve, it is possible that there is here an allusion to the promise of Genesis 3:15, to the promise of the one who would crush the serpent's head. If this were so, it would explain the reference to salvation in this verse. This suggestion is attractive in spite of the obscurity involved.

4. Another proposal is that the words should be taken to mean, 'she shall be saved, even though she must bear children', that is to say, she shall be linked with man in salvation, in spite of the penalty of her misdemeanour imposed on her. In that case the statement would be a kind of apology about what has just been said about women (cf. Scott). This view has the advantage of showing Christian women the way in which the original curse on their race is mitigated by Christian salvation, but it imposes an unnatural meaning on the Greek preposition *dia* (*through*).

Pastorals put a different construction on it is not borne out by a comparison between 2 Cor. 11:1–3 and I Tim. 2.

It is difficult to reach a conclusion, but the third suggestion is perhaps faced with less difficulties than the others.

In this verse the verbs change from the singular 'she shall be saved' (*sōthesetai*) to the plural *if they continue* (*meinōsin*). NIV gets over the difficulty by translating the former as generic and therefore plural (*women*). This means that the former part of the verse must be interpreted in the light of the latter part. This would make good sense of the verse, but some other interpretations have been given. Some suggest the plural refers to husband and wife (*cf.* Brox) or that the writer is quoting a separate source (*cf.* Hanson). But neither is convincing, for Paul is dealing here with the wife not the husband, and the source suggestion seems an act of desperation. It is much more likely that the plural refers to Eve and her successors.

There is a quartet of Christian virtues which women are expected to develop – *faith, love, and holiness with propriety*. These terms suggest the quality of Christian living expected from women. They imply a continuing state. The preposition *en* (*in*) points to the woman's sphere as being pre-eminently in the fostering of these Christian graces. The inclusion of holiness in the list demonstrates that such a quality is possible in the married state, and gives no support to the view that the celibate life is indispensable for the attainment of holiness as some sections of the church have supposed.[1]

C. THE QUALIFICATIONS OF CHURCH OFFICIALS (3:1–13)

i. *Overseers* (3:1–7)

1. There is some question whether the initial formula should be attached to the preceding words, as the statement about an overseer's office seems to lack sufficient theological weight. Since, however, in all probability this was a popular or proverbial saying, it is more likely to have referred to the office of an overseer than to the obscure allusion to Eve in the previous chapter. The opening formula, *Here is a trustworthy saying*, draws

---

[1] For a careful survey of 1 Tim. 2:8–15 as it affects the role of women, *cf.* M. J. Evans, *Woman in the Bible* (Exeter, 1983), pp. 100–107.

strong attention to the importance of the overseer's office. It may seem strange that such an underlining of the office was necessary, but it is best seen as Paul's way of bringing out the dignity of the office before introducing the particular qualifications required. The formula is used four times elsewhere in the Pastorals to introduce doctrinal sayings. The more practical use here is exceptional.

The statement, *If anyone sets his heart on being an overseer*, makes use of a word *episkopos*, which later came to be used for bishops (RSV has 'bishop'). In its original usage, at least until the time of Ignatius, it was restricted to those who exercised oversight in the local church. In the proverbial saying in this verse, the office referred to is quite general and might encompass any position, secular or ecclesiastical, where 'oversight' was necessary. There is no hint here or elsewhere in the Pastorals of the monarchical episcopacy so much lauded by Ignatius (see Introduction, pp. 31ff.). It is possible that Paul may here be referring to a proposition submitted for his adjudication (*cf.* Simpson). The aspirant to the office of overseer is said to desire *a noble task*. Wherever spiritual values have been rightly assessed there has always been a high estimate of the Christian ministry within the church. However, the nobility of the office has not always been recognized in the secular world.

The first verb used in this verse, *sets his heart on*, is *oregomai*, which means 'to stretch oneself out', hence 'to aspire to', but not in a bad sense; the second verb, *desires*, is *epithymeō*, which expresses strong desire. Clearly there must be a decisive sense of call.

2. With precise detail Paul proceeds to list the qualities required in an overseer. In Greek circles parallel lists were current for various occupations, such as kings, generals, midwives. The qualities required for Christian administrators are strikingly similar in many particulars. It is surprising that the required standards, particularly the negative ones (*e.g. not given to much wine, not quarrelsome*) do not lead us to suppose that the usual aspirant for office was of a particularly high quality, since no exceptional virtues are demanded. Yet this in itself accurately reflects the earliest state of the Christian church, when the majority of converts probably came from a background of low moral ideals.

There seems to be no special reason for the order in which the qualities are mentioned, a lack of system which also pervades Hellenistic lists. The first, *above reproach* (*anepilēmptos* means not only of good report but deservedly so), suitably stands in this position as being indispensable to the Christian minister's character. The next words, *the husband of but one wife*, have been variously interpreted. Some have taken the words to be a prohibition of second marriages (*e.g.* Tertullian), supported by the parallel phrase in verse 9. Others have suggested that they enforce monogamy for Christian ministers as opposed to the polygamy often practised in the contemporary heathen world. Yet no Christian, whether an overseer or not, would have been allowed to practice polygamy (*cf.* Bernard). The only occasion for such an injunction would be to exclude from office any who before their conversion had been polygamists. There is no need to suppose that Paul is making a general suggestion that any Christian man who had more than one wife before his conversion should put away all but one of his wives. If, as here, church leaders only are in mind, they would themselves be worthy examples for monogamous marriage and would serve as patterns for all new converts. Further acts of polygamy would be prevented among church members. A third suggestion is to regard the words in a more general way as meaning that an overseer must embrace a strict morality.

Among the next virtues listed, the first three are closely akin (*temperate, self-controlled, respectable*) and describe an orderly life. The fourth, *hospitable*, would have particular point in the early church, since without the willing hospitality of Christian people expansion would have been seriously retarded. The fifth quality, *able to teach*, involves mental skills. An overseer must certainly have the propensity to pass on advice and doctrine to enquirers. The church has been at its weakest when this basic requirement has been absent in its leaders.

3. Some of the qualities required amount to denials of extreme cases of excess: *e.g. not given to much wine* which combats drunkenness; *not violent* (*plēktēs* means 'a striker') which refutes lashing out irrationally; *not quarrelsome* which advises against contentiousness; *not a lover of money*, which warns against devotion to materialism. Such excesses are clearly quite alien to the Christian spirit, which is particularly exemplified by contrast in the sole positive quality mentioned in this verse, *i.e. gentle* (*epieikēs*). This portrays a spirit diametrically opposed to the negatives. It points to a considerateness and patient forbearance that would not tolerate any violent methods. It recurs in Titus 3:2 in the Pastorals. It is enjoined in Philippians 4:5. The cognate noun is used in 2 Corinthians 10:1 of Christ, who provides *par excellence* as example of this quality.

4–5. A most important principle, which has not always had the prominence it deserves, is next propounded. Any man unable to govern his children graciously and gravely by maintaining good discipline, is no man for government in the church. The principle is universal, for potential skill in a larger sphere can be indicated only by similar skill in a lesser sphere (*cf.* the rewards granted in the parable of the talents, Mt. 25:14ff.). The parallel between the church (in the expression *God's church* the local community is clearly in view) and the home brings impressive dignity to Christian home-life, a dignity as imperative in the twentieth century as in Paul's day. The apostle is here dealing with church officials in whom such worthy home-life is indispensable (*cf.* verse 12). Yet his words must not be taken to mean that the same standards are not expected of Christians generally (*cf.* Eph. 5 and 6 and Col. 3 and 4).

The Greek phrase rendered *with proper respect* (*meta pasēs semnotētos*) involves an element of dignity, yet without sternness. It is important for a leader to command the respect of his children as well as commanding the respect of others. The parenthetical question in verse 5 is in complete accord with Paul's style (*cf.* the three examples in 1 Cor. 14:7, 9, 16), giving rhetorical support to the point just made. The answer to the question is obvious. Lack of proper management of home-life disqualifies the person from leadership in the church. It is significant that the same verb used here for fathers ruling their children (*prohistēmi*) is used later for elders ruling the church (5:7; *cf.* also 1 Thes. 5:12 and Rom. 12:8).

6-7. The aspirant to office must not be *a recent convert* (*neophytos*). This expression is evidently used here of one recently converted. It is often supposed that such a proviso must indicate a late date for the Pastorals, since in a recently established church all the members would necessarily be recent converts. It is significant that this particular feature is omitted from the directions for the Cretan church, whose more recent establishment no doubt rendered it inappropriate. In itself this provision is most reasonable, as too rapid promotion may easily lead to excessive pride and instability. The Greek word translated *become conceited* (*typhoō*) means literally 'to wrap in smoke' (Abbott-Smith) and suggests that a new convert would find himself 'beclouded' (*cf.* Brox). Pride gives a false sense of altitude, making the subsequent *fall* all the greater.

It is not clear what is meant by the words *fall under the same judgment as the devil*. It may mean (a) the condemnation reserved for the devil, *i.e.* the judgment meted out for the sin of pride; or (b) the condemnation wrought by the devil, *i.e.* the condemnation brought about by the further intrigues of the devil when a man is once lured into his grasp through pride; or (c) the condemnation of the slanderer, taking *devil* in its original sense, and understanding by the phrase the malicious attacks to which an arrogant neophyte is subjected as a result of his vanity. The use of the word in 2 Timothy 2:26 in the sense of 'devil' and the rarity with which *krima* (judgment, condemnation) means 'slander' (as Calvin noted) makes the third suggestion improbable, while of the other two the more natural interpretation seems to be the first, since pride is clearly a pressing danger for a promoted new convert.

The next requirement, *a good reputation with outsiders*, may at first sight seem impossible in view of the lack of favour shown towards Christianity in the contemporary world. Yet the injunction was essential to protect the church from unnecessary abuse, for the non-Christian world has generally respected the noble ideals of Christian character, particularly ministers and leaders, but has persistently condemned professing Christians whose practice is at variance with their profession. It is not that outsiders are arbiters of the church's choice of its officers, but that no minister will achieve success who has not first gained the confidence of his fellows.

The devil's trap is again ambiguous, for it may either mean the trap laid by the devil into which a man unpopular with non-Christians will easily fall; or it may refer to the devil's sin of pride. The mention of *disgrace* suggests that the former is to be preferred, although the latter forms a better parallel with the previous verse.

ii. Deacons (3:8–13)

The earliest allusion to a class of people especially appointed for practical work is found in Acts 6, although the word 'deacon' is not there used. Their function was probably temporary to deal with a pressing problem. Since the seven were particularly concerned with the distribution of the church's charities it was essential for them to be morally equipped for the task. Although there is no clear evidence of continuity between the seven in Acts 6 and the deacons here, there is a parallel in the need for worthy men in both instances. There is no need to suppose that the office of deacon was a late development in view of Philippians 1:1. On that occasion deacons are specially linked with bishops, probably because a gift is under consideration, for which no doubt they had been mainly responsible.

8. The list of qualities specified is closely akin to the preceding, but there are significant variations. Once again an element of seriousness is prominent, for such a quality would naturally call out a due measure of respect. The word translated *sincere (mēdilogos)* could mean 'not double-tongued', in the sense of not speaking one thing to one person and something different to another. But it could sustain the meaning 'tale-bearer' suggesting the idea of gossipers, a tendency which would be all too easy yet damaging for the holder of the deacon's office. The former is to be preferred, in the sense of sincerity as in the NIV rendering.

The two further comments forbidding *wine* addicts and men of insatiable appetites for *dishonest gain* are both expressed in stronger terms than in the case of the overseers. Perhaps this was no doubt because they may have been involved in visitation in homes which would expose them more pointedly to these evils. But we have no precise evidence of what their functions were.

9. The deacons are to be men not merely of practical acumen, but also of spiritual conviction. They have a possession described here as *the deep truths of the faith*. This translation somewhat veils the significant use of the word *mystērion*, which is a common Pauline expression denoting, not what is beyond knowledge, but what, having been once hidden, is now revealed to those with spiritual discernment. Some scholars see a difference here from Paul's normal usage, assuming that mystery has now become a conventional term, in the sense that men can accept the gospel in faith without understanding it. But it is difficult to see how anyone can hold these deep truths *with a clear conscience* without any understanding of what it is all about. To Paul the word always conveys a sense of wonder at God's plan of salvation (Rom. 16:26), and he cannot conceive of other Christians lacking the same realization. The whole phrase might mean (a) the mystery, the substance of which is the Christian faith (the use of the article supports this); or (b) the mystery appropriated by faith. In view of other occurrences in the Pastorals of the *faith* representing a body of doctrine, the former interpretation seems most consistent.

10. The testing which is here regarded as necessary must be understood rather as an examination of the required qualities than as a period of probation. The verb for testing (*dokimazō*) means to test in the hope of being successful (*cf.* Abbott-Smith). Appointments of deacons, as of every officer in the church, demand careful scrutiny. Spicq rightly appeals to Acts 6:3 to show that the proving is carried out by the assembly of believers. Only when adequate testing has been made and it is found that *there is nothing against them* are they eligible to serve as deacons. The requirements are demanding, for the word used (*anenklētos*) means 'blameless'. The demand itself enhances the high regard for the office.

11. In this special injunction to women, some understand a reference to the deacon's wife and there is much to be said for this in view of the probable share such a wife would have in her husband's visitation work. Others have postulated an order of deaconesses, but there is difficulty in view of the special section later in the Epistle devoted to women workers. Yet the word *hōsautōs* translated *In the same way* shows a close connection between the women and the deacons, and would support the contention that a new class is introduced analogous to the preceding order of deacons. Another argument in favour of deaconesses is that no special requirements are mentioned for the wives of overseers. Yet a third possibility is that an order of women deacons is in mind analogous to Phoebe (*cf.* Rom. 16:1). The reference is too general to postulate with certainty a distinct order of deaconesses or of women deacons, but some feminine ministration was necessary in visitation and in attending women candidates for baptism. For such work certain moral qualities would be essential whether for deacons' wives or for deaconesses or deacons in their own right. These qualities all contain a serious note, befitting the character of their task. The warning against *malicious talkers* is basic, for no-one in God's service can be allowed to indulge in slander. Of the other necessary qualities the first, *temperate*, echoes verse 2 and is again a basic requirement, but the second, *trustworthy in everything*, is again one of those demanding requirements which makes a person stand out in an age when reliability and honesty are at a premium in the non-Christian world.

12–13. Domestic orderliness and parental control are as necessary in a deacon as in an overseer and the requirements stated are in this respect identical with the previous list. A different reason, however, is given, perhaps by way of encouragement to the lesser officials of whom so high a standard is demanded. It is not quite clear what the words *gain an excellent standing* signify, but three different suggestions have been made. The word for 'standing' (*bathmos*) means a 'step', and is taken to mean (a) a step in promotion to a higher office; (b) 'standing' or 'vantage ground' (as in NIV, RSV), relating to the influence gained in the esteem of the Christian community; (c) 'standing in the sight of God'. The first seems quite out of keeping with the context and would make the previous instructions ridiculous if this were the main aim of the deacon's office. The second makes good sense and fully accords with the context, since influence is a by-product of character (Simpson). But the third possibility cannot be ruled out in view of the concluding phrase, *great assurance in their faith in Christ Jesus,* which is linked with 'standing' as objects of the same verb *gain.* Both parts may therefore legitimately be understood in a spiritual sense. Yet the transition of thought from moral qualifications to spiritual status is more difficult than that required for solution (b). Boldness seems primarily towards man, though it could include the notion of boldness in approach to God.

The expression *in their faith in Christ Jesus* has been much discussed. Some have objected that this application of the usual Pauline phrase 'in Christ Jesus' is in fact non-Pauline because Paul used it almost invariably to describe persons and not qualities. But whereas this particular application is unusual for Paul, it is surely not inconceivable that the apostle should use his favourite expression when describing faith, since he is here concerned with the exercise of faith and not the body of Christian doctrine.

D. THE CHARACTER OF THE CHURCH (3:14–16)

This section marks a pause in the apostle's instructions in order to put them in a right perspective, to give the reason for them, and to give a reminder of the wonder of the Christian revelation which must never be divorced from practical arrangements. It is not unlikely that this passage should be regarded as the high doctrinal point of the Epistle (as Spicq maintains).

14. Although the apostle hopes soon to meet Timothy he writes the preceding instructions in case of delay. The major problem is why the apostle did not give Timothy the necessary instructions before leaving him at Ephesus. It might appear on the one hand that Paul lacked sufficient foresight to prepare his deputy, or on the other hand that he needed to give elementary instructions in view of Timothy's immaturity. But neither of these solutions seems likely in view of what we know of the two men from other sources. If, however, we assume the semi-official character of the letters, there is no necessity to suppose these instructions were entirely new to Timothy (*cf.* Jeremias). Indeed, the explanation may well be that the present Epistle is confirmatory of oral advice given to Timothy on Paul's departure and is sent before his arrival to buttress the authority of his deputy. It is also possible that Paul was obliged to leave Ephesus hurriedly, and for this reason has had to supply Timothy with authorized instructions. The elementary character of the instructions reflects an early state in the development of the church.

15. In the Greek text, except for a few Western authorities, the subject of the verb *conduct* (RSV, 'behave') is omitted and could, therefore, refer to men generally or to Timothy himself. It probably refers to Timothy since he is the subject of the main verb, but it has been contended that a general reference is more in keeping with the preceding injunctions. On the other hand these injunctions are directed to Timothy to ensure that suitable appointments are to be made, and an allusion to his own official behaviour cannot be deemed alien to the present context. The Greek verb *anastrephō* ('conduct oneself') could well apply to the discharge of official duties. It was a particular concern of Paul that everything should be done in a dignified and efficient way.

The idea of the *church* as a household has already been introduced in verse 5. God's household here is defined precisely as *the church of the living God*, which is clearly no material building but a spiritual assembly. The image is a favourite one in Pauline thought (*cf.* 1 Cor. 3:9–17; Eph. 2:20–22). The absence of the article before *ekklēsia* (church) suggests that the local community is again primarily in mind, yet conceived of as part of a larger whole.

The phrase *the pillar and foundation of the truth* has caused difficulties mainly because it appears to give greater eminence to the church than to the truth. The uniform New Testament teaching is that the church is grounded on the truth, not vice versa. To avoid the difficulty the following suggestions have been made.

1. The whole phrase relates to Timothy and not to the church.

But Timothy could hardly be described as *the pillar* or 'prop' of the truth, and in any case the Greek construction would not naturally suggest such an antecedent.

2. By rendering the word *hedraiōma* as 'bulwark' instead of *foundation* the major difficulty disappears, for the church has in varying degrees been the custodian of spiritual truth, and was in any case intended to be so (*cf.* Hasler).

3. A third suggestion is that the phrase should be attached to the subsequent words and be regarded as a description of the *mystery of godliness* (so Bengel), but this is ruled out by the awkwardness of such a construction in the Greek and the anti-climax involved in the thought (*cf.* Scott). It is important to notice that no articles are used with either *pillar* or *foundation* in the Greek. And this must be considered intentional. A building needs more than one pillar. The pillar in fact stands for each Christian community (*cf.* Hort), unless it is an allusion to the Old Testament pillar of cloud (so Hanson, who regards the passage as a midrash). As with every figure of speech the analogy is imperfect, but the main idea is clearly of strength and support. There may also be here the idea that other agencies are used equally by God in the preservation of the gospel (*e.g.* Scripture, conscience).

16. The Christian hymn contained in this verse is introduced by a formula intended to intimate something of the grandeur to follow. The adverb translated *Beyond all question* (*homologou-menōs*) means by common consent, which draws attention to what all Christians hold. There is no room for manoeuvre regarding the basic facts of the faith. Some comment is needed on the expression *the mystery of godliness*, since this occurs nowhere else. The word *mystery* has already been met in verse 9 in the phrase *the deep truths of faith*, but here it is qualified by a word which in 2:2 appears to denote religion in general, although clearly the Christian religion is in view. But why does Paul use this unusual expression here? Perhaps the answer may be found in the implied comparison between the practical godliness previously enjoined on church officers and the inner character of its revealed secret described here.

The AV, based on the Received Text, reads 'God was manifest

in the flesh', but modern editors reject this reading in favour of 'Who was manifest'. NIV translates *He appeared in a body*, based on the second reading. In this reading the masculine relative is taken to refer to Christ. This is most probable. It has been suggested that Christ may have been mentioned in an earlier part of the hymn which has not been preserved in the citation. It was evidently well known and the reference would be beyond dispute.

Much of the lyrical quality of this hymn is missed in the English translation, but it is most impressive in the Greek. The first phrase celebrates the incarnation and presupposes the pre-existence of Christ, a magnificently succinct statement of a profound Christian truth. The mystery has been made known, yet how incomprehensible we discover it to be! The next line, *was vindicated by the Spirit*, may be regarded as parallel to the previous phrase. In that case, as the phrase *en sarki* (*in a body*) denotes the sphere of operation of the verb *appeared*, so *en pneumati* (*in the Spirit*) denotes the sphere of the verb *vindicated*. By translating the preposition *en* as 'by', NIV does not follow this parallelism. If however the parallelism is correct, 'spirit' could refer to Christ's human spirit (as in Rom. 1:4), in which case the meaning would be that God had vindicated Christ in the spiritual realm, *i.e.* when he declared him to be his son. If the parallelism is not enforced, the Greek preposition *en* could be understood instrumentally (as NIV), in which case the Holy Spirit would be declared as agent in vindicating the cause of the crucified, rejected Messiah, and this idea would connect well with the first phrase. But the former interpretation on the whole seems preferable, especially in view of the repetition of the preposition *en* throughout the hymn.

The next phrase, *was seen by angels*, is obscure, for it is not certain in what sense the word *angels* is to be understood. If the reference is to the principalities and powers believed to rule the unseen world (*cf.* the word 'elements' used in Gal. 4:3, 9 and Col. 2:8, 20 and *cf.* also Col. 2:15 and Eph. 6:12), the idea would be that the triumphant Christ showed himself to his spiritual enemies. But the words may also be taken as a reference to the hosts of unfallen angels, which seems to be supported by such statements as 1 Peter 1:12 and Ephesians 3:10. The hosts of heaven are depicted as eager to receive back the exalted Son of God, but this latter thought is more clearly gathered up in the sixth phrase. At the same time the idea of angelic worshippers of the Son was a popular theme among early Christians as the book of Revelation shows. It has been suggested that an emphatic antithesis exists between the third and fourth phrases, between the revelation to *angels* and to *the nations*, both together indicating the extent of Messiah's manifestations (*cf.* Bernard). But it is probably better to link the fourth and fifth phrases as parallel. The universalism of the gospel is classed next among the wonders of this *mystery*, and this factor would have special point for Paul, the apostle to the Gentiles. It must never be forgotten that a Hebrew Christ had become a Christ for the nations. As this expression focuses on earth, so does the next, which celebrates the response to the preaching *in the world*. Some understand the words to mean 'throughout the world' and take them as indicating the consummation of gospel preaching as the previous phrase shows its commencement. But they may indicate no more than the fact that the proclaimed Messiah is received by faith in the sphere of the world (here used without moral connotations) as contrasted with the ascension in glory with which the hymn concludes.

The refrain *was taken up in glory* in line 6 may be regarded as parallel to *was seen by angels* in line 3. But if the latter phrase is understood to refer to hostile agencies, the former refrain with its triumphal allusion to the ascension would form a fitting conclusion to the whole hymn. In any case there seems to be some thread of thought linking the fifth and sixth phrases, for Christ's triumph on earth (in the faith of his people) is concluded by his triumph *in glory*. The hymn could not close more suitably than with the humiliated Messiah's exalted entry into the heavenly sphere. It is noticeable that nowhere in the hymn is the death or resurrection of Christ mentioned, a surprising thing if this letter is Paul's own work. But if he is citing a current hymn and citing only a part, it is at least possible that the part not cited contained these great truths. The part preserved can hardly represent a complete Christian creed, and indeed is not intelligible apart from some doctrine of the cross and resurrection being assumed.

E. THREATS TO THE SAFETY OF THE CHURCH (4:1–16)

Having pointed out the exaltation of Christ and the future prospects of the church, the apostle next comes to opposing elements. Whenever truth flourishes error will raise its head, and the apostle is concerned that Timothy should deal rightly with this insidious opposition.

i. *The approaching apostasy* (4:1–5)

1. The ministry of *the Spirit* in apocalyptic revelations is emphatically brought out by the word *clearly* (*rhētōs*, 'in specific terms'), indicating that these elements of future events have been distinctly made known. At the same time no precise citation can be identified, and it is necessary, therefore, to apply the words to the general tenor of apocalyptic passages, especially in the teaching of Jesus (as *e.g.* Mk. 13:22). Paul himself has more than once prophesied such risings of false teachers (*e.g.* 2 Thes. 2:1–12; *cf.* Acts 20:29).

In later times (*en hysterois kairois*) is a phrase which suggests a more imminent future than 'in the last days' (used in 2 Tim. 3:1). Here the apostle is thinking of times subsequent to his own, but he foresees that Timothy needs to be cognisant of them. Indeed, as often in prophetical utterances, what is predicted of the future is conceived of as already operative in the present, so the words have a specific contemporary significance.

The apostasy is specified in a twofold manner. On the one hand the apostates *follow deceiving spirits*. The verb means 'to devote oneself to', suggesting a definite allegiance. The spirits concerned are evidently supernatural evil spirits whose existence and influence Paul has vividly described in Ephesians 6:11ff. Such spirits of error are contrasted with the Spirit of truth. In addition, reference is made to *things taught by demons*, which puts more emphasis than the former expression on the teaching than on the teachers. This has particular point as a contrast to the 'sound' doctrine so much stressed in the Pastorals.

2–3. The main elements in the character and teaching of the false teachers are now brought out in order to leave no doubt in

Timothy's mind about the precise nature of the heresy. The Greek construction demands that the words *through hypocritical liars* be understood of the human agents of the demons. Grammatically the phrase could describe the hypocrisy of the demons, but this is impossible in view of the following two clauses. The meaning seems to be that the demons and deceiving spirits find particular allies in hypocritical liars. These people have no sense of the wrongness of their actions for their *consciences have been seared as with a hot iron*. The force of the verb used here is that their consciences are cauterized (the literal meaning of *kauteriazō*), with the result that they are no longer able to fulfil their true function. They have become hardened. The apostle's description of some who had 'lost all sensitivity' (Eph. 4:19) supports this medical understanding of the term. Another interpretation is that the consciences have been branded as by a hot iron to show that their true owner is Satan. But this fits less aptly into the context, for the real point is that the consciences of these false teachers have ceased to warn them of the falseness of their teaching. Hanson speaks of them being 'anaesthetized'.

The false teachers insisted on two prohibitions: marriage and the eating of certain foods. There is no doubt that these point to an incipient gnosticism with its dualistic view of matter, which found its climax in the heretical teachers of the early second century (*cf.* Introduction, pp. 43ff.). The apostle's strong opposition to these practices is due to their dangerous implications. He argues that prohibitions such as these are in conflict with the divine ordinance. Here he strikes at the roots of dualistic gnosticism, which denied that God created matter. Quite apart from this the forbidding of marriage could never lead to a healthy society as God had planned it, and food-taboos were in direct opposition to the bountiful provision of God and could only lead to legalism.

The insistence on the reception of God's gifts *with thanksgiving* is a typically Pauline theme. Such a note must never be absent from the believer's attitude either to material or to spiritual realities. What is at stake is our whole conception of God. The false teachers were acting as if God were niggardly and were losing sight of his largesse. Those who cannot thank God have no real knowledge of him.

The concluding words of verse 3 are not to be taken as prom-ising any special material benefits for Christians (*i.e. those who believe and who know the truth*), but as demonstrating that what was created for all men must therefore be legitimate for Christians.

4–5. The apostle next supplies a reason for his previous statement. It involves a fundamental principle that what a good Creator creates must be *good*. The word translated *to be rejected* (*apoblētos*), which occurs nowhere else in the New Testament, means literally 'to be thrown away'. It is here used in the sense of taboo. Such taboos should have no place in an intelligent Christian's approach, in strong contrast to the many systems of taboos in heathen cults. The repetition of *thanks-giving* here is significant for what is thankfully received could not be rejected for ritual reasons.

There is some obscurity about the meaning of verse 5. What-ever is gratefully received is *consecrated*, *i.e.* it becomes 'holy' to the user in contrast to heathen taboos. The Christian idea of holiness embraces such mundane matters as 'meats', the least obvious subject for sanctification. The act of consecration is achieved through *the word of God and prayer*. There have been several proposed interpretations of the word of God here. (a) It may be a reference to the use of Scripture in the 'grace' before meals. This would fit reasonably well into the context and is favoured by several scholars (Bernard, Jeremias, Kelly, Spicq, Brox). (b) It could refer to divine revelation, or more specifically to the incarnate Word. But this seems out of keeping with the context and the connection with prayer is against it. (c) It could refer to the creative word of God as in Genesis 1:31 which would link directly with the word *good* in verse 4 (*cf.* Easton, Houlden). But again the linking of it with prayer seems strange. (d) Another suggestion is that the consecration is a reference to the eucharist (*cf.* Hanson) supported by a parallel in Justin. But the first suggestion makes the best sense in the present context. If correct it emphasizes the importance of the practice of prayer before meals and gives a timely reminder to modern Christians who tend either to neglect the practice altogether or else minimize its significance. The word of God has a sanctifying influence, as we are reminded in the words of Jesus in John 15:3.

ii. Methods of dealing with false teaching (4:6-16)

6. The apostle now begins a personal directive to Timothy which serves at the same time all ministers of the gospel who are called to deal with similar situations. It is significant that the approach is not mere denunciation, as so often alleged, in contrast with Paul's constructive approach in Colossians. In fact the words *If you point out* translate the Greek word *hypotithēmi* which means 'suggest' which is mild as compared with 'command'. The root meaning is 'to place under' and it is an interesting idea that the picture here may be stepping stones placed under the feet over treacherous ground (*cf.* Scott).

The minister of the gospel has a responsibility to lay before his people the positive answers to negative doctrines, and anyone who fails in this respect forfeits the right to be accounted worthy of the ministry. When Paul says *brought up in the truths of the faith*, he uses a present participle (*entrephomenos*) which suggests a continuous process. The article with the word *faith* indicates a body of Christian doctrine. There is no better means of spiritual nourishment than a constant dwelling on the great truths of the faith, which Timothy had had the inestimable privilege of receiving at first hand from the apostle.

In the concluding phrase *that you have followed*, the verb (*parakoloutheō*) suggests as the meaning either 'which you have closely investigated' or 'which you have followed as a standard'. The former is paralleled in Luke 1:3 and might very well fit Timothy's position. In 2 Timothy 3:10, however, the alternative sense of the same verb seems more probable. Both interpretations have this in common, that they focus attention on a pursuit of *good teaching* as contrasted with false teaching. That the best refutation of error is a positive presentation of truth is a principle which the church in every age constantly needs to learn.

7-8. By way of contrast to the good doctrine the apostle describes the false teaching as *godless myths*. The word used here (*bebēlos*) means 'profane', from a root meaning 'permitted to be trodden' with the idea that nothing remains sacred. The word has already been used in 1:9 in the list of law-breakers coupled with 'unholy men'. The use of this word to describe professedly religious people shows the utter bankruptcy of their religion. The addition of the epithet *old wives* brings out forcibly the frivolous character of the false teachers' *tales* (*mythoi*). The whole teaching lacked substance and must be vigorously rejected. The verb (*paraiteomai*) emphasizes the strong nature of the refusal (*cf.* Tit. 3:10 and 2 Tim. 2:23).

Again the apostle is quick to balance a negative with a positive injunction. He turns to athletics for his illustration, probably to emphasize the contrast between manly exercise and *old wives' tales*. There is a further comparison between physical and spiritual discipline. The apostle admits a place for the former but sets a strict limit on its exercise. The description of it in the NIV as *of some value* does not bring out the force of *oligos* which means 'little or slight' and which seems to suggest only a limited value for physical exercise. It is contrasted with spiritual training, which on the other hand is of *value for all things*; or perhaps 'in all directions' (Moffatt). Its range is immeasurably greater for it embraces not only this life but the life to come. The *promise . . . for the present life* is not an equivalent for worldly prosperity, but sums up the blessedness of godliness. Irrespective of his present earthly circumstances, the Christian may fairly be said to have the best of both worlds.

9–10. There is some doubt whether the *trustworthy saying* formula of verse 9 relates to the statement of verse 8 about godliness, or to the following statement giving the reason for our present toil. Many commentators prefer the former alternative because verse 8 sounds more like a proverbial saying than verse 10, and because the conjunction 'for' (not clearly brought out in NIV) gives the reason for the trustworthiness of the saying. Yet the subject matter of verse 10 is more theologically weighty than verse 8 and would therefore be admirably adapted for current catechetical purposes. Since in 2 Timothy 2:11 the conjunction forms part of the saying, it seems preferable, therefore, to connect the formula to the subsequent verse.

The word translated *labour* (*kopiaō*) suggests strenuous toil, and is used by Paul in Philippians 2:16 to describe athletic fatigue. The idea is therefore a continuation of the metaphor used in verses 7 and 8. The strong toil is further linked with the challenge to *strive* (*agōnizometha*), which is a much more likely reading than that used by the AV (*oneidizōmetha*, 'suffer reproach'). The former not only has weightier manuscript support, but also accords better with the context. The race of godliness demands every ounce of energy a person possesses.

The reason given for this particular striving is the constancy of the believer's hope. The word *hope* points to more than 'trust'. The perfect tense is used (*ēlpikamen*), implying a continuous state of hope (*we have put our hope in the living God*). The idea is of an ongoing and certain hope. The linking of *the living God*, who is seen as the ground of our hope, with *the Saviour of all men*, is significant. As already noted in 1:1 in this Epistle, God rather than Jesus is seen as Saviour. The expression *Saviour of all men* should probably be understood as 'Preserver' of all men, in line with the common meaning. Nevertheless, when used in a Christian sense it would convey more than the providential care of God. In fact the last part of verse 10, which singles out believers as special objects of God's saving power, suggests that the word *Saviour* is here used in a double sense. There is a clear development in the thought, since the believer's special confidence in God is reinforced by the knowledge that the divine mercy is universal in its scope (*cf.* 2:3–4).

11–12. The next advice is more directly concerned with Timothy himself. There is to be a note of authority in Timothy's teaching, as the word *Command* (*parangelle*) shows: and the author's purpose is clearly to inspire his timid representative to display such firmness. The reference to Timothy's youthfulness has led many scholars to imagine him as a mere stripling, but the word *neotēs* (NIV has *because you are young*) may indicate any age up to forty years old (*cf.* Lock). It must therefore be regarded relatively. Many of the Ephesian Christians, and especially the elders, were almost certainly of maturer years; and if for some time they had served under the leadership of the veteran missionary apostle Paul, it is by no means inconceivable that some would look with disfavour and contempt on the younger Timothy. As a counter-balance to contempt Timothy is to live in an exemplary manner (for the use of the same word *typos* for Paul's own ethical example, *cf.* Phil. 3:17; 2 Thes. 3:9). The qualities in which Timothy is to excel are those in which youth is so often deficient. Yet for that reason they would stand out the more strikingly. It would become evident to the Christian believers that authority in the community is contingent on character, not on age. Every young man called to the ministry or to any position of authority in the church would do well to heed Paul's five-fold enumeration here. The first two, *speech* and *life* (*i.e.* manner of life, or behaviour) apply to Timothy's public life, while the other three are concerned with inner qualities (*love, faith* and *purity*) which nevertheless have a public manifestation.

13. The three pursuits to which Timothy is bidden to devote himself until the apostle's arrival are concerned with his public ministry, although the verb translated *devote* (*prosechō*) implies previous preparation in private. The *public reading of Scripture* was important because it was the means of a large number of people being able to hear the text, whereas only a few would have had personal access to the text, or have been able to read it. For a considerable time to come the scarcity of manuscripts would make the public reading of Scripture essential to the life of the church. The Old Testament Scriptures must here be in mind. The church carried on the synagogue practice and made it a basic element of Christian worship. As in the synagogue so in the church, the reading of Scripture was followed by an exhortation (*paraklēsis*, NIV *preaching*) based upon it, but in Christian worship a special place was reserved for *teaching* (*didaskalia*) which consisted of instruction in the great truths of the Christian faith.

14. The *gift* (*charisma*) which Timothy must not *neglect* appears to be the spiritual equipment received at the time of ordination (*cf.* Calvin). This use is thoroughly Pauline and draws attention to the most primitive stage in church development, when charismatic ministry was of greater importance than official positions. Although the word *gift* draws attention to the part played by the Holy Spirit in Timothy's ministry, the exhortation not to neglect it brings out equally emphatically the human responsibility. God's gifts, like the talent, must never be left unused.

There were two distinct yet complementary confirmations of Timothy's commission. The first, *a prophetic message*, has already been mentioned in 1:18, where it refers to some prophetical indication of Timothy's call, and undoubtedly it must be here understood in the same sense. This was accompanied by an outward indication when the elders *laid their hands* on Timothy. No difficulty need be entertained over the fact that in 2 Timothy 1:16 Paul speaks exclusively of his own part in such a ceremony, for there are two possible solutions: either the elders were associated with Paul in the ceremony, and are specifically mentioned here to draw attention to the corporate attestation of Timothy's commission; or else the two references to laying on of hands refer to different occasions. The former on the whole seems the more likely explanation. The idea of the impartation of the gift of the Spirit through the laying on of hands is frequently found in Acts (*e.g.* 8:17; 9:17; 19:6), and provides a significant object lesson in the divine-human co-operation in the early church.

15–16. The methods by which the gift may be nurtured are carefully delineated. The first requisite is diligence (*Be diligent in these matters*). The verb used (*meletaō*) can also mean 'to ponder', implying careful reflection on the matter in hand. Diligence would fit in well with the athletic metaphor which seems to have been in the writer's mind. But the idea of reflection would be quite apt since *these matters*, referring back to verse 13, would need a constant application of mind. Whichever was Paul's intention, it is clear that Timothy is to become so closely acquainted with these injunctions that they become second nature to him. He is to *give* himself *wholly to them* (*en toutois isthi*, literally 'be in them', a construction which vividly brings out absorption in anything), a fitting reminder of the exacting nature of the Christian calling. The mind is to be as immersed in these pursuits as the body in the air it breathes.

The Christian minister's *progress* as on a journey is under public observation (note the significance of *everyone*) and for that reason demands the most careful thought. Timothy is to ensure that what most impresses other people is his true Christian development, and not some lesser thing such as brilliance of exposition or attractiveness of personality.

It is significant that in the next injunction the teacher and his teaching are intimately linked. He must first 'give attention to himself', *i.e.* keep a strict eye on himself (NIV has *watch your life*, which does not so well bring out the meaning). Moral and spiritual rectitude is an indispensable preliminary to doctrinal orthodoxy. Timothy must also have continually in mind (*persevere in*) either the advice just given, or the more general injunctions of this letter, according to what interpretation is given to the words *in them*.

` In following out the previous advice Timothy will achieve a double purpose. He will not only be working out his own salvation (in the sense of Phil. 2:12), but will also be assisting others to do the same. The danger of neglecting one's own salvation is greater in the Christian minister than in others, and even the apostle Paul himself could fear lest he became a castaway after preaching to others (1 Cor. 9:27). Calvin suggestively comments that although salvation is God's gift alone, yet human ministry has an important place in the way God works, as is here implied.

III. DISCIPLINE AND RESPONSIBILITY (5:1 – 6:2)

Almost the whole of the remainder of the Epistle contains specific directions to Timothy to assist him in dealing with various classes of people within the church. It may seem surprising that so much attention is given to the problem of widows, but no doubt this was a constant source of anxiety in the early church as Acts 6 shows. Since some were recipients of the church's bounty it was fitting that careful regulations should govern their selection. It must be remembered that in those days there were few ways in which a widow could earn her living.

A. VARIOUS AGE GROUPS (5:1–2)

1–2. The same word is used here for *older man* as is used later on of the church officials called 'elders'. But Paul's advice here concerns older members of the congregation. The verb *rebuke harshly* (*epiplēssō*) is a strong one meaning 'censure severely', and those advanced in years should be spared such treatment. If correction is necessary Timothy is to *exhort*, a less rigorous approach than harsh rebuke. The same applies to the *older women*, who are to be regarded in their role as *mothers*. Towards the younger members there must be true fraternity, but a special phrase, *with absolute purity*, is added to safeguard Timothy's relations with the younger women.

B. WIDOWS (5:3–16)

i. Widows in need (5:3–8)

3. The Greek word *timaō* which is rendered *give proper recognition to* conveys more than the normal idea of respect, for it here includes material support as is clear from the subsequent passage (*cf.* Mt. 15:5). It is worth noting that in approaching the theme of poverty as a matter of honour, the Christian removes some of its disgrace. The kind of widows who are here in mind are those *who are really in need*, having no other means of support. It was seen as a Christian duty to care for those who were genuinely destitute.

4. The apostle makes it quite clear that where widows have close relatives, those relatives must relieve the church of the responsibility to support them. It may be that the advice here has some continued modern relevance in spite of the provisions of the welfare state. The wide-spread break-up of the family unit has not left the church unaffected, but the elderly where possible should still be the responsibility of relatives. The expression *repaying* means to make a worthy requital (M & M). Children have a definite obligation towards *parents and grandparents* to do something to recompence the often sacrificial care given in their upbringing. Such an essentially practical procedure is nevertheless linked with spiritual example, since *this is pleasing to God.* Paul makes clear that the responsibility for parents which is carried over to the second and third generations, has the divine endorsement. *These should learn* could refer to the widows, but the context favours a reference to the descendants.

5–8. The characteristics of the kind of widow that Paul is concerned about are next specified. (a) She is a person *really in need and left all alone* (the word *memonōmenē* means left entirely alone); (b) she also is one who *puts her hope in God,* which at once distinguished her from non-Christian widows; she is to be a woman of prayer, who continues in an attitude of prayer *night and day.* The verb *continues* (*prosmenō*) is in the present tense and emphasizes still more the idea of continuity. There was to be a high spiritual standard expected of those to be cared for by the church.

In the contemporary world many widows were tempted to resort to immoral living as a means of support, and that is probably in the apostle's mind when he uses the verb *lives for pleasure* (*spatalaō*). Moffatt renders it as 'plunges into dissipation'. To be dead while still living is a thoroughly Pauline paradox (*cf.* Rom. 7:10, 24), and Timothy is here reminded that widows supporting themselves illicitly are attempting to support what is already dead ('a religious corpse', according to Simpson). Such people clearly have no claim whatever on the church's care. The *instructions* which Timothy is to give must refer to the responsibility of children to support their forbears (verse 4), and the responsibility of widows to fulfil the requirements mentioned in verse 5. The verb used is strong, involving 'command'. The command was necessary to ensure that *no-one may be open to blame* (*anepilēmptos,* 'irreproachable', *cf.* 3:2).

Provision for one's own *relatives* and *especially for one's own immediate family* is so clearly a Christian duty that to fail to do it amounts to a denial of the Christian *faith.* In the contemporary pagan world there was a general acceptance of obligation towards parents, and it was unthinkable that Christian morality should lag behind general pagan standards.

ii. Widows as Christian workers (5:9–10)

Whether there was at this time a distinct order of widows performing functions among women members, comparable to those of the elders, is a much disputed question (*cf.* comment on 3:11). While the following passage clearly points to some kind of register with a specific age qualification, there is not sufficient data to conclude for an 'order of widows'.

9–10. The proviso of so high an age as sixty presents a difficulty as to whether *widow* should be understood in the same sense as in verses 3–8 (*i.e.* of genuinely destitute Christian widows) or in the sense of widows belonging to an order. In the former case it is inconceivable that the church would set an arbitrary age in dispensing help to destitute widows, while in the latter case it is difficult to believe the entry age to an ecclesiastical order would be as high as sixty, in the contemporary world a relatively more advanced age than in our own. It seems preferable, therefore, to suppose that special duties in the church were reserved for some of the older widows receiving aid, and that some official recognition of this fact was given. Although the verb *katalegō*, translated *put on a list*, is used in Greek literature of the enrolment of soldiers, it can also mean 'reckon', a sense which would support the explanation given above.

In addition to the age-restriction there are two further requirements: (a) The widow must have been *faithful to her husband* (literally 'wife of one husband'), which can only mean that she has not remarried after her husband's death; it may be that a woman who had been married twice was likely to have more relatives who could support her and would be less in need of being enrolled on the church's list. (b) She must also be well reported for her conduct in the home and elsewhere. The order in which the *good deeds* are mentioned is significant: child-care ranks first, hospitality next, humble service towards believers third, and general sympathy and benevolence fourth. All these *good deeds* are not only essentially practical, but are even commonplace in character. A Christian woman well versed in these would be of inestimable value in caring for orphans, entertaining visiting Christians, attending to the many practical details, some very menial, such as feet-washing (a reminiscence of the Lord's own action, Jn. 13:1–7) and visitation among needy people. Moreover, the widow to be chosen must be known as *devoting herself* to these pursuits. She must be thoroughly established in well-doing.

iii. Younger widows (5:11–16)

11. *Younger widows*, who would presumably be eligible for relief when in genuine distress, are not, however, to be allowed to discharge any official function, because of the strong possibility of remarriage. The Greek verb *katastrēniazō* translated *when their sensual desires overcome their dedication to Christ* suggests the metaphor of young oxen trying to escape from the yoke. The younger women would not wish to be tied to church duties if further opportunities came for marriage. That some official functions must here be meant is evident from the fact that the sexual desires are set over against their loyalty to Christ. It follows that any widow who had undertaken church duties would be regarded as disloyal if she wished to remarry, a situation which Paul wished to avoid.

12. The *judgment* which the widows would bring on themselves is in the nature of censure. The AV rendering 'damnation' is far too strong. Nevertheless they are described as having *broken their first pledge* and this cannot be regarded lightly. Any who did this would deserve *judgment* and Paul would not expect the matter to be glossed over.

13. An awkward Greek construction makes the meaning of the first part of the verse uncertain. The statement *they get into the habit of being idle* suggests that they become increasingly idle once they have disregarded their pledge. Another possible interpretation is that 'they learn by idleness', but this does not fit the context so well. The verb used here is *manthanō* which means 'learn' and dispenses with any suggestion that the idleness comes on unconsciously. There are two unpleasant fruits of this idleness. Those concerned gad about (*going about* *from house to house*). This may mean that younger widows were misusing their opportunities in visitation, an interpretation borne out in the second result – that they become *gossips and busybodies*, repeating in one house what they had heard in another. The additional words *saying things they ought not to* may indicate a publicizing of private matters, a betrayal of confidences. It is not particularly evident, at first sight, why the younger widows would be more susceptible to this danger than the older, but the apostle clearly thinks that women of maturer years would be the less liable to gossip.

14. In order to avoid such problems the apostle urges the *younger women to marry*. There is a clear connection between this statement and the preceding statement, and the advice must be applied to young widows, not to young women generally. No contradiction need be supposed with 1 Corinthians 7:25–26, where Paul states a definite preference for the unmarried state, for the widows under review are those whom he would class as 'incontinent'.

Rather than become idle scandal-mongers these women should devote themselves to the bearing of children and the managing of homes. Paul sees the mother's task as involving the ruling of the household. This common-sense advice is in striking contrast to the penchant for celibacy which developed in the later history of the church. The apostle is once again most anxious that unnecessary reproach from any non-Christian opponent should be avoided. The word for *opportunity* (*aphormē*) is a military term for 'a base of operations', a favourite Pauline metaphor (*cf.* Rom. 7:8, 11; 2 Cor. 5:12; 11:12 and Gal. 5:13).

15. The apostle's injunctions to strict discipline are occasioned by the example of some who have already *turned away* from their true course in order *to follow Satan*. This latter expression probably means that they have given themselves to immoral practices. The result is the antithesis of what is expected of a Christian.

16. Some difficulty arises here over the Greek text, for the best attested reading has *if any woman . . . has widows*, but the alternative reading 'if any man or woman' would seem to accord better with the sense, for it is difficult to believe that the exhortation to relieve the church of its responsibility to care for widows would be confined to women. The verse is closely parallel to verses 4 and 8, but Paul is here particularly concerned with widows not eligible to be enrolled.

C. ELDERS (5:17-20)

17. Attention is next focused on the officials of the church with special advice about their remuneration. There is no doubt that *honour* should be understood in this sense, in view of verse 18. The adjective *double*, descriptive of this honour, would appear to have the sense of ample or generous provision, but this would depend on efficiency, as the adverb *well* indicates. It has been suggested that *double* refers to both age and office, or that it shows an advance on the honour due to widows; but the interpretation adopted above seems preferable. The word translated *direct the affairs* (*prohistēmi*) means general superintendence, and describes the duties allotted to all presbyters. But special consideration is due to those whose *work is preaching and teaching*, which may point to a particular class within the presbyterate.

18. The proposition is supported by two citations linked together under the formula *For the Scripture says*, precisely in the Pauline manner (*cf.* Rom. 4:3; 11:2; Gal. 4:30). The first citation is from Deuteronomy 25:4, and the second is exactly paralleled by Luke 10:7, where the words are attributed to Jesus. The same passage from Deuteronomy is cited by Paul in 1 Corinthians 9:9 under the caption, 'For it is written in the law of Moses'. With this the apostle links the Lord's command (1 Cor. 9:14), but does not as here cite his words. The two sayings were evidently closely associated in the apostle's mind, and there is no need to suppose that he is quoting from the canonical gospel, although that cannot be entirely ruled out. He may be citing from a collection of the words of Jesus, and if so it is clear that such a collection was placed on an equality with the Old Testament, at least as far as the authority of each was concerned. To the apostle the words of Christ would naturally assume an importance proportionate to his conception of Christ's Person. It cannot be maintained, on the contrary, that both Jesus and Paul cite from a current proverb, for Jesus did not describe it as such and Paul here classes it as Scripture, which he could never have confused with a proverbial saying. Scholars who maintain the non-Pauline authorship of the Pastorals claim that their position presents less difficulty, for the later writer might actually be using Luke's Gospel, which could not be said of Paul if the prevailing estimate of the date of Luke's Gospel is correct (*i.e.* AD 80–85). There would be less difficulty if Luke's Gospel is dated around AD 60, and indeed there is no compelling reason why Paul should not have been acquainted with it.

Whatever the apostle is here citing, he intends Timothy to understand that a divine sanction underlies the principle of fair provision for those who serve the church. Too often a niggardly attitude has been maintained towards faithful men who have laboured for Christ in the interest of others.

The apostle has already deplored money-grubbing (3:3), but he equally deplores inadequate remuneration. If God ordained ample provision for oxen treading out corn, it is incumbent upon Christian communities to see that those who devote time and energy to their service are adequately rewarded.

19–20. It was of utmost importance to safeguard innocent men from false accusation, and as Jewish law required the agreement of two witnesses before a man might be called upon to answer a charge (*cf.* Dt. 19:15), so it must be in the church (*cf.* Mt. 18:16; 2 Cor. 13:1), especially when *an elder* is implicated. He must be protected against malicious intent; but if there are real grounds for accusation, then disciplinary action should be taken before the whole church (NIV has *are to be rebuked publicly*). It is possible to understand the 'all' (*pantōn*) to relate to all the elders, but the NIV is probably right in referring it to the whole church. Such public action could not fail to have a salutary effect on the community (*so that the others may take warning*), by drawing attention to the need for Christian purity. The abuse of discipline has often led to a harsh and intolerant spirit, but neglect of it has produced a danger almost as great.

When faced with sinning elders a spineless attitude is deplorable.

D. TIMOTHY'S OWN BEHAVIOUR (5:21–25)

21. The sudden and solemn charge delivered to Timothy at this juncture throws a flood of light on the young man's character. He needs stiffening up and the apostle finds it necessary to use a strong expression – *I charge you, in the sight of God and Christ Jesus and the elect angels*. A similar adjuration is used in 2 Timothy 4:1, but without reference to angels. The mention of these *elect angels* is surprising, but may be due to the belief that they are commissioned to watch over men's affairs. There may also be an eschatological reason, reminiscent of the Lord's words in Luke 9:26. The same phrase occurs in the apocalyptic book of Enoch 39:1.

These instructions that Timothy must *keep* are all the careful instructions already given. RSV suggestively translates 'keep these rules'. This must be done both *without partiality, i.e.* without any prejudging or prejudice, and without *favouritism, i.e.* without any inclination towards one rather than towards another. This is a difficult objective, but is indispensable for any Christian leader.

22. There is difference of opinion whether the ordination ceremony is here in view, or the restoration of penitents after due discipline. It has been suggested that Timothy would not alone be responsible for the ordination of elders (*cf.* 4:14), yet the directive given to Timothy may have been intended also for the elders. If he presided it would fall to his lot to exercise restraint. Such an interpretation certainly suits the context better if the whole section from verse 19 onwards concerns elders, but there is much support for the contrary opinion. The laying on of hands needs careful consideration and Paul urges against doing this too hastily (*tacheōs*).

The second half of the verse, *do not share in the sins of others*, seems to mean that whoever lays hands on an unworthy man must take responsibility for the man's sins. It is difficult to believe, however, that this could apply generally to penitents, although it would have some relevance to penitent elders. It seems preferable, therefore, to take the act of laying on of hands in the sense of setting apart for specific service, as elsewhere in the Pastorals (*cf.* 2 Tim. 1:6). Undue haste in Christian appointments has not infrequently led to unworthy men bringing havoc to the cause of Christ.

The rather abrupt personal charge to Timothy, *Keep yourself pure*, must primarily be understood in the general sense of honourable and upright behaviour. It is as if the apostle had said – make sure you appoint 'pure' men and keep yourself 'pure' in the process.

23. Expositors who look for some close connection between this verse and the preceding are faced with a knotty problem, but the solution might lie in the precise meaning of 'pure' in verse 22. It may be that the apostle feared lest his injunction 'keep yourself pure' might be interpreted too rigidly as an exhortation to ascetic practices and he wished to make clear that 'purity' was not synonymous with abstention. Possibly Timothy was naturally inclined towards asceticism. On the other hand there may be no connection with the previous verse intended, and this advice may be interjected because the apostle calls to mind Timothy's weak health, and thinks it helpful to draw attention to the medicinal value of wine.

Stop drinking only water clearly means not that Timothy is to cease drinking water, but is to cease from doing so exclusively. It may be that contaminated water had contributed to Timothy's indigestion and so the apostle suggests a remedy. The verse shows Timothy to be a man of delicate health, and is one of those incidental touches which help the modern reader to feel greater sympathy with him. It is an intimate touch quite natural to the apostle when writing to a close associate, but strange indeed if written by a later pseudonymous writer.

24–25. It is best to regard verse 23 as parenthetical and to make these last two verses resume the thought of verse 22. A distinction is drawn between men and women whose sins are clearly evident (*prodēlos*, *obvious*) and those whose sins are not immediately apparent, but who will ultimately be pursued by them (*apakoloutheō*, to follow after). *The judgment* could be the estimate of Timothy and his associates, but more probably the judgment of God is in mind. This seems even clearer in verse 25 where conspicuous and concealed good works are set side by side, the latter, however, ultimately becoming known. These parallel observations, viewing human potentialities both negatively and positively, bring out forcibly the complexities involved in selecting suitable candidates for God's work. Hasty action relies on first impressions, but these impressions are often deceptive. Unworthy men might be chosen, whose moral culpability lies deeper than the surface; and worthy men, whose good actions are not in the limelight, might easily be overlooked. The whole situation demands extreme caution.

E. SERVANTS AND MASTERS (6:1–2)

In communities where membership included numerous slaves together with some of their masters, the relationship between them was a pressing problem. Slaves enjoyed equality of status within the church, but a decided social inferiority in their respective households, an irreconcilable antithesis which found its only solution in the ultimate abolition of slavery. But since the time was unpropitious for overturning this deeply rooted system, interim Christian rules were indispensable.

1. The apostle envisages two kinds of situation. In this verse Christians *under the yoke of slavery* (*douloi* should be rendered as slaves rather than as servants as in AV) who belong to non-Christian *masters* are in mind, but in verse 2 the masters are *believing*. The resultant dangers in each case differed. A Christian slave who had found liberty in Christ might be tempted to maintain less respect for his master than he ought, particularly if the latter were harsh and tyrannical. But in such circumstances the cause of Christ is served best by an attitude of respect. The expression *under the yoke of slavery* draws attention to the fact that many masters regarded their slaves as little more than cattle. It focuses on the social conditions of the contemporary world. In such conditions it was more important where possible to avoid reproach against *God's name and our teaching* than to make an abortive revolutionary attempt to reform the social structure. The *teaching* here is the Christian faith.

2. A danger to which Christian slaves with believing masters were particularly exposed was to neglect their obligations. They must not *show less respect* for those whose discipline has become less taxing, because it has been tempered by the love of Christ, and because they are prepared to regard their own slaves as *brothers* for Christ's sake. Rather the slaves should render better service to such masters in return for the better treatment received. *Those who benefit from their service* may refer to the masters or to the slaves. The grammatical construction favours the former, in which case the reference is to the advantage gained by the master in the increase of the slave's goodwill. To apply the phrase to slaves would mean that they reap the benefit of having a master who is a believer and is *dear to them* (*agapētos*). Perhaps the ambiguity was intentional to remind both masters and slaves that the *benefit* which would acrue if both were 'faithful and beloved' was mutual.

IV. MISCELLANEOUS INJUNCTIONS (6:3–21)

The concluding portion of the Epistle contains no clear sequence of thought, and it is best therefore to deal with it in self-contained sections. There are further reflections about false teachers, and two separate passages dealing with wealth enclosing a personal note to Timothy, concluded by a majestic doxology. The letter then ends with another exhortation telling Timothy how to deal with the heresy, almost like a postscript adding weight to what had already been given in the earlier part of the letter.

A. MORE ABOUT FALSE TEACHERS (6:3–5)

3. The words, *These are the things you are to teach and urge on them*, are in the NIV (and AV) attached to the end of verse 2, but seem more illuminative when regarded as introductory to what follows (as RSV). Timothy is to stand out in obvious contrast to those who teach *false doctrines* (the same word is used as in 1:3). The *things* intended are probably all the subjects mentioned in the Epistle.

The verb translated *agree* (*proserchomai*) literally means 'approach' with the derived sense of 'attaching oneself to' (*cf.* Simpson's lexigraphical discussion). The true teacher is to adhere to *sound instruction*, which is further defined as being *of our Lord Jesus Christ*. The definition may itself be understood in two different ways: (a) it may refer to the sayings of Jesus, or (b) it may indicate words about Jesus, descriptive of Christian truth. The latter is more in keeping with the context and with the general usage in the Pastorals. It is further supported by its connection with the concluding clause, *i.e. and to godly teaching*, although this could also apply to some of the sayings of Jesus to bring out their essential contrast to the ungodliness characteristic of the false teaching. Spicq, who considers that Luke's Gospel is here meant, favours Schlatter's opinion that it is difficult to believe that Paul could so speak of the words of Jesus if no gospel existed in the community, Acts 20:35 furnishing an illuminating parallel.

4-5. The descripton of a teacher throws revealing light on the nature of his teaching, a principle applying as much to true as to false doctrine. The characteristics of these false teachers make an unenviable list. For a comment on the word translated *conceited* (*typhoō*), see 3:6. The true state of these puffed-up teachers is nothing short of abysmal ignorance, as the apostle points out.

The next words are not easy to represent clearly in English. NIV renders them *He has an unhealthy interest in controversies and quarrels about words*. The literal meaning of the verb (*noseō*) is 'to be sick', which is obviously intended as a contrast to the healthy words of verse 3. The controversies and arguments have impaired their mental health to such a degree that they have become diseased. This is a noteworthy example of the processes by which intellectual wrangling so often ends in moral deterioration.

All the evil results mentioned are mental activities, with some discernible progression, for dissension is bound to follow *envy*. In fact, on every occasion except one where *eris* (the Greek word translated *strife*) is used in the New Testament, it is linked with a word for *envy* (three times with *phthonos* as here and elsewhere with *zēlos*). It is significant that Paul alone uses *eris* and includes it in all his lists of the works of unrighteousness. *Malicious talk* and *evil suspicions* are a pair that go naturally together. The *constant friction between men of corrupt mind* points to the inevitable irritability which results from communication among those of depraved minds, for they are predisposed to think the worst about each other. When reason is morally blinded all correctives to unworthy behaviour are banished, and the mind becomes *robbed of the truth* (rsv has 'bereft of the truth'). The picture is of an intruder snatching away the truth, but with the mind doing all in its power to aid the despoilation of its own priceless possession. The sheer folly of it is apparent. The concluding phrase, *and who think that godliness is a means to financial gain*, is well rendered by Moffatt as 'they imagine religion is a paying concern'. But true godliness must never be commercialized for it is a matter of the heart and not the pocket. Whether the meaning is that these false teachers charged high fees for their specious teachings, or used their garrulous religious profession as a cloak for material advancement is not clear.

B. THE PERILS OF WEALTH (6:6–10)

Because money was a chief concern of the false teachers the apostle proceeds to deal with some of its dangers and lays down principles of universal significance.

6. The dictum of the false teachers is first of all admitted, yet with an all-important proviso. The notion of self-mastery inherent in the word translated *contentment* (*autarkeia*) is singularly Pauline (the noun occurs elsewhere only in 2 Cor. 9:8 and the adjective in Phil. 4:11). Godliness will only be true *gain* when independent of circumstances, and the apostle himself provides an admirable pattern of this in Philippians 4:11. To the Stoic notion of self-mastery Christianity brings the essential quality of a contented mind.

7–8. The thought contained in verse 7 has many parallels both biblical and classical and is cited here as axiomatic (*cf.* Jb. 1:21; Ec. 5:15). The thrust of what the apostle is saying is that material possessions are equally irrelevant at our entrance into and exit from the world. The second part of the statement points to the controlling factor, for it shows the folly of the constant quest to amass possesions which must be left behind at death. The saying also highlights the transitoriness of human life. Contentment in the present depends on a belief in a future which is independent of material things. Real living is infinitely more than the gaining of what is merely transitory.

Verse 8 gives a definition of Christian contentment. If we have no more than the bare necessities such as *food and clothing* (*skepasma* literally means 'covering material', which may represent shelter as well as clothes) contentment should result. The Stoics provide some parallels to this approach to life. The words are a timely reminder of the weakness of a consumer society which is based on the assumption that possessions are a symbol of status. The credit boom would take a considerable bashing if this teaching were taken seriously. The fact is contentment does not come from owning whatever we want, for there is no end to what we want. A Christian approach to life can never make a central feature of the acquisition of material things.

9. Strong words are used in the description of those whose desires are set upon the acquisition of wealth. The words apply to all whose aims are controlled by the passion to increase material possessions, yet there is here no condemnation of such possessions in themselves. The apostle is not so much thinking of those already rich, as of those ever grasping to become so. On the two other occasions in the Pastorals where the word *trap* is used, it is described as the devil's, and this is suggested here by its close association with *temptation*. Three clear steps of decline are discernible: first the lure, then the lust, and finally the total moral ruin. The verb translated *plunge* (*bythizō*) vividly represents the desire for wealth as a personal monster which plunges its victim into an ocean of *ruin and destruction*. The linking of the two words (*olethros* and *apōleia*) suggests an irretrievable loss.

10. A well-known maxim is next quoted to justify the strong language just used. The Greek does not contain an article before *root*, hence the NIV inserts *a*. Even without the article the position of the words in the Greek throws emphasis on the word *root*, and parallels could be found to justify the definite article in English (as AV, RSV). This makes the expression more sweeping, but the apostle's mind is so absorbed with the snares of riches that he addresses himself to extreme cases. Certainly for those mentioned in verse 9 the root of all their evils was *love of money*, but it must not be deduced from this that love of money is the sole root of all evils, for the New Testament does not support this. Such graspers have been led to take a wrong turning, they *have wandered from the faith*. The passive form of the verb (*apoplaneō*) used here suggests that they are helpless dupes in the grip of a merciless deception. At the same time the process of piercing is laid to their own charge, for they *pierced themselves with many griefs* (*odynē*, 'distress'). There is much pain in self-inflicted pangs of disillusionment.

C. A CHARGE TO A MAN OF GOD (6:11–16)

11. The apostle addresses Timothy as a *man of God* in striking contrast to the previous description of a man of material desire (the opening words *But you* (*sy de*) are emphatic). Yet the things which Timothy must *flee from* must be given a wider connotation than the dangers of wealth. There is probably an extended reference to all the vices mentioned from verse 4 onwards.

The antithesis in the words *flee . . . pursue* is in the characteristic manner of Paul. It is repeated exactly in 2 Timothy 2:22. Of the objects of pursuit the first two describe a general religious disposition, *righteousness* being used in its widest sense of conformity to what is right towards both God and man, and *godliness* of general piety. This double pursuit is also found in Titus 2:12. The two following virtues, *faith* and *love*, are fundamental to Christianity and cardinal in Paul's teaching. It has been suggested that for Paul faith and love were sufficient to stand alone without needing to be linked with other virtues. But in Galatians 5:22 the same two virtues occur with others in a statement about the fruit of the Spirit.

The concluding virtues, *endurance and gentleness*, link together two very different qualities. The first has an element of strength, a patient stickability. But the second is softer, a gentleness of feeling, which in itself is a somewhat rarer quality. It is a precious target for the man of God.

12. The command to *Fight* (*agōnizō*, lit. 'to contend for a prize') is generally supposed to be an allusion to the Olympic Games and this seems supported by the cognate use of the noun *agōn* (*fight*). It may by this time have become stereotyped as an athletic metaphor, or it may still have retained its military meaning. Whether in contest or in conflict, the verb implies a disciplined struggle already begun, but the following verb *Take hold of* (*epilabou*) denotes a single complete event. This thought does not exclude the idea of *eternal life* as a present possession in the Johannine sense, but points to its perfect appropriation.

The *good confession* is taken by most commentators to refer to Timothy's baptism, although some have seen an allusion to ordination, but the close link with the quest for eternal life suits the former occasion better than the latter.

13. Timothy's own confession is compared with Christ's confession before Pilate, and a solemn charge is delivered, conditioned by the character of the witnesses (*i.e.* the life-giving God and the confessing Christ). The reason for describing God in this context as the God *who gives life to everything* is to bring out the the ever-present character of the divine witness. The notion of Christ as a witness is more characteristic of the Johannine writings (*cf.* Rev. 1:5 and Jn. 18:37) than Paul's, but the latter often invokes God as witness (*cf.* Rom. 1:9; 2 Cor. 1:23; Phil. 1:8; 1 Thes. 2:5, 10).

14. The *command* which Timothy is urged to keep spotless is probably Timothy's baptismal commission. It may, however, refer to the charge in verses 11 and 12, which is invested with sufficient solemnity to be termed a commandment. This latter view seems more in keeping with the context, especially if these verses refer to ordination. It is strange to find such words as *without spot or blame* applied to a commandment and this has led some scholars to construe it with the subject of the verb (*i.e.* that Timothy himself is to be without spot or blame), but this suggestion involves an awkward Greek construction. Nevertheless the context seems to demand the application of the words to Timothy himself and it is preferable to understand them in this way.

There is a distant forward look in this verse, which may mean that the *appearing* (*epiphaneia*) of Christ was no longer considered imminent. The coming is envisaged as a definite historical event still in the future (*cf.* 1 Thes. 3:13; 5;23; 1 Cor. 1:8; Phil. 2:15–16 for the Pauline idea of blamelessness at the coming of Christ or in the day of Christ).

15–16. It is not unlike Paul to launch suddenly into a magnificent doxology, but some scholars have questioned whether the doxology itself is not more like a Christian hymn than a spontaneous Pauline production. The titles used of God cannot be precisely paralleled from Paul's writings, while the ascription of the adjective *blessed* to God is found only in the Pastorals in biblical Greek, although Hellenic parallels exist (see note on 1:11).

It has been suggested that this doxology may be reminiscent of a formula in use in synagogue worship because of its strong Jewish flavour (*cf.* Kelly). If so it may well have been a doxology which sprang readily to the lips of the apostle when his mind was centred on God's sovereign disposition of the events of time. The word translated *Ruler* (*dynastēs*) in contemporary usage meant a prince or chieftain as distinct from a king exercising sovereignty in his own power. But the description *only* makes clear that the apostle was not referring to a delegated authority (which in God is inconceivable), but a unique and princely dignity. The same title is applied to God in Ecclesiasticus and 2 Maccabees, but in the New Testament it is found elsewhere only in the Lucan writings (Lk. 1:52; Acts 8:27) where it applies to human officials.

In the Apocalypse (17:14; 19:16) the double title *King of kings and Lord of lords* is twice used of Christ, which suggests that it was probably an accepted Christian ascription. There are parallels in the Old Testament (Dt. 10:17; Ps. 136:3; Dn. 4:34; LXX) and in the Apocrypha (2 Macc. 13:4).

Already in 1:17 the quality *immortal* is applied to God, although there the adjective *aphthartos* is used, while here the noun *athanasia* (immortality) occurs. Both words are found in parallel clauses in 1 Corinthians 15:53–54 with apparently no difference of meaning. The expression *who alone is immortal* does not deny it to any other, but brings out the uniqueness of the divine immortality in that God alone inherently possesses it, being himself the source of all life. Linked with this characteristic of eternity are two qualities which equally distinguish God from all others, his transcendence (*who lives in unapproachable light*) and his invisibility (*whom no-one has seen or can see*). Undoubtedly the background of the apostle's thought is Exodus 33:17–23 which graphically portrays the awful majesty of God. The more usual conclusion of a doxology is an ascription of glory (*doxa*) to God, but here the words *honour* (*timē*) and *might* (*kratos*) are probably called forth by the present use of the word *Ruler*. Other Pauline uses of the word *kratos* in the sense of God's power are found in Ephesians 1:19, 6:10 and Colossians 1:11).

D. ADVICE TO WEALTHY MEN (6:17–19)

The preceding section was parenthetical for the theme of riches is now resumed, although with a different purpose. The earlier section concerned those aspiring to be rich, whereas this deals with those already rich. It should be noted that such a digression is characteristic of Paul's style.

17. The approach to wealth is strikingly moderate. There is no suggestion of denunciation. Rich men must carefully avoid two perils: (a) loftiness of mind, and (b) too much dependence on wealth. One suggestion is that the parable of the man who built his house on the sand may lie beneath this warning (*cf.*

Scott). In face of the increase in materialism the reminder of the uncertainty of riches is relevant to our modern age. There is the danger of trusting in material security instead of in God, the Giver of all things. These words would incidentally provide an answer to excessive abstinence, for if God has ordained everything for enjoyment (*who richly provides us with everything for our enjoyment*) the ascetic approach cannot be right.

18–19. Positive and practical demands are made upon rich men. Their actions are to be characterized by goodness and generosity, both of which are described actively and passively. They are *to do good* and *to be rich in good deeds*. They are further to be generous and to share with others.

Because of the mixture of metaphors involved in laying up *treasure* as a *firm foundation*, some have suggested a textual emendation. Moffatt, for instance, changes to 'amassing right good treasure' (assuming *thēma lian* instead of *themelion*). But because the emendation not only lacks any MS support but also involves an awkward Greek construction, it is better to assume a mixture of metaphors. At least, the thought is clear, and is reminiscent of the words of Jesus (Mt. 6:20 and Lk. 18:22).

The concluding clause (*so that they may take hold of the life that is truly life*) is closely linked with the similar phrase in verse 12, but with an interesting variation. The Greek *tēs ontōs zōēs* must be rendered *life that is truly life* (as NIV) or 'life indeed' (as RSV), bringing out its contrast with life propped up by so uncertain a support as riches.

E. FINAL ADMONITION TO TIMOTHY (6:20–21)

20. The Epistle closes with another exhortation urging Timothy to *guard* the faith as a fixed deposit (*parathēkē*), a word which occurs only here and in 2 Timothy 1:12, 14 in the New Testament. This deposit cannot be distinguished from the frequent objective use of such terms as 'the faith', or 'the commandment', but its particular significance is found in the preciousness of what is to be guarded. It is like treasure deposited in a bank for safe keeping. The metaphor must not, of course, be pressed too far, for the minister of the gospel does not keep the 'deposit' from others, but encourages them to come and share in its precious secrets.

Timothy is to guard the deposit by deliberately turning away (the same verb *ektrepomai* as is applied in 1:6 to the false teachers' defection from truth) from the false teaching, here described as *godless chatter* and *opposing ideas*. The meaning of the first expression is clear from parallels in the Pastorals (*e.g.* 1 Tim. 4:7; 2 Tim. 2:16), throughout which the futility of the false teachers' jargon is frequently stressed. The second word (translated *opposing ideas*) has occasioned much discussion because of Marcion's use of the same term *antitheseis* as a title for his gnostic speculations based on the alleged opposition between the Old Testament and the Christian gospel. Only scholars who date the Pastorals very late can claim that Marcion's work is here specifically referred to, but there is no evidence to show that Marcion was the first to use the word in this sense, nor is there sufficient support in the scattered references in the Pastorals to prove that Marcion's teaching is in mind. For further discussion of this see Introduction, pp. 43ff.).

The *falsely called knowledge* that Timothy must shun should be understood in the light of the empty and godless chatter of which the apostle has already spoken. The false teachers were claiming quite naturally that their teaching was the true *knowledge* (*gnōsis*), a characteristic certainty not confined to second-century gnosticism. It is evident in all the modern cults which claim an exclusive grasp of true 'knowledge'.

21. This parting shot at the false teachers significantly uses the same word (*have wandered*, *astocheō*) to describe their defection as was used at the beginning of the Epistle (1:6).

The concluding benediction is interesting because *with you* is in the plural. This may mean that the Epistle was designed for others besides Timothy, although examples in the papyri of the plural used for individuals are not uncommon.[1] Both 2 Timothy and Titus close with the same plural greeting, while the conclusion to the Epistle to the Colossians furnishes an exact parallel from Paul's earlier letters.

[1] *Cf.* Moulton, *Expositor*, 6th series, 7:107.

2 TIMOTHY: ANALYSIS

I. SALUTATION (1:1–2)

II. THANKSGIVING (1:3–5)

III. ENCOURAGEMENT FROM EXPERIENCE (1:6–14)
A. THE GIFT OF GOD (1:6–10)
B. THE TESTIMONY OF PAUL (1:11–12)
C. THE CHARGE TO TIMOTHY (1:13–14)

IV. PAUL AND HIS ASSOCIATES (1:15–2:2)
A. THE ASIATICS (1:15)
B. ONESIPHORUS (1:16–18)
C. TIMOTHY (2:1–2)

V. DIRECTIONS TO TIMOTHY (2:3–26)
A. THE BASIS OF ENCOURAGEMENT AND EXHORTATION (2:3–13)
  i. *Various examples* (2:3–6)
  ii. *Further reminiscences* (2:7–10)
  iii. *A Christian hymn* (2:11–13)
b. METHODS OF DEALING WITH FALSE TEACHERS (2:14–26)
  i. *Positive action: what to promote* (2:14–15)
  ii. *Negative action: what to shun* (2:16–18)
  iii. *Ultimate certainties* (2:19)
  iv. *Degrees of honour* (2:20–21)
  v. *The teacher's behaviour* (2:22–26)

2 TIMOTHY: COMMENTARY

I. SALUTATION (1:1-2)

1. As in the other Pastorals, Paul claims the title *apostle of Christ Jesus* (*cf.* note on 1 Tim. 1:1). The formal opening to this Epistle, although in conformity with ancient practice, seems rather stiff when addressed to Paul's closest associate. It is argued by many who dispute the Pauline authorship that it is unthinkable that Paul would use such solemn formality to his tried lieutenant, but he is clearly not informing Timothy of his apostleship or even reminding him. It is rather that he can never forget the noble work to which he was so impressively called. The phrase *by the will of God* reflects Paul's deep consciousness of the divine purpose for his life, and springs from his constant wonder at the catastrophic encounter near the gates of Damascus.

Unlike the opening of 1 Timothy, the phrase *by the will of God* is here qualified by the words *according to the promise of life*, which give the purpose of Paul's apostleship. He is sent to proclaim a gospel of life, and Timothy is reminded at the commencement of this Epistle of the apostle's high calling.

The concluding words, *that is in Christ Jesus*, qualifying *life*, conceive of the Christian's life as being centred in Christ, an idea reminiscent of Galatians 2:20, where Paul says, 'I no longer live, but Christ lives in me'. This use of the formula *in Christ* accords, therefore, with Paul's thought.

2. A greater intimacy is introduced in the description of Timothy as *my dear son*, and there can be no doubt that this young man was held in the most affectionate esteem by the great apostle. As in the salutation in 1 Timothy, *mercy* is added to the more usual *grace* and *peace* (*cf.* 1 Tim. 1:2).

II. THANKSGIVING (1:3–5)

Here only in the Pastorals does Paul follow his frequent procedure of including thanksgiving and intercession immediately after the salutation, a practice which had become an accepted convention in contemporary letter-writing.

3. The same formula is used to denote thanks as in 1 Timothy 1:12 (*cf.* note there), although it is not the usual Pauline formula. The apostle mentions his service to the same God as his ancestors, in order perhaps to draw attention to what he is about to say concerning Timothy's own forebears. The words *whom I serve, as my forefathers did* must be understood to mean that Paul thought of Judaism in such close connection with Christianity that his present worship of God is in a sense a continuation of his own Jewish worship. Although possessing such firm convictions about the superseding of the Jewish law, he never speaks of it with disrespect and sometimes even expresses pride in its observance (*cf.* Rom. 7:12; Phil. 3:4–6).

This service must be carried out with a *clear conscience* (an expression parallel to that occurring in 1 Tim. 1:5). As a Jew the apostle would know that morality and worship and service go hand in hand. When worshipping God the believer must have no ulterior motives, his mind and purpose must be untainted.

When Paul says *as night and day I constantly remember you*, this constancy in prayer for the Christian communities whom he served may be amply illustrated from Paul's other letters (*cf.* Rom. 1:9; Phil. 1:3; Col. 1:3), and he would be even more diligent in praying for his closest associates. Whenever Paul remembered Timothy he gave thanks to God for him.

The mention of *night and day* brings out the seriousness of the apostle's purpose, reminiscent of Acts 20:31. The same expression, applied to prayer, is found in the directions to genuine widows in 1 Timothy 5:5, and since in that case it concludes the clause, there is justification for the NIV (and AV) connecting it with the preceding words in this case. It stresses the continuity of prayer and gives added strength to the Greek word *adialeiptos* (*constantly*), a word found elsewhere only in Romans 9:2 in the New Testament. The RSV, however, following the RV, attaches the words to the next clause, 'I long night and day to see you'. In either case the frequency of prayer for Timothy would intensify the longing to see him. Such expressions as these illuminate the spiritual stature of the apostle who in constant and hazardous journeyings could maintain an attitude of continuous intercession. His practice provides an example for all servants of the gospel.

4. The apostle's intensity of feeling frequently comes to the surface in his letters, and the words *I long to see you* are reminiscent of the strong yearning found in Romans 1:11; 1 Thessalonians 3:6 and Philippians 1:8, where the same verb (*epipotheō*) is used. A particularly intimate touch is the memory of Timothy's tears (*recalling your tears*), which appears to be a reference to their last time of meeting (*cf.* Acts 20:37). In modern times convention restrains men's tears, but in Paul's time the expression of strong emotion was less inhibited. Timothy, who seems to have been a sensitive type of man and who was deeply attached to the apostle, obviously felt the parting keenly.

The apostle does not disguise his own pleasure at the prospect of seeing his friend. In the Greek the word for *tears* and the word for *joy* are closely juxtaposed. Though partings are often painful their very tears are a pledge of greater joy at the possibility of reunion. The words *so that I may be filled with joy* are characteristic of the apostle's wholeheartedness, for he uses the verb 'fill' (*plēroō*) no less than twenty-three times.

5. When Paul says *I have been reminded*, it may be that he had just had news of Timothy (so Bengel). The expression in the Greek would support this (*hypomnēsin labōn* literally meaning 'having received a reminder'). It is striking to note that four different expressions are used in verses 3–6 to denote memory. *Remember* in verse 3 is paralleled in 1 Thessalonians 3:6; *recalling* in verse 4 is used in 1 Corinthians 11:2; *I have been reminded* in verse 5 is not used elsewhere in Paul (but *cf.* 2 Pet. 1:13); and *I* *remind you* in verse 6 is paralleled in 1 Corinthians 4:17. This rich variety of wording emphasizes the apostle's reminiscent mood, and his desire that Timothy himself should have stores of memory on which to draw.

It is Timothy's *sincere faith* which prompts some further reflections. A similar description of faith has already been met in 1 Timothy 1:5, although it is not found elsewhere in Paul. There is no need to imply from the use of the qualifying adjective *sincere* that faith here means no more than religious feeling. A profession of faith, understood as commitment to the Christian doctrine, could certainly be unreal. In this case the sincerity of faith was transparent and there was good reason, therefore, for its special mention. Paul refers in the Pastorals to some of Timothy's weaknesses, such as his timidity, but there was no deficiency in his faith.

The indwelling of faith is paralleled by the Pauline ideas of the indwelling God (2 Cor. 6:16), the indwelling Spirit (Rom. 8:11; 2 Tim. 1:14), the indwelling word (Col. 3:16) and indwelling sin (Rom. 7:17). The metaphor of a building and its inhabitants was well suited to express this inner character of Christianity.

The thought of Timothy's faith stimulates the memory of his grandmother's and mother's faith. But there is difference of opinion among commentators whether the Christian or Jewish faith is here meant. The use of the word *first* (*prōton*) in this context has been supposed to indicate that Lois was a devout Jewess and was the first to incalcate religious faith in Timothy; in other words from his earliest days he had been surrounded by religious faith. Yet if Christian faith is intended, *prōton* may mean that Lois was the first to become a Christian, followed by Eunice and her son. The reference to Timothy's parents in Acts 16:1 is little help in solving this question since the word 'believer' used of Eunice could apply equally to both Jewish and Christian believers. Since by her marriage to a Greek Eunice cannot have been a strictly orthodox Jewess, it seems more probable that Christian faith is meant (*cf.* comment on 3:15). The lack of mention of Timothy's father, who according to Acts 16:1 was a Greek, was probably because he was not a Christian (*cf.* Jeremias). Such personal details bear a genuine stamp and some scholars who dispute the authenticity of the Pastorals as a whole list this passage among the genuine fragments (*e.g.* Falconer). It is difficult to believe that a pseudonymous writer would have thought of mentioning Timothy's forebears by name if the Epistle was directed to some 'Timothy' of a later age.

The apostle was not only deeply conscious of the powerful home influences which had shaped his own career, but was impressed by the saintly atmosphere of Timothy's home. Lois and Eunice were perhaps well known in the Christian church for their domestic piety. The apostle closes this personal reminiscence by the assertion of a strong conviction (*I am persuaded*), in thoroughly characteristic style, the verb *peithō* being used twenty-two times in Paul's writings. There is no doubt in his mind about Timothy's faith.

III. ENCOURAGEMENT FROM EXPERIENCE (1:6–14)

There is no real break between this section and the last, for it is thankfulness over Timothy's faith that leads Paul immediately to give his first personal charge to his lieutenant. The terms of this passage suggest that Paul recognizes that Timothy's character requires some moral stiffening.

A. THE GIFT OF GOD (1:6–10)

6. The opening words *For this reason* (an unusual Greek expression for Paul), connects with the apostle's assurance regarding Timothy's faith. Because of this, Timothy is first encouraged by being reminded of God's commission to him. For his heavy responsibilities he needs no new gift but a rekindling of that already received. The words *fan into flame* (*anazōpyreō*) can be understood either in the sense of 'kindle afresh' or 'to keep in full flame' (Abbott-Smith). There is no necessary suggestion, therefore, that Timothy had lost his early fire, although undoubtedly, like every Christian, he needed an incentive to keep the fire burning at full flame.

As in 1 Timothy 4:14, *the gift of God* (*charisma*) is certainly more than natural ability and has the character of a supernatural operation of the Spirit. In both cases the endowment is connected with the laying on of hands, and must be understood in the light of the special tasks to which Timothy was commissioned on that important occasion.

It is noticeable that the gift is specified as being *in* (*en*) Timothy, making quite clear that the true gift of God is an internal grace and not an external operation. Every Christian minister needs at times to return to the inspiration of his ordination, to be reminded not only of the greatness of his calling, but also of the adequacy of the divine grace which enables him to perform it. Indeed, every Christian worker engaged in however small a task requires assurance that God never commissions anyone to a task without imparting a special gift appropriate for it.

7. The gift is now defined more precisely since the connecting particle *For* links this verse closely with verse 6. The words *God did not give* focus attention on the event when it took place. This may indirectly refer to the outpouring of the Spirit on the Christian church at Pentecost, in view of the collective pronoun *us* (*hēmin*). But it seems better to assume that the plural is here used to soften a direct personal criticism and that the occasion of Timothy's own commissioning is in view. It may be that his besetting sin was timidity, and this was Paul's tactful way of dealing with it.

The negative statement, *not . . . a spirit of timidity*, serves to heighten the positive. The word for 'timidity' or 'cowardice' (*deilia*) is used only here in the Greek Testament, although frequently in the LXX. The statement is reminiscent of Romans 8:15, although it must be noted that the purpose of each passage is different. It was unthinkable to the apostle that Timothy could have received a spirit of cowardice at ordination. The Christian gospel could never be furthered by men of craven spirit. Instead, the Christian minister receives a triad of graces, *i.e. power*, *love* and *self-discipline*. The spirit of *power* means not that the servant of God must of necessity be a powerful personality, but that he has strength of character to be bold in the exercise of authority. The power of the Holy Spirit within him has enabled many a naturally timid man to develop a boldness not his own when called in the name of God to fulfil a difficult ministry. The spirit of *love* is indispensable to all Christians, most of all to the chosen ministers of Christ, and none understood its power more clearly than the apostle who wrote the incomparable hymn of love in 1 Corinthians 13. The third feature is *self-discipline* which is equally necessary in ministry for no-one can have discipline over others who has not first subdued himself. The apostle here has more in mind that stoical self-effort, for the self-mastery is part of the divinely bestowed gift.

8. In virtue of these special endowments Timothy is told *So do not be ashamed*. There is no need to suppose that Timothy had already shown symptoms of shame, but the apostle is evidently intent on strengthening his mind should the temptation arise. Natural timidity quickly breeds shame; and calls to courage are not out of place even for many who have proved stalwarts of the faith. The words translated *to testify about our Lord* could be translated to mean 'the testimony borne by our Lord'. But the former has the support of 1 Corinthians 1:6 and is favoured by most commentators. It would refer to the Christian message as a whole. Such a message would bring ignominy to its preachers, especially in a Greek environment where the preaching of the cross was foolishness (1 Cor. 1:23). Timothy might also be tempted to be ashamed of Paul's chains, since imprisonment for the sake of the gospel carried with it a social stigma. The apostle is so deeply conscious of the Lord's purpose in his present affliction that he can describe himself as *his prisoner*, as in Ephesians 3:1 (*cf.* also Phil. 1:12–14). Men might imprison his body, but they could never enslave his spirit. To Christ alone he acknowledged himself a captive.

The exhortation, *join with me in suffering for the gospel* (RSV has 'take your share of suffering'), is a development of the previous prohibitions. It denotes a readiness to share, if need be, the same afflictions that others have endured for the sake of the gospel. A new word seems to have been coined to express this thought, *synkakopatheō*, which means 'to take one's share of ill-treatment' (*cf.* Abbott-Smith; *cf.* also 2:3). It may be that the prefix *syn* (with) is used to urge Timothy to recognize that he must be prepared to share some of the apostle's sufferings. The evil treatment meted out to Christ's ministers is a recurring theme in this Epistle, for the uncompounded verb is also used (2:9; 4:5). The concluding words *by the power of God* are intended to assure Timothy that the sharing of suffering for the gospel's sake is never undertaken in one's own strength. 'Stronger than all suffering is the power of God' (Jeremias). This is the complement of verse 7 where a spirit of *power* is included in God's gifts.

9. This verse and the next are considered by some scholars to be cited from a Christian hymn, but if so the language and thought are thoroughly Pauline, and it would be necessary to suppose either that the apostle had written the hymn himself or that he had used an existing hymn which expressed exactly what he wanted to say.[1] First he makes a double assertion about God's relation to us. God *has saved us and called us*. His saving activity is prominent in the Pastorals, especially in the sixfold use of the title 'Saviour', and although this designation occurs only twice elsewhere in Pauline writings, the idea of divine agency in human salvation is more prominent in Paul than in any other New Testament writer (*cf.* 1 Cor. 1:21).

The Christian's vocation is attributed to God, as usual in Pauline writings (*e.g.* Rom. 8:28; 1 Cor. 1:9; Gal. 1:6). There is a close connection between salvation and vocation. Christians are saved not only from a life of sin but to a life of holiness. As Spicq well puts it, 'The consequence of salvation is a consecration of Christians'. God has called us *to a holy life* because he himself is holy. His activities partake of his own character. The same idea is found in 1 Thessalonians 4:7 where the call to holiness is set over against uncleanness.

The apostle then makes clear the controlling factor in this calling. It was not on the basis *of anything we have done* (Gk. *ou kata ta erga*), as Paul so constantly stressed and as he himself had so poignantly experienced (*cf.* Tit. 3:5 for the same negation of works in the Pastorals). It is a process of God's *own purpose and grace*, which provides a solid ground for assurance. No words could sum up more characteristically the Pauline approach to

---

[1] See my monograph, *The Pastoral Epistles and the Mind of Paul*, pp. 17-29, for a fuller discussion of this point.

Christian calling than the phrase *because of his own purpose and grace*. For the same idea of divine purpose, see Romans 8:28; 9:11; Ephesians 1:11. The focus on the sovereign choice of God is unmistakable. This grace is not earned but *given us in Christ Jesus*, another typically Pauline phrase, if we understand the words in the sense that Christ is the medium for the imparting of grace. This gift was determined *before the beginning of time* (RSV has 'ages ago'). For the same idea, *cf.* Titus 1:2. The phrase is introduced here to bring into greater relief the historic appearance of Christ (verse 10). This may be a reference to the earliest promise of triumph to the woman's seed (Gn. 3:15), or to the grace of the pre-existent Christ.

10. The thought moves from eternity to time. Though the idea of God's eternal purposes of grace may be beyond comprehension, at least the fact of the incarnation is capable of being understood. The grace, *which has now been revealed through the appearing of our Saviour, Christ Jesus*, is echoed again in Titus 2:11–13, where the same word *epiphaneia* is used for *appearing*. In the Titus passage, however, the word refers to the second and not the first advent as here. Because of the use of the same word and also the title 'Saviour' in the mystery cults and in the emperor cult, some scholars have claimed that we have here a Christian protest against a pagan doctrine. But a more probable explanation is that the Christians were echoing terminology being used in its pagan surroundings. In any case the word *epiphaneia* is used by Paul in 2 Thessalonians 2:8. Moreover, the contrast between a mystery once hid but now revealed is the thought of the doxology in Romans 16:25–27, a passage whose language is closely akin to this.

The word translated *destroyed* (*katargeō*) here used to describe the abolition of death is a favourite with Paul. In 1 Corinthians 15:26 he speaks of death as the last enemy to be destroyed (the same verb as here), and although his thought there is clearly future whereas the tenses of the verbs here denote a complete event, no contradiction need be assumed. Here the whole range of Christ's work is envisaged as an accomplished fact, but there the attention is focused on its consummation. Although Christians are not absolved from physical death, their approach to it means its virtual abolition since it is no longer to be feared (Heb. 2:14–15) and has lost its sting (1 Cor. 15:55).

But Christ is not only a great destroyer. He is also a great illuminator. *Life and immortality* had been obscured until the gospel, but now they are flooded with light. The same thought is found in Ephesians 3:9 where Paul describes the grace given him to bring to light the mystery hidden for ages. By linking *immortality (aphtharsia)* with *life*, the apostle defines more closely the quality of *life*. Because Christians possess a life which cannot decay, anticipation of the accident of physical death can do nothing to destroy their confidence.

By the *gospel* is meant the entire revelation of God in Christ. It is noteworthy that nothing is said of the manner in which death is nullified and life illuminated, but since the channel of revelation is the *gospel*, the action must be understood in the light of Christ's life and death and teaching. This verse lends no support, therefore, to the gnostic view of salvation by illumination.

B. THE TESTIMONY OF PAUL (1:11–12)

11. For the passive form of the verb *was appointed* see the comment on 1 Timothy 2:7, where Paul also expressed his awareness of the divine origin of his commission. The same three designations of his work are repeated here, but without any strong assertion of veracity (*cf.* 'I am not lying' in 1 Tim. 2:7). It is reasonable to enquire whether such a reminder was necessary for Timothy, who would certainly be well acquainted with Paul's commission. Some scholars see here a pointer to non-Pauline authorship. But it need not be taken that Paul is informing his lieutenant, which would admittedly be inconceivable, but that, as in 1 Timothy 2:7, his mind is so carried away by the thought of the greatness of the gospel that the wonder of his own call to preach it dominates him here.

12. Timothy is reminded that Paul's present sufferings are entirely due to the fact that he is a preacher of the gospel. The same Greek expression, which is here translated *That is why*, is used in verse 6 and again emphasizes the connection with the previous statement.

As Paul contemplates his present unenviable position he is led to make a great personal affirmation calculated to encourage Timothy in his own sufferings for the gospel. He is *not ashamed* of his bonds, even if others are, and this personal claim is probably intended to reinforce the advice given to Timothy in verse 8.

In spite of the constant appeal to sound doctrine in the Pastorals generally and in this context in particular, there is no justification for the view that personal faith has given place to a formulated creed. It is significant that the apostle's affirmation in this verse is so intensely personal. *I know whom I have believed* draws attention to the intimate relationship between himself and God. The statement would have lost immeasurably if Paul had said 'what' instead of 'whom'. His persuasion here is reminiscent of his persuasion in Romans 8:38 that nothing can separate us from the love of God (*cf.* also verse 5 where the same verb is used in the passive for virtual certainty). The perfect tense used in this context brings out the continuous assurance that the apostle enjoys.

The words *what I have entrusted to him* represent an expression (*parathēkē mou*) which literally means 'my deposit'. The noun is used in verse 14 and 1 Timothy 6:20, where in both cases it describes the deposit committed to Timothy for safe keeping. But the present verse focuses attention on God's ability to guard. The 'deposit' could be understood either of what God entrusted to Paul or what Paul entrusted to God, but since in the other occurrences in the Pastorals the word *parathēkē* is used in the former sense, it is most probably used in the same sense here. In that case the reference is to the work which the apostle was commissioned to do or the doctrine entrusted to him. Some scholars dispute that the word here is used in the same sense as in the other cases. One suggestion is that Paul is referring to himself or his 'soul', or else everything that he has committed to God, himself, his work, his converts.

That day, used again in this undefined manner in 1:18 and 4:8, must be understood of the Parousia (the second coming) as in 2 Thessalonians 1:10 (*cf.* also in 1 Cor. 3:13). A suggestion worth considering is that there is an allusion to the parable of the talents. The deposit in this case is likened to the talents which were committed to the different servants and Paul sees it as of paramount importance to be able to give a good account of his stewardship.

C. THE CHARGE TO TIMOTHY (1:13–14)

13. An interesting word is used to denote *the pattern of sound teaching* which Timothy is urged to *guard*. *Hypotypōsis* means an outline sketch such as an architect might make before getting down to the detailed plans of a building. The importance of this pattern cannot be over-emphasized. It means that the apostle claims his own teaching to be no more than a starting-point. It was to be a guide-line rather than a stereotyped form of words. It would allow for growth within that guide-line (*cf.* 1 Tim. 1:16 for a discussion of the word *hypotypōsis*). Timothy is not told merely to repeat what Paul taught, but to follow that teaching as a basis. Its description as *sound teaching* has been previously noticed as characteristic of the Pastorals, but nowhere is the link between sound words and what Paul himself taught so clearly specified as here.

The Greek construction makes clear that what Timothy has heard is *sound teaching* and not the 'form' or *pattern* underlying it. The content must always be considered of greater importance than the shape. The exhortation calls for some effort on Timothy's part, for he is to *guard* the deposit. It is better to treat *pattern* (without the article) as a predicate and to understand the words to mean, 'Hold as a pattern of sound words what you heard from me'. In this case the words *with faith and love* would qualify the act of holding and would not be attached to *sound teaching*. The manner in which Timothy maintained his orthodoxy was as important as the orthodoxy itself. Had all loyalty to sound words been tempered by these great Christian virtues, *faith and love*, the bitterness of much ecclesiastical disputation would have been impossible. The two virtues must go together, as Paul eloquently shows in 1 Corinthians 13. The recurrence of the favourite Pauline phrase *in Christ Jesus* shows that an intimate union with Christ is necessary before faith and love are possible. Neither Easton's translation 'in Christian faith and love', nor Moffatt's 'in faith and love of Christ Jesus' does justice to the mystical connotation of the expression. It is true that in Paul's other writings the phrase 'in Christ' is mostly applied to persons and not virtues, but there is no necessity to suppose a discrepancy here. The meaning clearly is that faith and love follow from abiding *in Christ*.

14. This verse is an amplification of the last with special emphasis on guarding the *good deposit*. We have noted above that the same word is used as in verse 12, but whereas in the former case the deposit is kept safe in God's hands, here Timothy himself must guarantee its security. Although the human element is more stressed, it is immediately recognized that Timothy unaided could never achieve it. It can come only *with the help of the Holy Spirit* (*dia pneumatos hagiou*). The Spirit is the one *who lives in us* (for the idea of indwelling, see note on verse 5). Paul states in Romans 8:9–11 that the Spirit dwells in every Christian, but a special endowment is given to those set apart for specific tasks, closely akin to the primitive *charismata* (spiritual gifts) mentioned in 1 Corinthians.

There is no support in these verses for the Roman Catholic doctrine of the ministry as the custodian of the church's traditions (*cf.* Spicq), for the words *in us* need not mean, as is widely supposed, that Paul and Timothy are alone intended. The indwelling Spirit performs the same function in every Christian, although the degree of operation varies with the work done. This is very different from the view that a hint of a later doctrine of the Spirit is there to be found (*cf.* Scott). Even many who deny Pauline authorship recognize here a genuine Pauline concept (*cf.* Hanson). It is better to assume the words to mean that since the deposit must be faithfully guarded, any man without the aid of the Holy Spirit is attempting the impossible. But although the Spirit of God dwells in Christians generally, he may certainly be depended on to give gifts of power to ministers set apart from the work of the gospel.

IV. PAUL AND HIS ASSOCIATES (1:15 – 2:2)

A. THE ASIATICS (1:15)

15. The defection of the Asiatics is spoken of as a fact well known to Timothy, and for that reason would provide a powerful object lesson. The verb translated *deserted* (*apostrephō*) is used in Titus 1:14 of the false teachers who turn away from the truth, but here the context demands no more than a defection from the apostle himself. Nevertheless this is painful enough from whatever cause; and the fact that *Phygelus and Hermogenes* are singled out for special mention suggests that these were the main cause of the trouble. Nothing more is known about them, and it can only be surmised that they were probably opponents of Paul's mission and authority. When Paul says that *everyone in the province of Asia has deserted me* he probably means that none of the Asiatics had come to his assistance in the present crisis. One scholar, however, speaks of the 'all' as the sweeping assertion of depression (*cf.* White). *Asia* is the Roman province comprising Mysia, Lydia, Caria, most of Phrygia and the islands off the coast. Another possibility is that Paul is referring to the failure of Asian Christians in Rome to give him support at his trial. In that case, however, the Greek preposition *ek* would have been preferred to *en*, which implies that the Christians were still in Asia at the time.

B. ONESIPHORUS (1:16–18)

16. In contrast to these, Onesiphorus is held up as a model of Christian kindness. Both here and in 4:19, there is mention of the *household of Onesiphorus* which suggests to some commentators that Onesiphorus is already dead. But there is an inseparable link between a man and his household, and there is no reason to suppose them to be separated here. It is true that this verse prays for mercy for the household, while verse 18 confines the prayer to Onesiphorus, yet in each case Onesiphorus himself is mainly in mind since it is he who is specially commended for kindness. In the Apocryphal *Acts of Paul and Thecla*, Onesiphorus is spoken of as a convert of Paul's who gave him hospitality on his first visit to Iconium. The particular help given by Onesiphorus is picturesquely described in the words *he often refreshed me*, conjuring up the idea that the presence of his friend provided a special tonic. Moffatt aptly expresses it, 'he braced me up'. Although Onesiphorus' help may have included material assistance, his fellowship was of much greater value. He seems somewhat sensitive to his chains, presumably because they had become an object of shame in the eyes of some (*cf.* verse 8). But one fellow-Christian at least, Onesiphorus, *was not ashamed*, and his example is probably cited as an indirect hint to Timothy.

17–18. In strong contrast to being ashamed, Onesiphorus had actually *searched hard for me until he found me*. Such earnestness in seeking was necessary because of the difficulties of tracking down prisoners in Rome.

The prayer of verse 18 is a reiteration of verse 16, but here an eschatological factor is introduced. *That day* is evidently the judgment day of Christ. It has been suggested that the first *Lord* with the article refers to Christ and the second without the article to God the Father, to whom the function of judgment is often attributed (so Spicq). This conforms to the LXX practice of applying the anarthrous form to God. Another suggestion is that the double mention of *Lord* springs from a mixed formula: (1) The Lord grant him to find mercy and (2) may he find mercy from the Lord (*i.e.* God; so Jeremias). A further possibility is to refer both to God, but this is most unlikely.

Since it is assumed by many scholars that Onesiphorus was by now dead, the question has been raised whether this sanctions prayer for the dead. Roman Catholic theologians claim that it does. Spicq, for instance, sees here an example of prayer for the dead unique in the New Testament. Some Protestants agree with this judgment and cite the Jewish precedent of 2 Macc. 12:43–45 (*e.g.* Bernard, who also appeals for support to early Christian epitaphs). Yet it is precarious to base a doctrine, which finds no sanction anywhere else in the New Testament, upon the mere inference that Onesiphorus was already dead. It is supposed that he must have been dead on three grounds: 1. only the house of Onesiphorus is here spoken of in the present tense; 2. in the closing salutations (4:19ff.) the same phrase is used coupled with the names of individuals; 3. the apostle's prayer for Onesiphorus himself relates to the day of judgment. But if the household was coupled with Onesiphorus in the apostle's warm affections, the difference of tense used would be explained as no more than a reminiscence of past events. Even if he were dead, however, the words need mean no more than that Paul is expressing a very natural feeling. The eschatological emphasis suggests that he is looking ahead and is keen that Timothy also should stand well in the judgment day.

The conclusion of the verse reminds Timothy of his familiarity with the solid Christian service Onesiphorus had done at Ephesus. The words *in how many ways he helped me* represent the Greek *hosa diēkonēsen* which contains no object and is therefore more general than the translation supposes. RSV rightly omits the *me* and calls attention to the wider extent of Onesiphorus' ministry. What this man had done in Ephesus he had continued to do in Rome.

C. TIMOTHY (2:1–2)

1. The personal exhortation to Timothy which follows contrasts with the general defection of the Asiatics, as the opening words *You then* show. The emphasis falls on *you*. The exhortation here is therefore re-inforced by the splendid example of Onesiphorus. Timothy is to *be strong*, a characteristic Pauline word (*endynamoō*) which occurs in the same sense in Ephesians 6:10.

The phrase *that is in Christ Jesus* qualifying *grace* shows not only that the grace comes from Christ alone, but also that all Christians possess it and may rely on its enabling power. There is no reason to suppose that *grace* here means power rather than favour, for any power which flows from union with Christ is through an act of grace. *Grace* here has the usual Pauline meaning of unmerited favour, but includes within it the divine enabling.

2. No doubt exists as to the precise nature of the tradition and doctrine to be transmitted, for Timothy had heard them from Paul's own lips (*cf.* 1:13). The next statement, *in the presence of many witnesses*, is somewhat obscure and has proved a perplexity to commentators.

1. It is sometimes explained by referring it to the occasion of Timothy's ordination, at which many would have witnessed the charges delivered by Paul to his child in the faith (*cf.* Lock). But in that case the preposition *dia* must be given the unusual meaning *in the presence of* as in NIV. This Greek usage is not impossible, but it is better to assign a more usual meaning if possible. Another difficulty with this view is that it appears to presuppose a charge too long to be feasible on a public occasion. In any case there is no supporting evidence for such a practice in primitive Christian records.

2. An alternative view is that the expression should be understood in a general sense and not restricted to a single event, in which case there would be no need to strain the Greek. The Greek would then need to be interpreted 'through the intervention of many witnesses', which presumably would mean that many witnesses could testify to what Paul had committed to Timothy.

3. Various attempts have been made to identify the witnesses. They could be the elders to whom Paul refers in 1 Timothy 4:14. Or they could be Timothy's mother and grandmother and others perhaps who had heard and seen the Lord (*cf.* Spicq), an idea which would well fit the context. If this view were correct, it would point to a greater breadth of mind on the part of the apostle who would not then restrict the deposit to his own transmission. It takes great grace for independent thinkers to acknowledge that truth can flow in channels other than their own.

4. Some have regarded the witnesses as impersonal representations either of the various forms and expressions of Paul's teaching, or, more generally, of all the evidences of apostolic authority. But neither of these interpretations belongs naturally to the context.

Of these various views the second seems the most natural and stresses for Timothy that what he is to pass on has a variety of witnesses to bolster up Timothy's own recollections. He is to *entrust* (*paratithēmi*) to others what he has heard Paul say. The verb used here has already occurred in 1 Timothy 1:18 for the committal of the charge to Timothy. It occurs in Acts 14:23 where Paul and Barnabas appointed elders and then committed them to the Lord, and also in Acts 20:32 where Paul similarly committed the Ephesian elders to God. The idea is clearly to entrust something to another for safe keeping, and in the present context this notion is of great significance. The transmission of Christian truth must never be left to chance, and is clearly not committed fortuitously to every Christian, but only to *reliable men who will also be qualified to teach others*. Two qualifications are demanded: a loyalty to the truth, *i.e.* a loyalty which has to be proved, and an aptitude to teach (*cf.* 1 Tim. 3:2).

Two important considerations arise out of this verse. First, the apostle is depicted as solicitous for the preservation of Christian teaching, and it cannot be imagined that he would ever have overlooked this necessity. He must at the end of his life have conceived of the teaching being in a form sufficiently fixed to be transmitted, in which case the claim that the stereotyped doctrine in the Pastorals is un-Pauline falls to the ground. Secondly it is evident that Paul recognized that the manner in which he himself had forged out the doctrines would not continue in the next generation, and that more normal methods of transmission would not only be resorted to, but would be essential. This passage gives no support for the Roman Catholic claim of a deposit of truth infallibly handed down, as in the ecclesiastical tradition.

V. DIRECTIONS TO TIMOTHY (2:3-26)

A. THE BASIS OF ENCOURAGEMENT AND EXHORTATION (2:3-13)

In verses 3–6 three suggestive illustrations are used to encourage Timothy in various aspects of his work. All three, the soldier, the athlete and the labourer, are taken from common life and are frequent literary metaphors, applied here in a specifically spiritual sense. From the soldier Timothy must learn endurance, from the athlete discipline and from the labourer perseverance.

i. Various examples (2:3-6)

3. Military metaphors are great favourites with the apostle Paul (*e.g.* Rom. 6:13; 7:23; 1 Cor. 9:7; 2 Cor. 6:7; Eph. 6:11–18). The soldier served as an admirable illustration of fortitude to Timothy who was probably anything but military in his approach to his unenviable task at Ephesus. The same verb which is translated *endure hardship* (*synkakopatheō*) was also used in 1:8. The root meaning is perhaps better brought out by the RSV 'take your share of suffering', for the hardship in mind is a part of the witness of the Christian. Every Christian must expect some measure of ill-treatment, as every soldier does. It may be that Timothy was over-sensitive about the evil treatment which constantly threatened him, but more probably the apostle is particularly burdened with the intensity of the spiritual struggle which he is about to lay down and which would naturally fall heavily on Timothy's shoulders. The allusion in Hebrew 13:23 to Timothy's release suggests that not long after Paul's decease his successor did, in fact, suffer imprisonment. The term *soldier of Christ Jesus* may well have been a current expression in view of the description of two of Paul's associates as 'fellow-soldiers' (Phil. 2:25 and Phm. 2).

4. The personal advice of verse 3 is reinforced by a general principle of soldiering. Anyone *serving as a soldier* has to be a man of one mind. When it is a question of priorities, the duties of military service must take precedence over *civilian affairs*. What is meant by this latter phrase is an open question among scholars, and the following suggestions have been made. 1. That ministers of the gospel should not be 'pre-occupied' with the things of this world. 2. That ministers should not engage in commerce at all. 3. That in Timothy's case he is not to attempt to emulate Paul in working to maintain himself, if by so doing the more important duties of the ministry are neglected. The first seems the most probable solution. The determining Greek word is *gets involved* (*emplekomai*) which envisages a soldier's weapons entrammelled in his cloak. The main point is therefore the renunciation of everything which hinders the real purpose of the soldier of Christ. There is nothing intrinsically wrong, in other words, about *civilian affairs* until they entangle. Then they must be resolutely cast aside.

The basic reason for such renunciation is added to reinforce the metaphor. A soldier must please his *commanding officer*, who would have been responsible for mustering an army to serve under him. This involves for the soldier a sinking of his own desires in a total effort to please his chief. No more admirable figure of speech could be found to illustrate the extent of Christ's claims upon his ministers.

5. The connecting link between the soldier and the athlete is found in the expression *according to the rules* (*nominōs*). In the Olympic games there were strict rules which had to be obeyed. Simpson cites Galen to the effect that this expression includes the idea 'in the correct style', applied to fully fledged athletes, professionals as opposed to amateurs. Each athlete for these Olympics had to state on oath that he had fulfilled the necessary ten months' training before he was permitted to enter the contest. Any athlete who had not subjected himself to the necessary discipline would have no chance of winning and would in fact lower the standard of the Games. There were severe penalties imposed on any who infringed the rules (*cf.* Spicq). It is worth noting that as the first metaphor owed much to Roman influence, so this one shows strong marks of Greek influence. Applied to the Christian ministry, this second metaphor stresses the absolute necessity for self-discipline. There may be a hint that suitable training is essential for the Christian ministry, but that idea can hardly have been in Paul's mind. It is better to assume that the apostle is here exhorting Timothy to keep strictly to the 'rules' fixed by the life and teaching of Christ. There is one important difference between the metaphor and its application; only one athlete may gain the *victor's crown*, but every Christian who strives loyally in the contest will be crowned (*cf.* 4:8).

6. The third of this triad of illustrations significantly places the emphasis on toil. *The hardworking farmer* has rights which the indolent man has forfeited. Clearly the right to a share of the crop that his toil has helped to raise is elementary, so much so that the illustration has been thought to be far-fetched (*cf.* Scott) and merely thrown in because of its occurrence in the passage in 1 Corinthians 9:10–11, which is supposed to be the source of the illustration. But there is real point in the illustration here, for the Lord's teaching that a labourer is worthy of his hire was understood by early Christians to mean that God's servants had the right to remuneration from the people whom they served. It may be that Timothy, emulating the example of Paul, had declined material assistance in the belief that it was more noble to do so, and needed therefore to be reminded of what he might fairly claim for himself.

ii. Further reminiscences (2:7–10)

7. There follows an exhortation to *reflect on what I am saying* (the verb *noeō* means to 'understand', 'to think over'). This can be taken in either of two ways – generally of everything that Paul has taught Timothy, or more specifically of the teaching contained in the illustrations just quoted. If Timothy seriously attempts to 'grasp the meaning' (White), *the Lord* will supply all needed wisdom. The Christian minister particularly needs to receive *insight* from the Lord concerning problems of self-discipline and of a right approach to material matters. There is strong conviction here that the Lord *will give* the needed insight. The matter of understanding is not left in doubt. As the Christian ponders and applies the exhortations to his own life, the Lord will increase his powers of understanding.

8. The apostle next strengthens the appeal to his own teaching by directing attention to his Master. As Bengel says, 'Paul, as usual, quickens (gives life to) his own example by the example of Christ'. The form of words here has suggested to some scholars that an early Christian formula is being cited, parallel to some interpretations of Romans 1:3–4. There are striking parallels between the two passages but there is no need to suppose that there is any literary connection. If Paul is citing an existing statement of primitive belief in Romans, there would be no reason why he could not be doing the same here. It is significant that the only other places where Paul uses the words 'according to my gospel' (NIV paraphrases as *This is my gospel*, RSV has 'as preached in my gospel') are found in Romans (2:16; 16:25), which may suggest that Paul intentionally used common elements of primitive teaching when appealing to *my gospel*, to show that what he preached was the common gospel.

The words *Remember Jesus Christ, raised from the dead*, draw attention to the present experience of the risen Lord, which would be particularly underlined by Paul's own conversion. It is not so much the resurrection as a fact of history, important as that is, but the risen Christ as the central factor of the Christian's ongoing experience. For Paul the resurrection is the most prominent Christian truth, containing as it does the guarantee of all other aspects of the work of Christ. It is strange, however, to find coupled with this the descriptive phrase *descended from David* (literally 'of the seed of David'), which although occurring in Romans 1:3 figures nowhere else in Pauline thought. It is considered by some though to be irrelevant here (*cf.* Ward), but it may be intended to highlight the historical descent of Jesus to root him firmly in history.

9. Having in verse 3 urged Timothy to endure hardship, Paul cites his own case as an example. The Greek construction *en hōi* underlying *for which* indicates the gospel as the sphere of Paul's sufferings. Another less probable interpretation is to find the antecedent in Christ rather than in the gospel, in which case Paul would be suffering as a member of Christ's mystical body (*cf.* Simpson). It is Paul's work 'in the gospel' that has caused him to be ill-treated by the authorities. The translation *for which* (both in NIV and RSV) may suggest that the gospel itself was the basis of the charge brought against the apostle. Yet it is more probable that Paul's bonds resulted from disturbances following his preaching than from his Christian beliefs.

The words *I am suffering even to the point of being chained like a criminal* may throw some light on the charge brought against the apostle. The word *kakourgos* was the contemporary word for a common criminal. The only other place where it is used in the New Testament is in Luke 23:32, 39, where it describes those crucified with Jesus. Ramsay[1] sees in the word a hint of the *flagitia* (shameful acts) imputed to Christians in the Neronian persecution, in which case this passing reference would support an early date for the Epistle, for Christianity would not yet have been regarded as in itself a forbidden religion.

In contrast to Paul's own bonds is the absolute freedom of *God's word*. The apostle's statement applies not so much to his own freedom to preach the gospel in prison, as to the fact that even when he is imprisoned others are carrying on the work of proclamation. The persecution of Christian leaders may hamper the progress of the gospel, but it cannot imprison the Word of God nor prevent its spread.

10. The apostle next states a reason for his endurance: it is *for the sake of the elect*, which seems to mean those who are elect but do not yet believe. They have to be won and every ounce of effort must be put into the present conflict, in which both Paul and Timothy are engaged. This is brought out more forcibly by the concluding clause *that they too may obtain the salvation that is in Christ Jesus*. All Paul's present trials are abundantly worthwhile in view of the priceless benefits to be obtained by those who receive the message of himself and his fellow-labourers. The descriptive words *in Christ Jesus* mark out not only the specifically Christian character of the salvation to be obtained, but also its sphere of operation, *i.e.* a salvation possessed by all who are 'in Christ' (see verse 1). The final phrase *with eternal glory* envisages the consummation of Christian salvation. This linking of *glory* with *salvation* is familiar in Paul's writings (*e.g.* 2 Thes. 2:13–14; *cf.* Rom. 5:1–2, 8:21–25), while the idea of suffering giving way to eternal glory is clearly brought out in 2 Corinthians 4:17.

iii. A Christian hymn (2:11–13)

11. Another *trustworthy saying* is added at this juncture, at least if we follow the majority of commentators and attach the formula to what follows. Some have attempted to apply it to the antecedent

---

[1] *The Church in the Roman Empire* (1893), p. 249.

passage but not convincingly (see Spicq for details). There is so marked a rhythmic pattern in the words that follow, that it must be considered more natural to attach the formula to verses 11–13. A difficulty occurs in the inclusion in the first line of the conjunction *gar* (for), which NIV and RSV omit. It would seem that some back reference is involved, but the explanation may be that part only of the original hymn has been preserved, and that the antecedent is therefore now lost. Most scholars agree that the words here are derived from a Christian hymn, although there is dispute among some scholars whether all of the words are authentic. Since the words form a rhythmic pattern there is no reason to regard them as anything other than a unity.

The connection of thought between the hymn and the preceding passage may possibly be found in the idea of glory. There are great things to look forward to in Christian experience even if hardship is the present lot. Some have seen in this hymn an encouragement to martyrdom (*cf.* Bernard), but the alternative view which holds that 'baptismal death' is in mind is much more likely (*cf.* Jeremias). This is confirmed by the close connection between this passage and Romans 6:8, in which baptism is used to illustrate the union between the exalted Lord and the believer. The idea is therefore in complete accord with Pauline thought, and seems to be brought in here to illustrate the worthwhileness of enduring *everything for the sake of the elect* (verse 10).

The tense of the verb translated *we died with him* (*synapothnēskō*) indicates that a past event is in view; and if this event was the moment of baptism, the apostle is reminding himself and Timothy of that experience of identification with Christ which forms the basis of Christian living and hence of Christian courage and endurance.

12. The next line follows on the thought of the last, for the believer having risen to new life must face the call to endurance. Paul has already referred to his own endurance in verse 10 and its recurrence in this hymn suggests that all Christians are called upon to *endure* in the same way as Paul has done. What is important is not so much the suffering as the attitude of mind towards it. Yet if endurance is the Christian's constant duty, much more will partnership in the kingdom be his constant enjoyment (*cf.* Rom. 8:17).

The possibility of disowning Christ seems so reminiscent of the Lord's own words (Mt. 10:3), that some have supposed that a Pauline church has worked into an existing Christian hymn these words of Jesus.[1] But there is no reason to suppose that Paul would not have agreed with the same sentiment.

13. The awful contemplation of being denied by Christ is offset by the concluding emphasis on his faithfulness. The words *if we are faithless* are in strong contrast to *he will remain faithful*. Christ's constancy to his own promises provides the believer with his greatest security. It is unthinkable that any contingency could affect the faithfulness of God, *for he cannot disown himself*. Nevertheless these words are not a charter for sin and apostasy, but rather a consolation for a frightened conscience (as Jeremias points out). The main thrust of this statement, however, may be that God's faithfulness implies that he cannot acknowledge those who disown him. Some think this conclusion was not an original part of the hymn, but the moral impossibility of self-contradiction in God forms the basis of his faithfulness and is therefore necessary to complete the hymn.

B. METHODS OF DEALING WITH FALSE TEACHERS (2:14–26)

Specific instructions are next given to Timothy to guide him in his unavoidable encounters with false teachers. There is little that is distinctive about the data in this Epistle as compared with false teaching denounced in 1 Timothy and Titus.

i. *Positive action: what to promote* (2:14–15)

14. The first necessity is maintenance of right doctrine. Timothy is to *keep reminding them of these things*. The things are either those contained in the previous hymn or perhaps more generally

---

[1] *Cf.* my monograph, *The Pastoral Epistles and the Mind of Paul*, p. 20. Hanson (*ad loc.*) considers the four lines from verse 11b to be a thoroughly Pauline Christian hymn.

of the teaching in the whole of the preceding part of the Epistle. The same strong word translated *warn* (*diamartyromai*) is found also in 1 Timothy 5:21, where Timothy himself is the object of the solemn charge. The seriousness of the position is impressive when viewed *before God*. This adds considerable solemnity to any warning.

The description of the futility and harmfulness of the false teachers is cryptic in the Greek. The words translated *against quarrelling about words* might be rendered 'not to engage in word battles, a useless procedure'. The content of these verbal bouts is immaterial, as is the attempt to discover in them obscure allusions to gnosticism. Whenever men waste time on trivialities they merit the same condemnation. But the more serious aspect is the effect upon others, for this method of futile argument *only ruins those who listen*. The Christian teacher must never forget his responsibility to those who listen. The word *katastrophē*, used here for ruin, which means literally 'turning upside down' is the antithesis of edification.

15. It is one thing solemnly to charge others and quite another to take oneself in hand. The danger of self-neglect was certainly not confined to Timothy, for its symptoms are universal. Yet the value of self-discipline cannot be too highly estimated, for the most effective refutation of error is for the teacher to be the living embodiment of the truth, with God's approval upon him. But this is not easy. The word lying behind *do your best to present yourselves* (*spoudazō*) contains the notion of persistent 'zeal'. The AV 'study' misses this sense of persistence. The aim is to *present yourself to God as one approved* (*dokimos*, 'accepted after testing'), as contrasted with the canvassing of men's approval so evident among false teachers. It is better to leave all wordy strifes alone and to seek the approval of God, whose estimate is always infallible.

The shame that any workman feels when the incompetence or shoddiness of his work is detected is used as a figure for the Christian ministry. *A workman who does not need to be ashamed* must, therefore, be understood in the sense of a Christian teacher who can unblushingly submit his work for God's approval, like the men in the parable of the talents who had gained other talents. This unashamedness is achieved when the workman *correctly handles the word of truth*, a phrase in which the verb (*orthotomeō*) is difficult to define with any precision because it occurs elsewhere only twice in the LXX (Pr. 3:6 and 11:5). In the latter instances it means 'to cut a straight road', and this has been applied in the present case to the road of truth, which is to be made so straight that all deviations of heretics will be evident. An objection has been raised to this on the grounds that *the word of truth* cannot naturally be understood as a road. If, however, the expression is applied generally to straightforward exegesis there would be less objection. The idea of cutting, inherent in the verb, is thought to mean the correct analysis of the word of truth, either in its separate parts or in its whole. But it is contended by many that the compound had probably lost the meaning from which it was derived and had acquired the more general sense of right handling. It was from this sense that the derived noun came later to denote orthodoxy.[1] In this context, however, the main idea seems to be that Timothy must be scrupulously straightforward in dealing with *the word of truth*, in strong contrast to the crooked methods of the false teachers. The term *the word of truth* is twice used elsewhere by Paul (Eph. 1:13 and Col. 1:5) and in both cases is defined as the gospel.

ii. Negative action: what to shun (2:16–18)

16. We have already met with a warning about *godless chatter* in 1 Timothy 6:20. This seems to have constituted a dominant element in the Ephesian heresy. The best way of dealing with this kind of situation is to *avoid* (*peri-istamai*) such teaching, although this is not a *carte blanche* for Christian isolationism, but a piece of sound practical wisdom. Time is too precious to be caught up in irrelevancies. As in verse 14, particular attention is paid to the devastating influence of godless chatterboxes, whose trivialities lead to increasing ungodliness (they *will become more and more ungodly*). The RSV applies the words to 'godless chatter' and translates it 'for it will lead people into more and more ungodliness'. On the other hand the RV 'for they will proceed further

[1]Clement of Alexandria; Eusebius, *Ecclesiastical History*, iv.3.

in ungodliness' focuses attention on the false teachers' own religious deterioration. Both of these interpretations are possible, and the ambiguity draws attention to the unenviable progress in ungodliness of both teaching and teachers.

17. The rapidity with which false doctrine spreads is most graphically illustrated from the medical world. *Their teaching will spread like gangrene* might be paraphrased 'Their teaching finds pasture (*i.e.* a grazing ground) as easily as a gangrene spreads in the human body'. Both the expressions *nomēn echein* (to have a pasture) and *gangraina* (gangrene) belonged to the current medical vocabulary. The metaphor illustrates insidiousness and nothing could more suitably describe the manner of advancement of most false teaching, whether ancient or modern.

The special case of *Hymenaeus* (see 1 Tim. 1:20) *and Philetus* is cited to give more point to the general injunction. Of the latter nothing else is known, while of the former the only other reference is in 1 Timothy 1:20, where he is delivered to Satan to learn not to blaspheme (*i.e.* he is excommunicated). There is no need to suppose that 2 Timothy must have been written before 1 Timothy on this account, since Hymenaeus might well have continued his subverting activities, even although he had been officially excommunicated. His sphere of activity had possibly changed, for Paul appears to be informing Timothy of something he did not know.

18. Underlying the words *who have wandered away from the truth* is the verb *astocheō* (to miss the mark), which is used on two other occasions in the Pastorals of the defection of the false teachers from the true path (*cf.* 1 Tim. 1:6; 6:21). That these men denied a future resurrection shows the serious extent of their error, for this is a basic element of Christian faith, as Paul so forcibly brings out in 1 Corinthians 15. In fact, 1 Corinthians 15:12 shows that at Corinth some were denying the reality of resurrection altogether, and the present allusion must be similarly understood. By treating the *resurrection* as a spiritual experience, these teachers had planned to dispose of it. No wonder *they destroy the faith of some*, since Christianity without a resurrection ceases to be a living faith.

iii. Ultimate certainties (2:19)

19. In contrast to the insecurity of the false teaching, the stability of Christian doctrine is brought into focus. The opening word *Nevertheless* represents the Greek particle *mentoi* and brings out the certainty of this part of the antithesis. In the statement, *God's solid foundation stands firm*, the emphasis falls on the immovable character of God's foundation. It is never in doubt. It forms a vivid contrast to the defection which the false teachers represent.

The metaphor of a building to represent the Christian church appealed strongly to the apostle (*cf.* 1 Cor. 3:10–15; Eph. 2:19–23; 1 Tim. 3:15), and in the present case was admirably suited to inspire Timothy with renewed confidence in the ultimate triumph of the church. The *foundation* may here be the church as a whole, or the Ephesian community in particular, or the truth of God, or the deposit of faith. The word seems to be used to represent the whole structure, in order to show that the major question was the security of the building as a whole and not a few isolated 'stones'.

It is generally supposed that the ancient practice of engraving inscriptions on buildings to indicate their purpose is alluded to in the phrase *sealed with this inscription* (*sphragis* is a word used twice elsewhere by Paul in the sense of authentication; see Rom. 4:11; 1 Cor. 9:2). God has put his own seal on his church by a double inscription. There may be a confusion of metaphors here and the thought may have passed from the building to the sealing of individual members. If so, this would bring it closer to the normal meaning of *sphragis*, but since verses 20 and 21 continue the metaphor of a building or household, the former view seems more probable.

The first *inscription* (*The Lord knows those who are his*) comes from Numbers 16:5, from the account of the revolt of Korah and his associates, in which the people are reminded that the Lord is well able to differentiate between the true and the false. This knowledge of God's infallible discernment is intended to provide strong encouragement to Timothy and all the others perplexed by unworthy elements in the church. It brings also its own restraint on all who take the responsibility of judgment upon themselves. Although it is not the primary purpose of this quotation to draw attention to the predestination of God, this thought cannot be entirely absent since the knowledge of God is so inseparable from his purposes. The writer's main intention, however, is to show what God unerringly knows his true children.

The second *inscription* (*Everyone who confesses the name of the Lord must turn away from wickedness*) is not a precise citation although it is possibly intended to express the sentiment of Numbers 16:26, from the same context as the first. But Isaiah 52:11 is nearer the sentiment and the LXX uses the same verb for *turn away* (*aphistēmi*) as here. The verb is in the imperative mood (*apostētō*), which as Bengel remarked implies the power to depart from wickedness, although this is somewhat obscured by the NIV translation *must turn away from wickedness*. The reading of the received text on which the AV 'the name of Christ' is based is not original since all the uncials and versions have the reading *Lord*. To name the name of the Lord implied for Israel identification with his covenant, and all true Israelites would wish to avoid what he abhors. The thought seems to be that since men like Hymenaeus and Philetus had not turned away from iniquity, as was clear from their injurious doctrine, they cannot be God's true children.

iv. *Degrees of honour* (2:20–21)

20. There is a close connection between the metaphor of an edifice to describe the church and the foundation referred to in the previous verse. Yet there it is not the external structure but the contents which are in mind, and Paul's purpose is to illustrate the variety of the people, some good, others unworthy, who are to be found in the Christian church. The language is certainly Pauline, as a comparison with 1 Corinthians 3:12 and Romans 9:21 shows. Some scholars explain this away as an example of the reproduction of Pauline patterns. But a simpler explanation assumes that the same association of ideas as in 1 Corinthians 3 is due to the workings of the same mind.

The train of thought does not follow quite as we should expect, for in a great house both types of vessels would be necessary and the wooden and earthern would never be considered worthless. The illustration in fact digresses in its application. The variety of vessels in the house is intended to show the variety of types in the church, but the application fastens on the people and the vessels are completely forgotten. The real contrast is between the honourable and dishonourable, the thought imperceptibly having moved back to the case of Hymenaeus and Philetus (verse 18). The phrase *for noble purposes* finds an exact replica in Romans 9:21–22 where the contrasting phrase is more specifically applied to 'objects of wrath, prepared for destruction'. The contrast is not so strong here. Since the words form a prelude to a personal exhortation to Timothy, it must be assumed that the word *ignoble* is intended to be understood relatively. Timothy's aim must be to attain the most honourable usefulness, of which there are varying degrees. The focus is upon the cleanliness of each vessel, and this seems preferable to the suggestion that the illustration indicates the presence of evil members within the church.

21. The indefinite subject of the verb *cleanses* shows that the following injunction is intended for all Christians. The action has been interpreted in two ways. Either the purging relates to the false teachers, especially Hymenaeus and Philetus, and the words mean that Timothy is to take strong action against them; or else it denotes inward purification. The latter idea would provide a fit sequel to the warning against *godless chatter* in verse 16. Yet the only other place in the Greek New Testament where the verb *ekkathairō* (to cleanse) is used is 1 Corinthians 5:7, where it combines the idea of cleansing out impurities (typified by leaven), with the need to deliver the person to Satan.

The *instrument for noble purposes* is carefully delineated in three ways. First, he is *made holy*, in the sense of being set apart for a holy purpose. Secondly, he is *useful to the Master* (*euchrēstos*, another word used elsewhere only by Paul). Both Mark and Onesimus are described by the same word as being useful to the apostle (see 2 Tim. 4:11 and Phm. 11), yet the Christian's serviceableness to Christ here is of much greater importance. And, thirdly, he is *prepared to do any good work*, which stresses the readiness for performing a good work rather than the good work itself.

v. The teacher's behaviour (2:22–26)

22. This direct advice to Timothy is closely linked with the general principles stated in verses 20 and 21. There is an implied contrast with the pursuit of good works, as the sequence *flee the evil desires of youth* and *pursue righteousness* shows. The rsv translates the latter expression as 'aim at righteousness', *i.e.* set right actions as a goal for living. It need not be supposed that Timothy was beyond the age to need such advice, for as compared with Paul he was still at a stage when adverse influences might lead him astray. One suggestion is that the apostle is here thinking of such passions as impatience, love of dispute and novelties, ambition (Spicq). This is supported by the contrasted virtues to be pursued, *righteousness, faith, love and peace*, the first three of which have already been urged on Timothy in 1 Timothy 6:11. To live at peace *along with those who call on the Lord out of a pure heart* is an indispensable requisite of the Christian minister, as indeed of every Christian, although all too often ignored. The secret is to be found in the concluding words *out of a pure heart* (*cf.* 1 Tim. 1:5), for peace and purity are never far apart.

23. The apostle again delivers a warning against foolish controversy. He uses the same verb (*paraiteomai*) as in 1 Timothy 4:7. The force of the word is 'have nothing to do with'. Something more than evasive action was required to deal with these *foolish and stupid arguments* (the word *apaideutos* means ill-educated, hence senseless). Timothy should know that these questionings *produce quarrels*, and the only sane approach is to refuse to have anything to do with them. The word translated *quarrels* (*machē*) is used also in Titus 3:9, where it applies to legal contentions (*cf.* the comment there).

24. Whereas every Christian is called to be a *servant* of the Lord, the term is used here in a restricted sense. Anyone called as Timothy was to care for a community of believers has a special claim to the title and for that reason must rule out all striving. It may be that the Servant passages of Isaiah have influenced the apostle's thought, for if Christ did not strive it is incumbent on his followers to cease from striving.

Again the negative is contrasted with the positive virtues enjoined. The first word *be kind to everyone* (*ēpios*) expresses a quality of kindliness and gentleness, which must be exercised irrespective of the response of the recipients. In addition to being *able to teach* (cf. 1 Tim. 3:2), the Lord's servant is to be *not resentful*. This latter word (*anexikakos*) denotes an attitude of patient forbearance towards those who are in opposition.

25. The right treatment of opponents is an urgent matter for all who hold responsible Christian positions, and the apostle's advice to Timothy to *gently instruct* those who oppose is calculated to win them over rather than to antagonize them. Instructing could be understood in the sense of 'correcting' (RSV), since these particular opponents are in mind, but the word used here (*paideuō*, 'teach') may be intended as a contrast to the *apaideutos* (ill-educated) in verse 23. Those who follow after empty arguments are certainly in need of instruction, both regarding the wrong teaching and the right doctrine. There can be no doubt that the false teachers mentioned elsewhere in the Pastorals are in mind here. It must be the aim of every Christian minister to lead to *repentance* those who are in opposition. Paul speaks of repentance as a work of God, but this does not absolve the offender from the responsibility of acknowledging his sin. This must be the aim of right instruction, for God is a God of mercy ever ready to forgive. It requires a change of mind to come to *a knowledge of the truth*. Repentance implies such a change of mind, which delivers a person from being in bondage to error. The same expression for recognition of the truth used here is found in 1 Timothy 2:4 denoting the divine desire for all men.

26. Graphic words are used to describe the reclamation of the devil's captives. *That they will come to their senses* means literally 'that they may return to soberness' (*ananēphō*), a metaphor implying some previous duping by evil influences. As in the case of intoxication, the devil's method is 'to benumb the conscience, confuse the senses and paralyse the will' (*cf.* Horton). But the metaphor becomes mixed when the *trap of the devil* is introduced (see 1 Tim. 3:7 for a parallel use of the phrase, and *cf.* 1 Tim. 6:9). The devil is portrayed in a double role. He is both intoxicator and captivator of men's minds. The second vivid verb *taken captive* (*zōgreō*) means 'to catch alive'; it is used elsewhere in the Greek Testament only in Luke 5:10 where it occurs in Jesus' promise to Peter that he would catch men.

Considerable discussion has surrounded the use of two different Greek pronouns in the concluding phrase – *to do his will*. There have been three different interpretations of the words in the Greek (*hyp' autou eis to ekeinou thelēma*).

1. Both pronouns apply to the devil (as in AV, RSV and NIV, where no distinction is made between them). This can claim the support of later Greek usage when the distinction between the personal pronoun *autos* and the demonstrative *ekeinos* was often disregarded. This rendering certainly makes good sense and fits in well with the context.

2. RV takes the *autou* to refer to an antecedent in verse 24 and the *ekeinou* to verse 25, rendering the words, 'having been taken captive by the Lord's servant unto the will of God'. This was favoured by Lock on the following grounds: it gives the full force to the verb *zōgreō* (take captive), it makes 'unto his will' parallel to 'unto recognition of the truth' (verse 25), and it ends the passage on a hopeful note. But these reasons do not seem to apply exclusively to this interpretation, for the devil also catches men alive, while the so-called parallel may equally well have been intended as a contrast, and the hopeful note is surely contained in the possibility of escape from the devil's trap after a period of submission.

3. A mediating view is that of the RV margin which has 'by the devil unto the will of God'. But this may be criticized on the grounds of its grammatical intricacy, involving as it does the assumption that *ekeinou* relates to the main subject of the sentence. Yet it has the considerable advantage of differentiating the demonstrative and personal pronouns, which it may justly be claimed was probably intentional, and it avoids the difficulty inherent in the second interpretation of imagining that God takes captive the devil's captives and they, so to speak, merely

exchange one snare for another. Whereas this is a possibility, it seems best to adhere to the first interpretation.

VI. PREDICTIONS OF THE LAST DAYS (3:1-9)

The apostle now turns his attention to the future and describes a time of general moral decadence. There appears to be a definite connection between the heresy referred to in the last chapter and elsewhere in the Pastorals, and the disastrous corruption of society so vividly described here.

1. *The last days* is a common New Testament phrase denoting the period immediately preceding the consummation of the present age. Yet in the apostle's thought this future time is not unrelated to his own, for from verse 6 onwards he uses the present and not the future tense. The statement that *there will be terrible times* (*chalepos*, 'grievous') must not be restricted, therefore, to an eschatological interpretation. The following description is, in fact, so generally applicable that it has been used effectively to denounce many periods of moral corruption throughout the history of the church.

2-5. The list itself seems to lack any premeditated order as was usually the case in the ethical lists used by the Greek moralists.[1] On the other hand, the Pastoral catalogues of vices, and especially this one, show many affinities with Jewish descriptions, and are particularly akin to Philo's lists (*cf.* Spicq). There is also the suggestion that this list may have been based on some previous apocalyptic (Lock). There are many similarities between this catalogue and the vices mentioned in Romans 1 (*cf.* Dibelius-Conzelmann, Brox), the main difference being that in the latter Paul is describing the contemporary Gentile world, whereas here a future condition is being envisaged.

The first two, *lovers of themselves* (*philautoi*) and *lovers of money*

[1] For a discussion of the Greek household ethical lists and their bearing on the situation in the Pastorals, *cf.* D. C. Verner, *The Household of God. The Social World of the Pastoral Epistles* (1983).

(*philargyroi*) supply the key to the rest of the list. Moral corruption follows from love falsely directed. Self-centredness, and material advantages, when they become the chief objects of affection, destroy all moral values, and the subsequent list of vices is their natural fruit. It is significant that the list ends with a similar pair of words compounded with *philo* – *lovers of pleasure rather than lovers of God* (verse 4). It has been suggested that this passage is based on the Hellenistic writer Philo because of a striking parallel of expression (*cf.* Spicq). The implication here is that pleasure is regarded as a substitute for God. Basically materialism is opposed to piety and is bound to end in irreligion.

A clear connection exists between *boastful* and *proud* (verse 2). The former word *alazōn* includes 'the bounce of swaggering' (Simpson), while the other word *hyperēphanos*, when used in a bad sense, conveys the idea of haughtiness or arrogance. The word *abusive* translates the Greek word *blasphēmoi*, but points to evil-speaking directed against others rather than against God. The last three vices in verse 2 are all specific denials of definite Christian virtues (in the Greek they all have the negative *a*-prefix) bringing out forcefully the idea of militant moral perversion. The same evident reversal of moral values is also seen in five of the six vices mentioned in verse 3, the only word without the negative prefix being *slanderous* (*diaboloi*). The word translated *unforgiving* (*aspondos*) literally means 'without a truce, and therefore 'implacable'. It describes an hostility so intense that a truce is impossible. *Without self-control* shows an attitude of mind that is dominated by outside influences, while *brutal* is the antithesis of what is civilized. The expression *not lovers of the good* really describes those who hate the good and have replaced it with something less demanding.

The similarity of form of the first two words in verse 4 (*prodotai, propeteis*) cannot be reflected in the English translation, but was clearly intended to link them together. NIV has *treacherous, rash*, the latter word meaning 'to fall headlong', hence precipitate or reckless. Closely allied to this latter word is the next which NIV renders *conceited*, which describes an unwarranted self-importance.

In verse 5 the apostle examines more exactly the religious

situation. Religion is not entirely denied, but it amounts to no more than an empty shell. There is an outward *form* (*morphōsis*) *of godliness*, but no *power*. Indeed it is not simply a matter of an organized religion which has ceased to function, but a religion which is not intended to function. Its adherents are *denying its power*, which suggests a positive rejection of its effectiveness. They have no conception of the gospel as a regenerating force. It is clear that moral decadents can hardly be expected to pay more than the most superficial lip-service to piety, and then only to maintain a cloak of respectability.

Though the full development of this state of affairs is still future, yet Timothy is even now given the warning *Have nothing to do with them*, which apparently means that he must exercise discernment to prevent the admission of such people into membership of the church. The Greek text includes a *kai*, which the NIV omits. If the meaning is 'also have nothing to do with them', the reference could be to those mentioned in 2:23.

6–7. The same influences are seen in the actions of certain men who take advantage of gullible women, as the opening words, *They are the kind who* (*i.e.* those mentioned in verse 5), show. The words *worm their way into* suggest insidious methods. The verb (*endynō*) is used only here in the New Testament in this sense. Evidently the false teachers, having sought out women of the weaker sort, exerted such powerful influence on them that the women lost their own freedom of thought. They had in fact been able to *gain control* over these women, who have become 'captives' (the word used to describe prisoners of war). The Greek word translated *weak-willed women* (*gynaikaria*) literally means 'little women' and is probably used contemptuously of those who are acting in a feeble manner. There is no necessary suggestion that these women lacked intelligence, for the emphasis is on their moral weakness. They *are loaded down with sins*, in the sense of being overwhelmed in their consciences. The verb used strictly means 'to be heaped up' and is used metaphorically to express a cumulation of sins which has become so unbearable that any solution offered is clutched at. The last phrase in verse 6 is well translated *are swayed by all kinds of evil desires* (RSV has 'by various impulses').

These women apparently desire to listen to other people's advice (*always learning*), but their minds have become so fickle and warped that they have become incapable of acknowledging the *truth* (cf. 1 Tim. 2:4). Their main quest is for sensational rather than serious information, and consequently they fall an easy prey to pseudo-Christian teachers.

8. An example of these teachers is found in *Jannes and Jambres*, who were, according to a work which probably circulated under their names and is referred to by Origen, two of Pharaoh's magicians who withstood Moses. While no mention of these names is found in the Bible, they are referred to in the Targum of Jonathan on Exodus 7:11 and in various early Christian literary works.[1] The *Zadokite Document* of the Qumran sect contains a reference (5:17–19) to the legend, in which Belial is said to set up Johana (Jannes) and his brother to challenge Moses. One view is that there is some link between this legend and Wisdom 15:18 – 16:1 (Hanson). Timothy would no doubt have been well acquainted with the legend and would draw his own conclusions from the allusion. The comparison with these legendary figures is based on the similar resistance to the truth on the part of both groups. There has always been a close connection between heresy and superstition. It is no less evident in modern times. It is noteworthy that both *truth* and *faith* have the definite article, and are therefore used in an objective sense.

The idea of depravity of mind is found also in 1 Timothy 6:5, where it even more strongly denotes men destitute of the truth. It is no surprise that they are described as *rejected* (*adokimos*), for when put to the test *as far as the truth is concerned* they have no hope of being proved acceptable.

9. The same verb expressing advancement (*prokoptō*) is used in 2:16 of the increasing impiety of the false teachers, and in 3:13 of their progressive degradation. Here, however, Timothy is assured that their apparent success is severely limited, for their true character (*i.e.* their *folly*) *will be clear to everyone*. The word translated *clear* (*ekdēlos*) is a strengthened form which means 'clearly evident'. The thought in this verse appears to be based

[1] *Cf.* H. Odeberg, *Theological Dictionary of the New Testament* 3, pp. 192f.

on the assumption that imposture is always tracked down in the end.

VII. FURTHER EXHORTATIONS TO TIMOTHY (3:10–17)

A. AN HISTORICAL REMINDER (3:10–12)

10. There is a strong contrast between Timothy and the false teachers as is clear from the emphatic *You*. The historical allusion that follows is particularly designed to encourage the apostle's rather fearful lieutenant. *You, however, know all about my teaching* (*parakoloutheō*) does not quite bring out the full meaning of the verb, which is 'to follow up' or 'to trace out as an example'. The same verb is used in the sense of investigate in Luke's preface (Lk. 1:3). It need not, therefore, imply that Timothy was an eye-witness of Paul's earliest sufferings as a missionary, for if it did this statement would then have to be considered an anachronism because Timothy is not mentioned in Acts until after these early persecutions. If Paul is mentioning what Timothy has already been informed of, regarding the earlier happenings on his missionary journeys, there would be no difficulty.

In a catalogue of nine features the apostle cites his own example, not for his own enhancement, but for Timothy's encouragement. Paul's life had borne rich testimony to God's faithfulness. It is significant that *teaching* is mentioned first, for throughout the Pastorals it occupies a prominent place. Timothy had been privileged to listen to Paul's expositions on many themes. But teaching must be linked with life, and so the next six virtues bring out the practical character of the apostle's impact on Timothy.

The word translated *way of life* (*agōgē*) denotes general behaviour, which a man's closest associates can never fail to know in all its aspects. Linked with this is the apostle's *purpose* (*prothesis*) or 'chief aim' in life. It is the same word that Paul uses of God's purpose in Romans 8:28. *Faith, patience, love, endurance* are all essentially Christian virtues, often referred to by Paul, of which all but *patience* (*machrothymia*) had been enjoined on

Timothy himself (1 Tim. 6:11). The last word *endurance* denotes a quality of fortitude in adverse conditions. If it be felt that the apostle lacks modesty in relating his own Christian graces, it should be remembered that a man, whose own race of life is nearly run, may draw out the main lessons of his experience for the benefit of younger aspirants without the least suggestion of egotism.

11. The appeal to the happenings at *Antioch, Iconium and Lystra* rather than to more recent examples of Paul's sufferings is prompted by Timothy's vivid recollections of these when he was still a youth at Lystra. The apostle's bearing during these trying events may even have been the major factor in influencing Timothy's attachment to the apostle. In any case the reminiscence of the earliest meeting of the two men is very natural for an ageing man in prison. The apostle brings into focus not only his own endurance, but the Lord's deliverances. There may possibly be an allusion to the words of Psalm 34:17 ('he delivers them from all their troubles').

12. After the apostle's visit to the places named in verse 11, he exhorted the believers, as recorded in Acts 14:22, 'We must go through many hardships to enter the kingdom of God'; so the present reference to the sufferings of *everyone who wants to live a godly life in Christ Jesus* is possibly due to the association of ideas in the apostle's mind. The principle that devoted Christians must expect persecution was explicit in our Lord's own teaching. The phrase *in Christ Jesus* points to the mystical sphere in which Christian life is to be lived, a concept well known from Paul's earlier Epistles.

B. AN EXHORTATION TO STEADFASTNESS (3:13-17)

13. A contrast to those who desire to live godly lives is now introduced. A progressive worsening of evil influences is prophesied, the same verb (*prokoptō*) being used as in verse 9 (see note there). The underlying idea is somewhat ironical – 'making progress in the direction of the worse'. Having set the worst possible goal in front of them they will make good head-way towards it by means of deception, but on the way they will fall a prey to their own methods. The word translated *impostors* (*goētes*) is literally 'wizards'. Its use here may probably be suggested by the earlier mention of Egyptian magicians (verse 8).

14. But against such a background of militant error, the Christian leaders must stand firm on what they know of the truth, like a rock resisting the increasing fury of the waves. Timothy is urged to *continue* in the sense of 'abiding' in *what you have learned and become convinced of* (RSV has 'firmly believed'). In contrast to the false teachers with their constant endeavour to advance to something new, Timothy may be satisfied with what he has already received. The basis of this confidence in the tradition is twofold. It is assured by Timothy's knowledge of the teachers and his knowledge of the Scriptures. The character of teachers closely reflects the character of what is taught; and since Timothy knew well the integrity not only of the apostle Paul, but also of his own mother and grandmother and others who had helped him arrive at an understanding of Christian truth, he may rest assured that he has not himself been deceived.

15. An unusual phrase here describes *the holy Scriptures* (*hiera grammata*). The RV more literally has 'sacred writings'. The question arises why this form was used here. Three possible answers have been proposed: 1. It may be used technically to draw attention to the way Timothy learnt to read, hence the significance of the words *from infancy*. 2. It may stress the sacred character of Timothy's learning in contrast to the varieties of doubtful literature used by the false teachers. 3. It may be designed to include other literature, such as apocalyptic and even Christian books. But there are many instances from early writers where the phrase is used of the Scriptures, apparently without special significance (Dibelius-Conzelmann).

The power of the Scriptures is directed to a particular end, *to make you wise for salvation*. RSV translates this, 'to instruct you for salvation'. The phrase *for salvation* (*eis sōtērian*) is frequently used in the earlier Epistles of Paul, while the notion of such value attached to the Old Testament is so thoroughly Pauline that Schlatter thinks it is difficult to think of anyone else speaking of it in such terms. That salvation is appropriated only *through faith in Christ Jesus* is also thoroughly Pauline. The mere reading of Scripture is ineffective in securing salvation unless faith is in operation, faith centred entirely in Christ. This was evident in the case of the unbelieving Jews.

16. There is a twofold problem in the interpretation of this verse. First, what is the precise meaning of *graphē* (*Scripture*), and second, should *theopneustos* (*God-breathed*) be rendered as a predicate (as AV, NIV and RSV), or as a qualifying adjective, 'every scripture inspired by God is also profitable' (RV)? The second problem cannot properly be settled until the first is decided, although in some aspects the two problems are inseparable. *Graphē* could mean any writing, but the uniform New Testament use of it with reference to Scripture (*i.e.* the Old Testament) determines its meaning here. But does it mean Scripture as a whole or separate passages within Scripture? The latter meaning is in accordance with the general use of the singular noun, and must therefore be given due weight in the present passage. Yet the crucial factor must be the meaning of *all* (*pasa*). The absence of the article may point to the sense 'every', but there are analogous cases where *pas* is used in a semi-technical phrase and where the meaning 'every' is ruled out, *e.g.* Acts 2:36 where all the house of Israel is clearly demanded (see also Eph. 2:21; 3:15; Col. 4:12). Yet it may well be that in all these exceptions the *pas* draws attention to the partitive aspect of the expression, and, if that is so, the present phrase may mean Scripture as viewed in each separate part of it.

The second problem cannot be decided purely on grammatical grounds for both the readings mentioned above are grammatically possible. It would be more natural for the adjective, if attributive, to precede the noun, *i.e.* 'every inspired scripture' rather than 'every scripture inspired', but the latter is not impossible. The context itself must decide. Simpson maintained that the adjectival interpretation 'presents a curious specimen of anticlimax'. It is difficult to see why the apostle should need to assure Timothy that inspired scriptures are profitable. On the other hand, it is not easy to see why Timothy should need to be assured, at this point, of the inspiration of the Scriptures. One explanation is that it is the profitableness not the inspiration which Paul is pressing on Timothy (*cf.* Bernard). After all he must have been assured of the inspiration of Scripture since his youth. The significance of the conjunction (*kai*) has some bearing on the matter. Its normal meaning is 'and' as in NIV *and is useful*, whereas the RV has to translate it as 'also' which seems in the context to be less meaningful. Comparison with the use of *kai* in 1 Timothy 4:4 would support the meaning 'and' here and this would seem to be the most probable. While not ruling out altogether the RV rendering, it is rather more in harmony with both grammar and syntax to translate as the NIV and RSV have done. Timothy is not therefore being informed of the inspiration of Scripture, for this was a doctrine commonly admitted by Jews, but he is being reminded that the basis of its profitableness lies in its inspired character.

Four spheres are now mentioned in which the usefulness of Scripture can be seen. The first two relate to doctrine and the other two to practice. *Useful for teaching* refers to positive teaching, while *rebuking* represents the negative aspect. The Scripture contains both encouragement and warning, and this double aspect is always present. On the ethical plane, the Scripture provides both *correcting* and *training*, again stressing both negative and positive aspects. All these uses of Scripture were admitted by Judaism; indeed the advanced ethics of the Jews was due to its basis in the Old Testament. Since the Christians took over the same Scriptures, the same profitableness applies. But for them each one of these uses became more comprehensive as the Old Testament teaching was illumined by the life and teaching of Christ.

17. There is a distinct objective in this profitableness of Scripture. The verse opens with a clause introduced by a word (*hina*) which indicates purpose or result. The Christian minister has in his hands a God-given instrument designed to equip him completely for his work. The phrase *thoroughly equipped* consists of two Greek words, an adjective *artios* which describes a man perfectly adapted for his task, and a cognate verb *exartizō* which adds further emphasis to the same thought. For a parallel use of *good works*, *cf.* 2:21.

The phrase *the man of God* appears to be applied specifically to the Christian teachers, rather than to Christians generally (*cf.* 1 Tim. 6:11). 'The man of God is before all the man of the Bible' (Spicq). There may be an allusion to the work of the prophets in the use of this title, for it was frequently applied to them in the Old Testament. The place of the Bible in the equipping of men for the ministry must always be recognized as the most powerful influence.

VIII. PAUL'S FAREWELL MESSAGE (4:1–18)

A. THE FINAL CHARGE (4:1–5)

1. The apostle has already used the solemn verb *diamartyromai* (to give a charge), with which this verse starts, in urging Timothy to exercise impartiality in dealing with church affairs (1 Tim. 5:21), and the adjuration here is couched in almost identical terms, yet without reference to 'elect angels' as in the former case. The solemnity of the present charge is doubly impressive as the parting advice of the aged warrior to his younger and rather timid lieutenant. It would be emptied of much of its meaning and dignity if it were no more than a fictitious attempt to represent what the real Paul might have said to the real Timothy. Particularly appropriate to Paul's closing instructions is the reference to Christ as the One who *will judge the living and the dead*, which may already have become a formula as part of a baptismal creed (*cf.* Lock) or confessional formula (*cf.* Brox). As the apostle contemplates his life's end the idea of judgment cannot escape his thought. He had often stressed it before (*cf.* Acts 17:31; Rom. 2:16; 1 Cor. 4:5).

Both the *appearing* and the *kingdom* are regarded as still future, yet they are so much the Christian's assured hope that they can form a basis for adjuration. Such future glories could not fail to inspire Timothy to present fortitude.

2. The five exhortations contained in this verse are as applicable to all Christian ministers as to Timothy. *Preach the Word*, in

the Greek is in the aorist tense, which together with the suc-
ceeding imperatives adds solemnity and decisiveness to the
injunctions. The apostle regards Timothy as being at a crisis in
which he must make definite resolves towards positive action.
He must preach the word in which he has been nurtured, as
never before. The verb behind the words *be prepared in season and
out of season* (*ephistēmi*) means 'to stand by, be at hand', hence
the meaning here seems to be that the Christian minister must
always be on duty. He must take every opportunity to serve,
whether the occasion seems opportune or not. This reference to
being prepared applies not only to preaching but also to the
many other responsibilities. The third exhortation is to *correct*.
Both Timothy and Titus are strongly urged to reprove (*elenchō*)
(*cf.* 1 Tim. 5:20; Tit. 1:13, 2:15), and no Christian minister must
shirk his responsibility in this respect. Christian discipline in our
modern age is so generally lax that the moral status of many
communities is greatly weakened. The fourth exhortation *rebuke*
(*epitimaō*), closely akin to the last, denotes in New Testament
usage the idea of censure. The last word *encourage* is a translation of *parakaleō*, which can also mean 'exhort'. Both these meanings are applicable to the preacher's work, but if this duty is
taken with the preceding two charges, the former meaning
would be more applicable.

All these imperatives must be effected *with great patience and
careful instruction*. The first denotes the manner and the second
denotes the method which Timothy must adopt; *makrothymia*
here translated 'patience' is a favourite Pauline expression, and
is generally used of God's forbearance. In Colossians 1:11 it is
used, as here, of the Christian's patience in trying circumstances. Christian reproof without the grace of long-sufferance
has often led to a harsh censorious attitude intensely harmful to
the cause of Christ. But the other requirement is equally essential, for correction must be diligently understood and hence
based on *careful instruction*. To rebuke without instruction is to
leave the root cause of error untouched.

3. Such attention to *sound doctrine* will become increasingly
urgent as the *time* (*kairos*) comes when there will be open opposition to the gospel. The apostle is looking ahead to times even

less favourable than his own, when *men will not put up with* such doctrine. Some have supposed that a post-Pauline author was describing his own day and attributing it to Paul's prophetic insight. But there is no need to deny that the apostle could foresee times in the not-too-distant future when the conditions he describes would apply. Christian history can furnish many examples of men's desires to *gather around them a great number of teachers*, who are not renowned for their ability to teach or their authority, but who seek the satisfaction of *their own desires* (RSV has 'to suit their own likings'). The emphasis here is on personal caprice. The absence of any serious purpose behind the amassing of 'teachers' is ironically summed up in the description of the hearers as having *itching ears*, which literally means 'having their ears tickled', as if what they heard merely scratched their eardrums without penetrating further.

4. Those with no more serious intentions than to satisfy their own desires will not only lack sufficient discernment to differentiate between *truth* and *myths*, but will, in fact, *turn their ears away from the truth*, which suggests a refusal to hear it. The reason appears to be the superficial fascination of myths; but the verb used (*ektrepō*) points to deviation from the true course, and suggests a wandering into counterfeits (RSV has 'wander into myths'), with no awareness that truth has been left behind.

5. The opening words bring the thought emphatically back to Timothy. *But you* well expresses the emphatic pronoun (which is obscured in the AV. The verb translated *Keep your head* (*nēphō*) means 'be sober' and urges moral alertness or 'coolness and presence of mind'. The same verb is used in 1 Thessalonians 5:6, 8 to denote a watchful and alert attitude towards Christ's second coming. The Christian minister must seek to cultivate an unruffled alertness in every aspect of his work. There is no circumstance in which this does not apply. It is particularly demanding. The Christian minister must also *endure hardship*, which recalls the earlier advice in 2:3, where the same verb occurs in a compound form.

The word *evangelist* is used of Philip in Acts 21:8, no doubt to distinguish him from Philip the apostle, and also in Ephesians

4:11 where it seems to denote an order of workers midway between apostles and prophets on the one hand and pastors and teachers on the other. There was probably a good deal of fluidity in the use of these terms describing various offices and there is no need to suppose that the terms were uniformly used. The function here implied is preaching the gospel and the term could equally well be used of Timothy or of any other Christian worker. The concluding words *discharge all the duties of your ministry* draw attention to the accomplishment (Gk. verb *plērophoreō*) of the whole range of responsibilities in the ministry. Timothy is putting his hand to the plough and must not look back until his ministry (*diakonia*) is completed.

B. A TRIUMPHAL CONFESSION (4:6–8)

6. There is a definite connection between the solemn personal assertions which the apostle is about to make and the last charge just given to Timothy. *For I* (*egō gar*) contrasts with the *But you* of verse 5. In stating that he is *already being poured out like a drink offering* (RSV has 'already on the point of being sacrificed'), Paul is repeating a figure of speech which he has used in Philippians 2:17, where the verb is found in a conditional clause, in which the apostle contemplates the possibility of his being condemned to death. Here the action is in progress. We can discount the objection that such a figure of speech could not have been stored in Paul's mind over a period of years, for the idea of a Christian martyr's life-blood being a libation or drink-offering was sufficiently striking when it had once caught the imagination of a man like Paul, to recur to his mind on many occasions.

Closely linked with the preceding statement are the words, *and the time has come for my departure,* which also draw attention to the imminence of death. But the word translated *departure* (*analysis*) triumphantly expresses the apostle's view of the end; it is a 'loosing, *e.g.* of a vessel from its moorings or of a soldier striking his tent' (Abbott-Smith). What might seem the end to Timothy appears to the apostle as a glorious new era when he will be released from all his present restrictions. The noun is used nowhere else in the New Testament, but the cognate verb is used by Paul in the same sense in Philippians 1:23.

7. The three perfect tenses convey a sense of finality; for Paul this is the end. In 1 Timothy 6:12 the apostle had appealed to Timothy to 'fight the good fight of the faith', and now he declares his own fight is over. It is probable that the responsibilities of his apostolic office are here graphically represented by the word *agōn*, meaning 'struggle' or 'contest'. It is generally supposed that *agōn* must be understood of an athletic contest in view of the next phrase. Yet if it bears a military meaning if would be more impressive (*cf.* Simpson) and this seems likely here.

I have finished the race (*dromos*) draws specific attention to the athletic arena as a metaphor of Christian service. It is significant that Paul makes no claim to have won the race, but is content to have stayed the course. This metaphor is a favourite with Paul and is particularly suited to express the idea of endurance in Christian service.

The third assertion *I have kept the faith* has been understood by some writers to refer to the athlete's promise to keep the rules, or to the military man's oath of fidelity (*cf.* Calvin). Since the apostle has urged his lieutenants many times to guard the deposit, it is possible that the same metaphor of a steward is here in mind. Deissmann considered the phrase to be no more than a business formula for keeping an engagement; but even if the apostle borrowed his phrase from contemporary commercial practice, he ennobles it in the process. *The faith* seems to be as objective as *the fight* or *the race*.

8. The apostle continues his thought into the future as is shown by the words *Now there is in store for me*. The first word in the Greek is *loipon*, which draws attention to what still remains to be realized as contrasted with those things already accomplished (verse 7). *The crown of righteousness* is reminiscent not only of the wreaths of honour awarded to Olympic winners, but also of the awards made to loyal subjects by oriental sovereigns for services rendered (Dibelius cites an example from an inscription of Antiochus I, where similar phraseology is used). There are two ways of understanding the phrase *crown of righteousness*.

If the genitive is in apposition with the other noun as in the parallel phrase 'crown of life' (Jas. 1:12; Rev. 2:10), then *righteousness* must be the crown. But if the genitive is possessive, the phrase would mean 'the crown which is the reward of the righteous man'. Most commentators prefer the second interpretation, which is the only one in harmony with Paul's doctrine of righteousness.

There may be an implied contrast between *the Lord, the righteous Judge* and the wrong judgments of the emperor Nero under whose perverted sense of justice the apostle is at the moment suffering. The idea, may, on the other hand, contrast with the not always impartial decisions of the Olympic umpires. If the Olympic Games (or Isthmian Games) supply the metaphor here there is a marked variation between the completion of the race and the receiving of the crown, which for the Christian is not immediate as in the Games, but must await *that day*. Already in 1:12 (see note there) the apostle has intimated his forward look to that glorious day of Christ's appearing and it is evident that this apocalyptic vision dominated his present reactions and his future hopes.

The apostle hastens to add that this *crown* is not a special reservation for himself alone. He seems sensitive about appearing self-centred and points out, no doubt for the immediate encouragement of Timothy, that a similar crown awaits all who fulfil the conditions. Those *who have longed for his appearing* probably describes all those who loved the Lord, for all the early Christians had an intense longing for Christ's complete triumph. The NIV does not bring out the true force of the verb here. RSV and AV translate as 'loved' and this is to be preferred. As the perfect tense suggests, they have loved his appearing in the past and will continue to do so to the moment of receiving the reward.

C. SOME PERSONAL REQUESTS (4:9–13)

9. The concluding section (verses 9–22) marks the climax of the Epistle, and shows the great apostle making his final personal arrangements before his departure. Twice (in verses 9 and 21) he urges Timothy to lose no time to come to him, and this reiterated desire proves not only the imminence of the end but also the strong attachment which existed between the two men. A problem has been raised about the appropriateness of the present request. It is argued that the earlier part of the letter has given the impression that Paul is writing because he does not expect to see Timothy again, and that this verse and the following section introduce a startling change. Yet 1:4 seems to suggest a possibility of reunion. The contents of this letter may be designed not so much to give Timothy new instructions about what he is to do after Paul's decease, but to confirm policies already verbally communicated. The fact that Paul urges haste shows that he is not too optimistic about the possibility of his request being fulfilled in time. Admittedly some months would elapse before Timothy could receive the request and travel to Rome, but this does not justify the conclusion that the request must be out of place in the present letter.[1]

10. The request for Timothy's presence is all the more significant in view of the defection of *Demas*. There is a note of solitariness as well as sadness in the statement *for Demas, because he loved this world, has deserted me*, for Paul clearly regards his action as related to him personally and not to the church at large. Demas is mentioned in Colossians 4:14 as one of Paul's close associates, but by this time he had perhaps found the apostle's demands too rigorous. There is, however, nothing to suggest that Demas became an apostate, although there was a later tradition to this effect.

The contrast between those who love Christ's appearing and *Demas* who *loved this world* is brought out not only by the use of the same verb (*agapaō*, 'love'), but also by the fact that *aion* (here translated 'world') denotes the world under aspects of time, thus emphasizing the difference between the present and future time sequences.

There is no other reference to *Crescens* in the New Testament, but there is a tradition which connects him with the churches of Vienne and Mayence in Gaul. The reading *Galatia* is changed in

[1]See Introduction, pp. 22ff., for a discussion of this point.

some MSS to 'Gaul', and this may have arisen either from the similarity of the two names in the Greek or from the fact that Gaul was widely called Galatia among first-century Greek writers (*cf.* Bernard). Since, however, the apostle's use of the term 'Galatia' elsewhere applies to Asiatic Galatia this seems the most probable here.

The despatch of *Titus* to *Dalmatia* would seem to indicate the cessation of his work in Crete. His new sphere was on the eastern shore of the Adriatic Sea.

11. *Luke* is also mentioned in Colossians 4:14, where he is styled 'the doctor'. He probably remained with Paul to minister to his weakness. The words *Only Luke is with me* (RSV 'Luke alone is with me') need not suppose that all the others had forsaken Paul as Demas had done, but that Paul had himself sent them on various missions, retaining only Luke. As in Colossians 4:10 *Mark* appears as a member of the Pauline circle, and, in striking contrast with the dissension he created by his early association with Paul (Acts 15:37–39), he is now commended for his usefulness. The word translated *helpful* (*euchrēstos*) means 'serviceable' and indicates general usefulness, while *ministry* (*diakonia*) is a comprehensive word which covers all Paul's many activities. Since Timothy is asked to *Get Mark and bring him with you*, this suggests that Mark was somewhere along Timothy's route.

12. The many references to *Tychicus* in Paul's Epistles indicate that he was a reliable associate. He was the bearer of the Epistles to both Colossians and Ephesians, and it is not improbable that he took the present letter to Timothy, if *apesteila* (*I sent*) is regarded as an epistolary aorist. The most likely explanation of Tychicus' mission to *Ephesus* is that he was to relieve Timothy during the latter's absence in Rome while visiting Paul (*cf.* Tit. 3:12).

13. The reference to the *cloak*, the *scrolls* and the *parchments* are so incidental that they bear strong marks of authenticity, and this fact is acknowledged in the various fragment theories, which all number this verse among the genuine passages.

The word used for cloak is *phailonēs*, which represents the

Latin *paenula*, an outer garment of heavy material circular in shape with a hole in the middle for the head. Paul had evidently left it on a recent visit to Troas, when Carpus, unknown elsewhere, was apparently his host. This cannot be the visit to the same city mentioned in Acts 20:6 for several years had elapsed.

It is impossible to say what the *scrolls* or *parchments* (*membranai*) were, but the latter word suggests documents of some value, since vellum was too expensive to replace the common papyrus for general purposes. It has been suggested that these were Paul's legal papers, *e.g.* his certificate of Roman citizenship. Another proposal is that they were parts, at least, of Scripture. But though there can be no more than speculation about their identity, the desire to receive them throws interesting light on Paul's literary pursuits, even while on missionary journeys. It is not impossible, at least, that Paul had in his possession some written account of the Lord's doings and sayings and that he wished to have them to hand in his present critical situation.

D. A PARTICULAR WARNING (4:14–15)

14–15. The mention of the opposition of *Alexander the metalworker* may be occasioned by the previous reference to the cloak and the books. There may have been some association of ideas which caused the revival of the memory. The words *did me a great deal of harm* mean literally 'showed forth many evil things against me'. The nature of this evil is further defined in verse 15, *because he strongly opposed our message.* Whether we take *message* (*logoi*) as the Christian doctrine which Paul preached, or Paul's defence at his trial, at which Alexander may have been a witness for the prosecution, it is clear that the evil was in the realm of mental and not physical violence. The use of the plural (*our*) for the singular is thoroughly Pauline.

Two other references to an Alexander are found in Acts 19:33–34 and 1 Timothy 1:20. In the latter case Paul links Alexander with Hymenaeus in a temporary excommunication and some have identified the *metalworker* (or coppersmith) with this man, and then have proceeded to argue that 2 Timothy must have preceded 1 Timothy. But even if the two Alexanders are the same person there is insufficient evidence that the present verse must describe an event prior to excommunication. The aorist tenses point to a specific act of opposition, but no indication is given as to how long ago the action happened. The other Alexander mentioned in Acts has some claims for consideration, for he attempted on that occasion to make a defensive speech but was prevented from doing so. It is possible, therefore, that on some later occasion he sought revenge at Paul's expense for the humiliation he suffered at the hands of the mob. It has been argued that it is inconceivable that Alexander would have nursed his grudge for so many years (*cf.* Harrison), but personal grievances have been known to survive a great deal longer than this theory necessitates. Even if we cannot with certainty identify this coppersmith, he was evidently well known to Timothy, who is urged *be on your guard against him*, or literally 'keep yourself away from him' (to bring out the force of the middle voice).

The apostle curbs his natural resentment by quoting the words of Psalm 62:12, which reads 'Surely you will reward each person according to what he has done'. Compare Paul's injunction in Romans 12:19.

E. THE FIRST DEFENCE (4:16–17)

16–17. *At my first defence* evidently refers to the preliminary investigation preceding the formal trial, which was sometimes delayed for a considerable period. There are three factors to be taken into account in attempting to reconstruct the historical situation. At his first defence *everyone deserted* Paul; the defence provided an opportunity for the preaching of the gospel; and it resulted in some form of deliverance. There are many points of resemblance with Paul's defence at Caesarea, and some have claimed on the basis of this that Paul is here calling to mind an earlier trial. But there is no mention of his being generally forsaken in Acts 24, and the situation there seems much less hostile than here. On the other hand, if these words describe the preliminaries to the second Roman trial, a serious difficulty has been imagined because of the alleged contradiction with verses 6–8. There the end is imminent and Paul sees no hope of any release. He is, in fact, already in process of being offered up. But here he speaks of a deliverance – *I was delivered from the lion's mouth*. The aorist tense of the verb suggests that the apostle is thinking of an historic occasion on which his defence was successful. Many solutions have been offered to account for the apparent contradiction.

Some who deny Pauline authorship of the Pastorals as a whole have recourse to one of two alternatives. Either verses 9–22 were part of a genuine fragment which belonged to a totally different context from verses 6–8; or the personal details were composed by a later author to give the conclusion of the letter a thoroughly Pauline flavour. The second alternative seems inconceivable, for the whole section contains incidental personal notes such as no later admirer of Paul would ever have thought of inventing. Would such a Paulinist portray all men forsaking his hero in the hour of his greatest need? And would the cloak and parchments ever have occurred to a writer wishing to append a characteristic Pauline conclusion? The first alternative raises the problem of the author's apparent awareness of the alleged conflicting statements which he places in such close juxtaposition.[1]

Those who maintain the Pauline authorship of the whole of 2 Timothy have generally supposed that verses 16–17 refer to an earlier examination which appeared to turn out favourably for the apostle and at least gave him the opportunity for witnessing in Rome, but that the position had since deteriorated, verses 6–8 representing the position at the time of writing. The alleged conflict between verses 6–8 and 18 is apparent only if the words of verse 18 (*The Lord will rescue me*) are understood to imply that the apostle optimistically expects release. But these words seem more intelligible if understood in a spiritual sense.

It was the custom for a defendant's friends to appear with him to give him moral support, but Paul complains that *no-one came to my support*. The RSV has 'no one took my part', which brings out the technical sense of the verb (*paraginomai*). It may mean

---

[1] See Introduction, pp. 29ff., for further difficulties in the fragment hypothesis.

that no-one officially acted on his behalf or that the Roman Christians, knowing nothing first hand of Paul's missionary journeys, were not in a position to assist. Yet Paul is not bitter against the desertion of either the local Christians or his closer associates as his words *May it not be held against them* (verse 16) show. The words in the AV 'I pray God' are not expressed in the Greek, although the wish is expressed in the form of a prayer.

Paul mentions the desertion of his friends to bring into greater prominence the divine assistance. *But the Lord stood at my side* brings out the contrast. The word *paristēmi* is here used in the same sense as in Romans 16:2 where it has the sense 'stand by for help'. This help is further described as a strengthening (*cf.* 1 Tim. 1:12 for the use of the verb *endynamai*) the meaning clearly being that the apostle received great moral courage to proclaim the gospel to his judges. *So that through me the message might be fully proclaimed* implies the completion of the apostle's mission. The verb used here, *plērophoreō* means literally 'to perform fully'. Paul seems to regard his mission as incomplete until the gospel has been proclaimed in Rome.

A difficulty arises over the next words, *and all the Gentiles might hear it*, for if the words are understood literally the reference cannot be to Paul's defence before his judges. It has been suggested that Paul may be thinking of a further period of missionary activity following a release. But even in that case the *all* would have to be understood in a very general sense. It is perhaps better to interpret the words metaphorically in the sense that to preach the gospel in Rome was to preach at the heart of the Gentile world. In the light of Matthew 10:17–33 it could be argued that witness before tribunals was one of the greatest forms of the preaching of the gospel (*cf.* Spicq). At the same time it should be noted that *all the Gentiles* is a phrase used in Romans 1:5 of the scope of Paul's apostleship, and in Romans 16:26 of the extent of the revelation of the mystery of the gospel. In each case the phrase is used generally in a sense equivalent to 'cosmopolitan'. If this is the meaning here the apostle is contemplating the cosmopolitan character of the audience he addressed on the occasion of his first defence.

When he adds *I was delivered from the lion's mouth* Paul is using a common metaphor to express deliverance from some extreme danger (*cf.* Dn. 6:20 and Ps. 22:21). This is more reasonable than to suppose that the lion is metaphorical for the Emperor Nero, or is an allusion to the amphitheatre, or symbolic of Satan, the roaring lion (1 Pet. 5:8).

F. THE FORWARD LOOK (4:18)

18. The key to the understanding of this verse lies in the obvious associations in thought between the aorist *I was delivered* of verse 17 and the future *The Lord will rescue me*. If these two verbs are both taken in the literal sense of deliverance in this life, there can be no doubt that Paul had a firm conviction that he would be released. But this seems contrary to the resignation to his fate in verses 6–8. The deliverance in this verse is reminiscent of the Lord's prayer, which is clearly intended in a spiritual manner, and it seems most reasonable, therefore, to suppose that a similar meaning is attached to the words here. The past physical deliverance reminds him of constant spiritual deliverances and raises his confidence for the future.

Not only is he confident that the Lord will deliver, but that he will also *bring me safely to his heavenly kingdom*. The verb used is the usual word 'to save' (*sōzō*), but here in the more specific sense of 'keeping safe'. The use of the adjective 'heavenly' (a characteristic Pauline word) draws attention to the emphatic contrast between God's kingdom and the present earthly circumstances of sorrow and suffering. It is strongly reminiscent of the Lord's teaching about the kingdom of heaven. It is no wonder that contemplation of it raises in the apostle's mind a doxology in which he ascribes eternal glory to the Lord. His mind is clearly centred more on eternal realities than on any hopes of further release.

IX. CONCLUDING SALUTATIONS (4:19–22)

19. It is interesting to note that Prisca (*Priscilla* is a diminutive form of the same name, used by Luke but not by Paul) is mentioned before her husband Aquila as in Romans 16:3 and

Acts 18:18, 26, although the reverse order is found in Acts 18:2 and 1 Corinthians 16:19. These facts are hardly sufficient to support the suggestion that Priscilla was either of higher rank or of stronger personality than her husband. All the references to them show a strong attachment to the apostle. The same is true of *Onesiphorus* whose *household* is so warmly commended in 1:16–17.

20. There is an *Erastus* mentioned in Romans 16:23, described as the city treasurer (presumably of Corinth). Another person of the same name, referred to in Acts 19:22, was an associate of Timothy when both were sent by Paul into Macedonia. Although no certainty can be established, it is more likely that this helper of Paul is to be identified with the Erastus mentioned here. Timothy may have been unaware of his location and if they were old associates would naturally be interested in his whereabouts.

The reference to *Trophimus* has occasioned difficulties, for it is evident from Acts 20:4 that he was with Paul when he went to Miletus during the closing stages of his third missionary journey and from Acts 21:29 that he went with Paul to Jerusalem, for he was seen with him in the city. The present intimation that Paul left him ill at Miletus cannot, therefore, refer to this visit. It must relate to a subsequent visit after the apostle's release from his first Roman imprisonment. Some scholars find difficulty in believing that history would repeat itself and that Paul would twice visit Miletus with Trophimus, but this does not seem a major difficulty when it is remembered that Trophimus was an Ephesian (Acts 21:29). It is not impossible, therefore, that on Paul's last journey from Asia to Rome Trophimus was to accompany him, but had to be left at Miletus due to illness, a fact of which Timothy could easily have been unaware.

21. The urgent request of verse 9 is repeated with the addition of the words *before winter*. For a period of some weeks the Adriatic would be closed to shipping and the apostle is therefore anxious that Timothy should hasten to reach Italy before transport delayed him. This is another intensely human touch which suggests the imminence of the apostle's trial.

The four whose greetings are coupled with Paul's are all unknown elsewhere in the New Testament, although there is a tradition which identifies *Linus* with the later Roman bishop of that name.

The inclusion of *all the brothers* in the salutation need not be thought to be in conflict with verse 16, *everyone deserted me*, for these latter words relate to the lack of support at the trial. This would not prevent these timid Roman Christians from sending greetings to the apostle's lieutenant.

22. The closing benediction is in two parts. Part one is directed personally to Timothy and the words used are reminiscent of Galatians 6:18 and Philemon 25. But a significant change is made. There it is 'The grace of our Lord Jesus Christ be with your spirit', but here the prayer is more directly personal. Bernard's comment is worth repeating, '*there* the presence of "the grace of the Lord", *here* the presence of "the Lord of grace" is involved'. Part two is directed to the Christians generally for the pronoun used is plural, as in the similar benedictions in 1 Timothy and Titus.

TITUS:
ANALYSIS

I. SALUTATION (1:1–4)

II. QUALIFICATIONS OF CHURCH OFFICIALS (1:5–9)

III. THE CRETAN FALSE TEACHERS (1:10–16)

IV. REGULATIONS FOR CHRISTIAN BEHAVIOUR (2:1–10)
A. THE AGED PEOPLE (2:1–3)
B. THE YOUNGER PEOPLE (2:4–8)
C. SLAVES (2:9–10)

V. THE THEOLOGICAL BASIS FOR CHRISTIAN LIVING (2:11–3:7)
A. THE EDUCATING POWER OF GRACE (2:11–15)
B. THE CHRISTIAN ATTITUDE IN THE COMMUNITY (3:1–2)
C. THE SUPERIORITY OF THE GOSPEL OVER PAGANISM (3:3)
D. THE APPEARANCE AND WORK OF THE SAVIOUR (3:4–7)

VI. CLOSING ADMONITIONS (3:8–11)
A. ABOUT GOOD WORKS (3:8)
B. ABOUT FALSE TEACHERS (3:9–11)

VII. PERSONALIA AND CONCLUSION (3:12–15)

TITUS:
COMMENTARY

I. SALUTATION (1:1–4)

This salutation is much longer than that in either 1 or 2 Timothy, and its formal character, addressed to so close an associate as Titus, has been considered a stumbling-block by many exponents of non-Pauline authorship. It is suggested that this introduction is more formalized than 2 Timothy 1:1–2, and that the writer strives to give as impressive a Pauline flavour as possible. But the difficulties of construction and slight obscurities of thought are more in favour of Pauline authorship than against it; and in the view of some the formal character of the introduction is due to the semi-official character of the contents.

1. On no other occasion does Paul describe himself as *servant of God*, although he calls himself 'servant of Jesus Christ' twice in salutations (*i.e.* Romans and Philippians) and in Acts 20:19 he referred to his service to the Lord. The more usual *apostle of Jesus Christ* is also appended to draw attention to the official character of his service.

There is some debate about the force of *kata* in the expression *for (kata) the faith of God's elect*. If *kata* has the force of 'according to' (as in the AV) this might suggest that Paul's apostleship was somehow regulated by the faith of others; but most scholars think such a meaning to be improbable and therefore suggest the meaning 'for' or 'in regard to' for *kata* (as adopted in NIV). RSV has 'to further the faith of God's elect'. Twice elsewhere the apostle Paul employs the phrase 'God's elect' (Rom. 8:33 and Col. 3:12), but no other New Testament writer uses it. It is a well-known Old Testament phrase, especially describing Israel as the Lord's servant. As used by Paul it stresses the idea of God's choice of his church. Faith must be linked with knowledge (the noun *epignōsis*, *knowledge*, literally means 'recognition') of the truth in a genuine apostleship, and this the writer claims for himself. God's servants are not intended to be ignorant in the field of truth, nor is their knowledge to be out of keeping with their religious profession (*that leads to godliness*, RSV 'which accords with godliness'). Moffatt translates 'that goes with a religious life'.

2. An apostleship, as any sphere of service for God, is not dominated by present circumstances alone, but has a distinct future reference *resting on the hope of eternal life*. The Greek preposition *epi*, translated 'resting on', suggests that such hope is the basis on which the superstructure of Christian service is built. This Christian hope is rooted in God's promises made *before the beginning of time* (RSV, 'ages ago'). There would seem to be a reference here to the same truth that John expresses in his Logos doctrine, the profound recognition that God's promises are grounded in his eternal purposes (*cf.* Kelly). The apostle applies to God the unusual epithet *who does not lie* (*apseudēs*, 'free from falsehood'), in order to bring out the absolute trustworthiness of the hope just mentioned. Even if it is true that Christians (and Jews) would take such a characteristic for granted, there is special point in its mention here to mark the validity of the Christian hope (*cf.* Paul's language in Rom. 3:4).

3. The *appointed season* (*kairoi idioi*) of the bringing to light of the word contrasts with the eternal aspect of the promise (*chronoi aiōnioi*, translated *the beginning of time*, v. 2). The *appointed season* refers to the appropriate events appointed by God for the revealing of himself in Christ. The word *kairos* denotes a suitable opportunity as compared with *chronos* which is used for duration or succession of time.[1] The plural (*cf.* AV) may either represent various points in the Lord's life, or is more probably used in the sense of the singular to describe the historic life of

[1]See Lightfoot's *Notes on the Epistles of Paul* (1895), p. 70.

Jesus as a whole (*cf.* Lock).

The *word* brought to light *through the preaching* must be a reference to the gospel, which formed the content of Christian preaching. The idea of having such ministry *entrusted* to him was a constant source of wonderment to Paul (*e.g.* Gal. 1:1; 2:7), and is reiterated in all the Pastorals (*cf.* 1 Tim. 1:11; 2 Tim. 1:11). The phrase *by the command of God our Saviour* is exactly paralleled in 1 Timothy 1:1, and draws attention once again to the divine character of Paul's commission.

4. The description of Titus as *my true son* finds a parallel in 1 Timothy 1:2. The word *true* (*gnēsios*) is found only in Paul's writings in the New Testament (*cf.* Phil. 4:3). No mention is made of Titus in the Acts of the Apostles but it is clear that he was a stalwart member of the apostle's circle of helpers, to whom, in fact, he refers several times in his letters (Gal. 2:3; 2 Cor. 2:13; 8:23; 12:18). It may be gathered from the Corinthian correspondence that Titus was selected for a particularly difficult and delicate mission and since the outcome appears to have been a happy one, it is clear that Titus was a man of unusual tact who possessed high qualities of leadership. His allotted task in Crete certainly demanded much wisdom and strength of character, and the apostle's confidence in him accords completely with what is known of him elsewhere.

In (*kata*) *our common faith* has a rather different emphasis from 'in (*en*) the faith' in 1 Timothy 1:2. The expression brings into prominence the catholicity of the gospel. Barrett thinks the reference is to the faith common to both Jews and Gentiles. The words of the salutation are almost identical with 1 Timothy 1:2 and 2 Timothy 1:2 except for the interesting variation *Christ Jesus our Saviour* for 'Christ Jesus our Lord' and the omission of 'mercy', which although included in the AV is rightly deleted in modern versions on the grounds of inadequate textual support. It is particularly significant that, whereas in 1:3, 2:10 and 3:4 the apostle applies the term 'Saviour' to God, here and in 2:13 and 3:6 the same title is applied to Christ. The apostle evidently uses it indiscriminately of Father and Son.

II. QUALIFICATIONS OF CHURCH OFFICIALS (1:5-9)

After the rather formal salutation the apostle moves directly to Titus' specific commission.

5. Paul had presumably visited Crete and left Titus there to carry on the work. But it is generally admitted that no room exists in the Acts framework for such a mission (but see Introduction, pp. 23ff.), and recourse must be had to one of two alternatives; either this visit occurred during a release period after the Roman imprisonment, or else this Epistle cannot be genuine. It has, however, been shown in the Introduction (see pp. 26ff.) that there are no intrinsic reasons for rejecting the release hypothesis. A further possibility is that the verb 'left' does not involve a personal visit by the apostle, in which case it may be capable of slotting into the Acts history, but the release theory seems more probable.

The church in Crete was in a more disorganized state than that at Ephesus, and Titus has therefore two important duties. He has to complete what Paul had left incomplete, *i.e. that you might straighten out what was left unfinished*, and to *appoint elders*. It has often been assumed that the appointment of elders shows an ecclesiastical organization too advanced for the time of Paul, but in order to maintain this view it has been necessary to regard Acts 14:23 as an anachronism (*cf.* Brox, who thinks the present reference was inspired by the Acts reference). While there does not appear to be any uniformity in Paul's practice, there is no reason to doubt that he appointed elders on his earliest missionary journeys where occasion arose. It is essential for Christian churches to possess some orderly scheme of government and the apostle had previously impressed this on his close associates. In the phrase *as I directed you* the *I* is emphatic, bringing out not Paul's egotism, but his authoritative endorsement of the elder-system. The close link between *elder* and *overseer* (bishop) in this context seems to show that the terms are virtually synonymous.

6. There is a measure of agreement between the list of qualifications required of an *elder* or *overseer* as given to Titus and the list

given to Timothy. While these similarities betray a common author, the divergencies reflect different but genuine historic situations. The same Pauline word for *blameless* (*anenklētos*) used to describe the Cretan elders is applied in 1 Timothy 3:10 to the Ephesian deacons reflecting the need for an irreproachable moral standard in all types of Christian office. For the phrase *the husband of but one wife* see the comment on 1 Timothy 3:2. Whereas in 1 Timothy the *overseer* must maintain an orderly discipline over his children, in Titus a further requirement is added. The children must be 'believing' and must not lay themselves open to the charge of *being wild and disobedient* (*i.e.* they must not be guilty of prodigality or insubordination). The former of these two words, *asōtia*, means literally 'inability to save', hence metaphorically of wasting money on one's own pleasures and so ruining oneself (*cf.* Lock). As in 1 Timothy, the home is regarded as the training ground for Christian leaders. Although it has been suggested that by referring to Christian children the author inadvertently lets us know that he belongs to the second generation of Christians, there is no need to suppose that Christianity had been long established. We need only suppose that elders who have children are expected to have a Christian household.

7. Because the list of qualifications appears to begin all over again, some scholars suppose that some secular ethical list underlies the text, and that this verse preserves its official beginning. But the repetition is not redundant for it gives the reason why an *overseer* must be *blameless*; he *is entrusted with God's work*. Paul here uses a metaphor drawn from contemporary life and pictures a manager of a household or estate (*cf.* Paul's use of it in 1 Cor. 4:1 and Gal. 4:2). Whoever holds a position of Christian responsibility must similarly be beyond reproach in order to serve as a true example to others.

The subsequent list sets out certain standards. Those who think that some secular ethical list has been used suppose that the writer has not been concerned about the appropriateness of this list in this particular situation. Nevertheless if Paul is writing to Titus, he would know how much care would be needed in the selection of officers for the church in Crete, where the character of the people is seen to be generally unstable. To our modern age the vices denounced may seem too obviously non-Christian to require mention in the description of a Christian minister, but many parallels to the contemporary Cretan situation could be furnished from modern missionary enterprise among primitive peoples. That the Christian minister must not be arrogant (*overbearing*) or hot-headed (*quick-tempered*) is timely, for such moral deviations have all too often wrecked the healthy progress of the church. The three following prohibitions, *not given to drunkenness, not violent, not pursuing dishonest gain*, which had relevance in first-century Crete (*cf.* 1 Tim. 3:3), are not without some point in modern times. Some who claim to be Christian ministers still need warnings about pursuing illicit material gains.

8. The more positive qualities are closely akin to those in 1 Timothy 3:2, but it is noteworthy that here there is no prohibition of novices. This suggests that the Cretan communities were more recently founded than the Ephesian church. The overseer must be both *hospitable*, which implies a real devotion to the welfare of others, and *one who loves what is good*. The word used in the latter phrase (*philagathos*) can include things as well as persons. It occurs in early Hellenistic inscriptions as exemplifying a quality singled out for special honour (*cf.* Dibelius). Calvin renders the word 'devoted to kindness' as a contrast to niggardliness. The absence here of any unusual or exceptional qualities shows again the realistic approach of the apostle (*cf.* 1 Tim. 3). Honest, upright, clean-living, social men are all that is demanded on the moral side, but it is significant that two specially religious words, *upright* and *holy*, are included here but not in 1 Timothy 3 To the word *self-controlled* (*sōphrōn*) which appears in the 1 Timothy 3 list is added the parallel virtue *disciplined* (*enkratēs*), which according to Lock involves more deliberate self-control than the former word.

9. Further qualifications are demanded on the doctrinal side, for a Christian official must cleave to the true message, *as it has been taught*. The message is described as *trustworthy*. In view of this, the minister must have clear convictions and an under-standing of the 'teaching' (presumably that which was passed on by oral tradition, although it may possibly refer to some written records (*cf.* Simpson), and he must be prepared to *hold firmly* to the truth even in face of opposition. Only so will he be able to perform the double task of exhorting others and correcting those who contradict the truth. By *sound doctrine* must be meant a body of teaching in which the Christians are to be instructed. There are three words in this verse which describe teaching and all presuppose in the original text some objective and authoritative system of doctrine. In a primitive community like Crete such authoritative doctrine was indispensable.

III. THE CRETAN FALSE TEACHERS (1:10-16)

10. The apostle proceeds to describe those who contradict. They are apparently numerous and are characterized by three undesirable qualities. They are *rebellious* (*anypotaktoi*), flouting the official rule of the church. Second, they are emptyheaded in their teaching, doing much talking but saying nothing (the word *mataiologoi*, *mere talkers*, may contain the idea of worthlessness associated in the Jewish mind with heathen idols, so Lock). Third, they are self-deceived and consequently *deceivers* of others. Such characteristics are dominant in all heresies, but were particularly evident among the Jewish teachers then active in Crete, as the mention of the *circumcision group* shows. There is no justification for the view that the reference here to Jewish influence was the invention of the writer (*cf.* Dibelius-Conzelmann). It is well known that there was a Jewish com-munity in Crete (according to Philo and Josephus, *cf.* Kelly *ad loc.*).

11. Strong medicine is prescribed for such teachers. *They must be silenced* (*epistomizō*, meaning 'bridled' or 'muzzled') to prevent their doing damage. This imagery would seem to be particularly suggestive in the light of the description of the Cretans in the next verse. It is significant that no question of expulsion from the church arises provided the false teachers are silenced, presumably by the skilful presentation of the true doctrine mentioned in verse 9.

By affecting one or two members of a family, the false teachers were able to ruin *whole households*. Presumably such families were Christian, and any movement which causes rifts in such family life must be most carefully watched.

By teaching things they ought not to teach these people are opposed to the *sound doctrine* of verse 9. There is also a prominent mercenary element about them which merits the apostle's strong condemnation. *And that for the sake of dishonest gain* vividly brings out the sordid character of these empty religionists. Wherever mercenary considerations dominate a religious movement the same strong condemnation is deserved.

12. The apostle supports his argument by appealing to a venerated Cretan critic of the Cretan character. The lines quoted are from Epimenides, a sixth-century philosopher whom many of his countrymen had raised to mythical honours. Many ancient writers (*e.g.* Aristotle and Cicero) mention him as a prophet and the apostle therefore cites him by this well-known description. There is some question whether the lines quoted are correctly assigned to Epimenides, although many early Christians regarded the lines as coming from an ode *Concerning Oracles*. Since part of the citation occurs in Callimachus' *Hymn to Zeus* (*c.* 270 BC) some scholars attribute the statement to him. It is most likely, however, that the hymn was earlier than Callimachus. Because a well-known Cretan condemns his own people the apostle cannot be charged with censoriousness for his exposures.

That Cretans were notorious for untruthfulness is strikingly confirmed by the Greek language containing a word *crētizō* meaning 'to lie'. The accompanying elements in their unenviable reputation give the measure of their sensuousness. *Evil brutes* represents a maliciousness akin to the more savage animal creation, while *lazy gluttons* describes their uncontrolled greed. The inclusion of such a lashing criticism of the Cretan character in this letter to Titus would seem to rule out the idea that the letter was semi-official. The apostle is about to urge Titus to take a strong hand with the unruly element in the church, and is priming him on the well-known characteristics of the people with whom he is dealing. This principle has constant relevance, for every minister of the gospel must of necessity be cognizant with the character of the people, however distasteful the facts may be.

13. The apostle endorses the veracity of the proverbial saying. It may have been the result of personal experience, or else by common report, that he knew the Cretans were a difficult people with whom to deal. The sharp *rebuke* is, of course, to be directed against the false teachers, not the Cretans generally. It is noteworthy that the adverb *sharply* occurs elsewhere in the New Testament only in 2 Corinthians 13:10. Such severe reproach has a saving purpose, *so that they will be sound in the faith*, which may either refer to the accepted body of doctrine, or their personal loyalty to Christ. The former would seem to be preferable in view of verse 9. Much vituperation would have been saved had Christians always had this saving purpose in mind when dealing with those erring from the faith.

14. There was a double strand in the false teaching. The *Jewish myths* were no doubt akin to those mentioned in 1 Timothy 1:4, and probably consisted of useless speculations based on the Old Testament. Since these myths are here described as Jewish as distinct from the general reference in 1 Timothy, it is a fair assumption that the Cretan heretics were more Judaistically inclined than their Ephesian counterparts.

The other strand, termed *the commands of those who reject the truth*, is strongly reminiscent of the ascetic tendencies in the Colossian heresy which are described as 'human commands' (Col. 2:22). That some ritual is involved is apparent from verse 15, which raises the problem of what is clean and unclean. False teaching and false practice are usually close companions, and find willing allies in men occupied in turning others from the truth.

15. In the true Pauline manner, an answer is given to the latter point raised in verse 14 by the enunciation of general principles. It is an echo of Jesus' own words in Luke 11:41 (*cf.* also Mk.

7:15), and Paul has partially expounded the same idea in Romans 14:20. Many scholars suggest that these words form part of a current proverb. Christianity exalts purity to the realm of the spirit, which automatically obviates lesser ceremonial purity. A pure mind cannot be contaminated by physical contact, and the purest minds will have no relish in seeking unnecessary defilement.

No stronger condemnation of the would-be purifiers could be made than the assertion that for *those who are corrupted and do not believe, nothing is pure*. Calvin argued that those defiled could touch nothing without defiling it, hence to them nothing could be pure. The unbelieving could refer either to weak Jewish Christians, who did not believe that Christ was the end of the law, or to those who, like the later Gnostics, refused to admit the divine creation of matter. Paul is in effect repeating our Lord's teaching that it is what comes out of a man that defiles him, not ceremonial impurity. The real seat of purity is the *conscience* and if defilement has entered there, *mind* and action are alike affected.

16. Those who make a false profession of religion often strongly avow their knowledge of God, and this was particularly true of those with Jewish tendencies. Some scholars see in this profession to *know God* a sure indication of gnosticism. But it can equally be maintained that what details of the teaching exist are sufficient to rule out second-century gnosticism. Since the Cretan heresy was strongly Jewish, it is more reasonable to suppose that Judaistic pride in monotheism is here in mind. Where profession and practice are as clearly conflicting as in the case of these Cretan claimants (*by their actions they deny him*), words of strong condemnation are richly deserved and the apostle uses three such terms to characterize their conduct. The first, *detestable*, is an expression of disgust at their hypocrisy. This word may here be used ironically, in the sense that those who claim to track down detestable things are themselves detestable. The second, *disobedient*, follows from their virtual denial of the true character of a holy God who also demands holiness. The third, *unfit for doing anything good*, which translates the word *adokimoi* (rejected after testing), is in striking contrast to the constant call to good works in the Pastorals, for in these cases good works are not even possible. All who profess must be tested, but these will be shown to be unfit for any kind of good deed.

IV. REGULATIONS FOR CHRISTIAN BEHAVIOUR (2:1-10)

Attention is now drawn to problems arising from the pastoral care of the churches, and the various classes of people with which Titus must deal are separately considered. Much of the apostle's advice is as instructive for modern times as for the contemporary situation.

A. THE AGED PEOPLE (2:1-3)

1. This verse is in contrast to the last. Whereas the false teachers are making empty professions, Titus is to be solicitous to *teach* (Gk. *lalei*, 'speak') *what is in accord with sound doctrine*. The word translated *in accord with* (*prepei*), which means 'to be suitable, fitting', is characteristic of Paul, who had a special sense of the fitness of things (*cf.* 1 Cor. 11:13; Eph. 5:3; 1 Tim. 2:10). The notion of sound doctrine has already been met in 1:9, and once again 'soundness' or 'healthiness' is set against the disease of heresy which was troubling the church. The pronoun *You* is intended to emphasize that Titus belongs to a very different category from the trouble-makers. It is hardly correct to claim, as many scholars do, that the writer merely denounces heresy, for in this case he clearly believes that truth is the best antidote to error.

2. The first practical outworking of such sound doctrine will be an insistence that behaviour should tally with belief. Older men are to act as becomes senior members of the community. The first three qualities are those generally expected from men of advancing age and may be paralleled in contemporary usage. The word *temperate* includes not merely restraint in the use of wine but general moderation. The adjective translated *worthy of respect* (*semnos*, literally 'grave, serious', as RSV) has already been met in 1 Timothy 3:8, 11, where it relates both to deacons and to their wives. A seriousness of purpose particularly suits the dignity of seniors, yet gravity must never be confused with gloominess. The next quality (*sōphrōn*), translated as *self-controlled*, literally means 'with sound mind, hence soberly', or 'sensibly' (as RSV). The word has previously been applied to overseers (or bishops) in 1 Timothy 3:2 and Titus 1:8.

But not only is self-restraint required of elderly Christians, as of all elderly men; they must exhibit also a triad of Christian virtues. The linking of *faith, love* and *endurance* is found not only in 1 Timothy 6:11–12 and 2 Timothy 3:10 but also in 1 Thessalonians 1:3. It is true that Paul in 1 Corinthians 13 links the *faith* and *love* with 'hope' rather than patience, but there is no need to see the *endurance*, as some have done, as a non-Pauline feature. There is not a great deal of difference between hope and patience, although patience may include some element of resignation. It may be for that reason that Paul chose 'patience' here since he is writing about elderly men. Yet patience is a quality highly prized at any time of life. It is interesting to note that the same Greek word (*hygiainō, sound*), which is here used of elderly men's pursuit of Christian graces, is used in verse 1 to describe doctrine. Both heart and mind for the Christian must function in a healthy manner. While this soundness is most applicable to faith, it may have an application to love and endurance, in that these latter virtues need to be kept healthy.

3. In introducing the subject of elderly women the apostle uses the adverb *Likewise* (*hōsautōs*), a favourite expression in the Pastorals, bringing out the closeness of the comparison with what precedes (*cf.* 2 Tim. 3:8, 11). The expression *reverent in the way they live* contains two words unique in the New Testament; *katastēma* (translated *the way they live*) means 'demeanour', describing a state of mind, while *hieroprepēs* means 'suited to a sacred character'. It has been suggested that there are parallels with this latter word being used to mean 'consecrated as priestesses', and that the meaning here is that they are to live in the manner of priestesses in a temple (*cf.* Dibelius, Lock). Some see a hint here of the priesthood of all believers (so Hanson). But these ideas seem too remote from the context.

The two prohibitions which follow, *not to be slanderers or addicted to much wine*, again vividly portray the contemporary Cretan environment. The first has already been met in 1 Timothy 3:11 and the second in 1 Timothy 3:8. Evidently in Crete the liability to these excesses was more severe than in Ephesus, especially among the women, for the verb (*douloō*) here signifies 'bondage' (RSV has 'slaves to drink'), a much stronger expression than the corresponding phrase in 1 Timothy.

To bring out the required Christian characteristics the apostle uses a unique compound expression (*kalodidaskaloi*) which is translated *to teach what is good*. Since elderly women in general are included in this category, the word cannot refer to public teaching, which was in any case mainly the responsibility of elders, but must refer to ministry in the home. Within this sphere experienced Christian women have throughout the history of the church performed invaluable service in the cause of Christ by their example and teaching.

B. THE YOUNGER PEOPLE (2:4–8)

4. Something of the nature of this service is now indicated. The senior women are to *train the younger women to love their husbands and children*. In other words, Christian matrons are to assist the younger women in the discipline of family love, not of course as interfering busybodies, but as humble advisers on problems of married life. It seems hardly necessary for Christian women to be trained in loving their own children, but again the exhortation may pinpoint some special weakness of the Cretan character. It would have a particular significance in view of the home-disturbing tactics of the false teachers mentioned in 1:11. Even our modern age is not without instances of Christian women lacking true maternal affection. For women who put their careers before the welfare of their own children are displaying a significant symptom of this weakness.

5. The same quality *self-controlled* (*sōphron*) is used of young women as of old men in verse 2. This is linked with that of being *pure*, which points to an upright moral character.

Timothy is urged to covet the same quality (1 Tim. 5:22).

A question arises about the correct reading of the next word. One reading has *oikourous*, which has the sense of 'keeping at home', but the alternative which is better supported has *oikourgous*, which denotes 'workers at home' and which NIV follows in translating *to be busy at home*. RSV has 'domestic', which amounts to the same thing. This latter word, however, is extremely rare and its exact connotation is uncertain. In any case, the apostle merely underscores what he has stated in principle in the previous verse, that a young married women's sphere is the home.

The next quality is *to be kind*. The adjective (*agathos*, 'good') is used in the same sense as in Matthew 20:15. That wives should be *subject to their husbands* is a sentiment expressed elsewhere by the apostle Paul (Eph. 5:22; Col. 3:18), and in all three instances he uses a verb (*hypotassō*) which properly means 'to be submissive to'.

Such care about behaviour, especially in home-life, has for the Christian a specifically religious purpose, *i.e. so that no-one will malign the word of God*. The substitution of 'word' for the more usual 'name' gives the phrase a special significance. Contravention of these Christian qualities would be a denial of the *word* or 'gospel', which they professed to believe. It would be an affront to the Christian message, suggesting that some women, emancipated by the gospel, were abusing their new-found liberty in ways which were not approved in contemporary society.

6. Attention is now focused on the *young men*, in whose case the special exhortation is once again directed towards self-mastery. Titus is to *encourage* them to be *self-controlled*, a much stronger directive than that found in verse 1. RSV has 'urge' which emphasizes the need for constant moral reminders. Because of the prevalence of this thought of self-control in the Pastorals and its dominance in Greek ethics, it has sometimes been supposed that there is nothing distinctively Christian about such advice as is given here. Nevertheless, self-mastery in the Christian sense has an element of humility lacking in the Greek moralists. It is, in fact, an essentially religious conception in the New Testament.

7. Titus, as a Christian minister, must be *an example by doing what is good*. The word *example* (*typos*), which is also applied to Timothy in 1 Timothy 4:12, literally means an impress of a die, and hence in a metaphorical sense an 'example'. The exhortations of Titus would carry no weight unless backed by the pattern of his life, a principle which has been amply illustrated in the history of the Christian ministry. It is a high demand to show an example *in everything*,[1] but no less than this is appropriate for the Christian minister.

Whereas the spotlight so far has been turned mainly on Titus' actions, it is next transferred to his teaching. The order is significant; example comes before precept, but the precept which accompanies it must be of the noblest kind. There is some question whether the word for *teaching* here (*didaskalia*) should be understood as 'the act of teaching' or as 'the content of teaching'. Although it could be either, the latter seems generally more in harmony with the context. Such teaching is described in a twofold manner as consisting of *integrity* and *seriousness*. The first word (*aphthoria*) is unique in biblical Greek and denotes 'untaintedness' in teaching as a direct contrast to the false teaching currently in vogue. The second word (*semnotēs*) has already been met in its adjectival form in the description of the deacons and their wives (1 Tim. 3:8, 11) and here the same note of seriousness is introduced. If the words of the Christian teacher are to earn respect he must teach in a serious manner.

8. As the manner of teaching must be untainted, so must the matter be sound. The word here used for *speech* (*logos*) is to be distinguished from the word used for teaching in verse 7. Here the teaching must be beyond condemnation. The word translated *that cannot be condemned* (*akatagnōstos*) is not found anywhere else in the New Testament. The teaching is to be of such a character *that those who oppose you may be ashamed*. Titus must take care to give no occasion for the opposition to level any accusation against himself or his teaching. By exemplary life and speech he can shame his opposers, for they will see so strong a

---

[1] Some scholars (*e.g.* Dibelius-Conzelmann, Jeremias) attach *peri panta* to the previous verse, as setting out the sphere in which soberness must be exercised.

contrast if they are at all sensitive to spiritual realities. Paul gives the reason why the opposers will feel shame – *because they have nothing bad to say about us*. This does not mean that they will be at a loss for words with which to abuse the Christian minister. The idea is that the Christian minister should present no legitimate opportunity for his opponents to use an evil report against him. The word translated *bad* (*phaulos*) means 'worthless', and is twice used by Paul in opposition to what is morally commendable (Rom. 9:11; 2 Cor. 5:10). It is used in the New Testament of both persons and of things, always in a moral sense.

C. SLAVES (2:9-10)

As in writing to Timothy (1 Tim. 6:1), so now in advising Titus the apostle finds it necessary to deal with the problem of slavery. He lays down the same principles governing the relationship between slaves and masters, but the injunctions are slightly varied.

9-10. It is significant that, whereas in Ephesians and Colossians Paul urges servants to obey (*hypakouō*) their masters, here he uses the verb *hypotassō*, meaning 'to be in subjection'. This latter word is rather the stronger, perhaps suggesting a greater tendency on the part of Christian slaves in Crete to abuse their new-found emancipation in Christ. Presumably the injunction applies primarily to slaves with Christian masters as in 1 Timothy 6:2, for no Christian slave could agree to submit to heathen masters if questions of conscience were at stake, as the Christian church recognized at an early age.

Slaves are *to try to please* their masters. The word here used for 'please' (*euarestos*) is an exclusively Pauline word, apart from Hebrews 13:21, in the New Testament, but is elsewhere always used of what is pleasing to God. If Christian slaves could introduce into their lives so high a principle as this, it would do much to lessen the evils of the system and to show the power of Christianity to transform the most difficult relationships. The prohibition *not to talk back to them* should probably be understood in the wider sense of 'opposition'. RSV renders the words 'not to be refractory', which brings out this sense.

The third requirement is little more than a straight demand for honesty. The word rendered *steal* (*nosphizō*) 'is the regular term for petty larcenies' (Simpson), a vice to which slaves would be particularly tempted. *To show that they can be fully trusted* presents the positive side of honesty, which must always include an element of good faith. The verb *to show* (*endeiknymi*) is, apart from two occurrences in Hebrews, an exclusively Pauline word expressing the idea of providing proof.

The concluding statement in verse 10 gives the dominating principle which raises the injunctions to slaves to a much higher level than contemporary Greek ethics. Slaves must act in such a way as to *make the teaching about God our Saviour more attractive*. The Greek word (*kosmeō*) is used here of the arrangement of jewels in a manner to set off their full beauty (*cf.* Bernard), and that idea is emphasized here. By exemplary Christian behaviour a slave has the power to enhance the doctrine and to make it appear beautiful in the eyes of all onlookers. Such a principle as this is by no means confined to slaves. It is applicable to Christians in all walks of life. The words *in every way* (*en pasin*) could possibly be masculine with the sense 'among all men', and this would illustrate the opportunity for slaves to permeate every part of society with their witness.

V. THE THEOLOGICAL BASIS FOR CHRISTIAN LIVING
(2:11 – 3:7)

The close connection of this section with the preceding bears out the relationship between theology and ethics in the New Testament. This imposing statement not only contains an epitome of Christian doctrine but also emphasizes the impossibility of giving practical advice apart from the eternal verities of the Christian faith. The appeal to a theological basis for action is the new factor in Christian ethics.

A. THE EDUCATING POWER OF GRACE (2:11–15)

11. The connecting particle *for* proves that this verse leads directly from the last. The mention of *God our Saviour* leads the thought to *salvation* and results in a concise statement explaining both the incarnation and the atonement. The expression *the grace of God* may fairly be said to be the key word of Paul's theology, and there is no reason for denying here its most characteristic Pauline sense. He cannot think of Christian *salvation* apart from *the grace of God* (*cf.* Eph. 2:8), and when he dwells on the divine intervention in human life he can find no more adequate term than this, expressive as it is of God's free favour in Christ in dealing with man's sin. It is this which gives the incarnation its significance.

When Paul says that the grace of God has *appeared*, he uses a verb (*epiphainō*) which apart from Titus is used only twice elsewhere in the New Testament (Lk. 1:79, a striking parallel to the present use, and Acts 27:20). When it is used in 3:4 in a similar sense as here, it is applied to the kindness and benevolence of God. The cognate noun (*epiphaneia*) is in the Pastorals a characteristic description of the second coming.

It is doubtful whether the words *to all men* should be attached to the verb *has appeared*, which implies the universality of the manifestation. This, if taken literally, presents a difficulty in view of the fact that many people have still not heard. It has been pointed out that the noun *sōtērios* (*salvation*) followed by the dative is a classical expression meaning 'bringing deliverance to' (Simpson) and the words *to all men* therefore naturally belong to the noun and demonstrate the universal scope of Christian salvation. An alternative interpretation understands 'all' in the sense of 'all classes of men'.

12. Grace is here almost personified in its task of educating us in the art of living, and, as so often in the Pastorals, attention is drawn to both negative and positive aspects of a Christian's 'education'. There must be a double denial, first of *ungodliness* (*asebeia*, the antithesis of the frequently repeated call to godliness), and secondly of *worldly passions* (*kosmikai epithymiai*), *i.e.* of all desires entirely centred in the present world system. While the Greek word translated *passion* (*epithymia*) is morally neutral, in the New Testament its context generally impregnates it with with a moral stigma. Again *kosmikas* (*worldly*) has no moral significance in itself, but in the New Testament it takes its ethical connotation from the use of the noun *kosmos* to describe the world apart from God (*e.g.* Jn. 7:7; 1 Cor. 1:21).

The positive elements, self-control, uprightness and a religious manner of living have already been emphasized. Self-mastery has been demanded of leaders, old men and young women (Tit. 1:8; 2:2, 5), and no less a standard could be required of Titus. *To live upright lives, i.e.* to live in conformity with God's requirements, is an ideal which Paul earlier claimed for himself and his companions when writing to Thessalonika (1 Thes. 2:10). The third requirement is the exact counterpart to the first denial. It is not enough to renounce ungodliness; life must be lived in a *godly* manner. Possibly this triad of adverbs expresses the Christian's ideal behaviour towards himself, his neighbour and his God.

13. The last verse closed with a reference to *this present age*, but the Christian looks also to the future. In the New Testament *hope* does not indicate merely what is wished for but what is assured. It is a particularly joyful possession for the Christian, hence the description *blessed*.

The content of the *hope* is given as *the glorious appearing of our great God and Saviour, Jesus Christ*. The force of the Greek is 'the appearing of the glory' (as in RV). The word *appearing* (*epiphaneia*) was commented on in verse 11, but its use here requires further discussion. It has been suggested that the whole expression is a citation from a credal formula or hymn (*cf.* Easton), and that throughout the whole section the emperor cult terminology is followed (*cf.* Dibelius). But the fact that such terms as 'Saviour of all men', 'grace', and 'appearing' were all part of the technical language of emperor-worship proves nothing in this context, which echoes sentiments which formed part of the very texture of primitive Christianity. In fact a difficulty here confronts exponents of a late date for the Pastorals, for the apocalyptic hope reflects a very early stage in Christian development. It is not acceptable to maintain that the primitive hope still lingers on from an earlier generation. There is no reason to deny that the statement here genuinely reflects a position relevant to the earliest Christian period.

The final words of the verse have perplexed commentators. There are two possible renderings: *of our great God and Saviour, Jesus Christ* (as NIV, RSV), or 'of the great God and our Saviour Jesus Christ' (as AV, RV mg.). The decision between these two renderings rests on a variety of considerations. Grammatically, the absence of the article before 'Saviour' supports the first translation, although the tendency to omit articles in technical terms and proper names lessens the weight of this consideration. The early versions all understand the words in the sense of the second, while the majority of Greek Fathers keep to the first. Of this double stream of evidence the former is probably more reliable than the latter, but neither can decide the matter. Doctrinally it is to be noted that only here is the adjective *great* applied to God, and for that reason the whole ascription must be regarded as unique. It may be considered more applicable to Christ than to God, since the greatness of God was assumed. Nor would it detract from the supreme greatness of God the Father if the adjective were applied to Christ. There is, moreover, no reason to suppose that the apostle would not have made such an ascription to Christ if the most reasonable interpretation of Romans 9:5 is followed (*cf.* Sanday and Headlam, Bruce, Metzger, Cranfield), or, indeed, if the general tenor of his teaching on the person of Christ is borne in mind. The use of the word *appearing*, which is never used of God, further supports the ascription of the entire phrase to Christ. Another factor which has influenced some commentators is the contemporary use of 'God and Saviour' for heathen objects of worship. There is a similar ascription applied to the Ptolemies, where one not two deities is meant (Moulton)[1]. This, at least, shows how the words would probably have been understood in contemporary Hellenistic circles. On the whole, therefore, the evidence seems to weigh in favour of the NIV/RSV rendering.

[1] *Grammar of New Testament Greek*, vol. 1, p. 84. *Cf.* also N. Turner, *Grammatical Insights into the New Testament* (1965), pp. 15–16.

14. A direct reference is now made to the self-sacrificial example of Christ and the words used are reminiscent of Christ's own words in Mark 10:45, where he speaks of himself as a ransom (*lytron*) (*cf.* note on 1 Tim. 2:6). The verb used here is *lytroō* (*redeem*), which literally means 'to release on receipt of a ransom' (Abbott-Smith). It seems most probable that the language is borrowed from Psalm 129:8 (LXX), where not only the same verb but the same phrase *from all wickedness* is found, although in the plural. In the qualifying clause *who gave himself for us*, which is thoroughly Pauline (*cf.* Gal. 1:4; 2:20), the use of the preposition *hyper* (as in 1 Tim. 2:6) brings out the sacrificial character of Christ's act. It may also suggest a substitutionary aspect in view of its connection here with *lytroō* and the close parallel in 1 Timothy 2:6.[1] It is on the basis of this self-giving that he delivers his people from sin, not merely 'out of' (as the *ek* of Ps. 129:8) but 'from' (*apo*) in the fullest sense.

Another metaphor, that of cleansing, is used to express the effects of the Redeemer's work. This is interpreted variously of sanctification, or baptism (White explains it in the light of 3:5). But the former is the most probable in the context, since the act of purification is performed by Christ himself. In fact, Ephesians 5:25–26, which also connects Christ's self-giving with his sanctifying work, contains the phrase 'cleansing her by the washing of water through the word', which although using the language of baptism, clearly refers to an inner rather than an outer purification.

The Greek words underlying the translation *a people that are his very own* (*laos periousios*) first occur in Exodus 19:5, and mean 'a peculiar treasure', *i.e.* something which belongs in a special sense to oneself. In this present context the words are particularly choice as expressing the attitude of the Redeemer towards the redeemed, whose main characteristic is said to be zealousness *to do what is good.* Paul uses the word *zelōtēs* (*eager*) in Galatians 1:14 of his own eagerness to maintain the traditions of his ancestors; and although this zeal was misplaced, he never

---

[1]Although *hyper* generally means 'on behalf of', it may on occasions have the more restricted sense of 'in the place of' (as *ante*). *Cf.* Simpson's note on classical instances of this limited meaning (*The Pastoral Epistles*, 1954, pp. 110–112).

lost his enthusiasm and envisages here a whole people noted for a rightly directed zeal.

15. This verse connects the present doctrinal section with what follows. Titus is told *these are the things you should teach*, by which is presumably meant all the practical exhortations contained in chapter 2. In addition to speaking, the Christian minister must engage in exhortation and reproof (*cf.* 2 Tim. 4:2). Some will require encouragement and others censure, but whatever the need Titus is to exercise *all authority* (*epitagē*). This word is found elsewhere in the New Testament only in the Pauline Epistles and always in the sense of a divine command. Here Paul no doubt means that the Christian minister is endowed with nothing less than a divine authority. Titus need not fear, therefore, to exercise jurisdiction over those entrusted to him. Some would no doubt attempt to *despise* him, but he is to demonstrate the seal of God upon his ministry (*cf.* 1 Tim. 4:12).

B. THE CHRISTIAN ATTITUDE IN THE COMMUNITY (3:1–2)

1. Christian behaviour in contemporary society was of utmost importance for the furtherance of the gospel. No new advice needs to be given to these Cretan Christians for Titus is to *remind the people to be subject*. This latter verb, which in Simpson's opinion implies 'loyal' subjection, shows clearly the Christian's duty towards the civil administration. The same descriptive words, *rulers and authorities*, are combined several times in Paul's writings, and generally refer to spiritual agencies. But here the apostle evidently fears that the turbulent Cretans might too readily implicate the church in political agitation which could only bring the gospel under suspicion. The Greek verb *peitharchō* translated *to be obedient* expresses generally conformity to the regulations of the civil authorities.

The Christian should *be ready to do whatever is good*, in the community in which he lives. Where good citizenship demands communal action, he must always be cooperative, provided no question of conscience is involved.

2. To refrain from *slander* requires considerable grace, but does much to commend the gospel. Christians must *be peaceable* (*amachos*), refraining from strife, and *considerate*, exercising moderation. These two words are coupled in the qualifications of bishops in 1 Timothy 3:3. The phrase *to show true humility towards all men*, is rendered in RSV 'to show perfect courtesy toward all men', although the word *prautēs* literally means 'gentleness or meekness' (Kelly renders it 'courteous consideration'). These qualities are perfectly reflected in the life of Jesus.

C. THE SUPERIORITY OF THE GOSPEL OVER PAGANISM (3:3)

As in 2:11–15, a theological statement is made to support the practical exhortations just given.

3. If Titus should despair of the Cretan character he should remember his own past experience, for retrospect is often salutary in helping us to understand the magnitude of God's grace. The past is described by means of a list of vices which may at first sight seem exaggerated, yet Paul, elsewhere, uses similar language of his own converts' pre-Christian experience (*cf.* 1 Cor. 6:9–11; 4:17–24). When the apostle says *at one time we too were foolish* (*anoētos*), he means that we were without spiritual understanding. Next in the list are *disobedient*, which is directed towards God, and *deceived*, which is related to man. The Greek word for *deceived* (*planaō*) suggests a false guide leading astray. The metaphor of slavery is then used to illustrate the Christian's former servitude to *passions and pleasures*. This combination is well known in Greek ethics, but for the Christian looking back on his pre-conversion state it would have greater meaning than for the Greek moralists (*cf.* the similar combination in Jas. 4:1, 2). Only the freed man can appreciate to the full the abjectness of his former state of slavery. The words *we lived in malice and envy* reflect the essentially anti-social nature of the former life, for both words emphasize malignity. The climax is reached in the concluding words *being hated and hating*. The former of these two words (*stygētoi*) is found only

here in biblical Greek and means 'odious'. Coupled with hating one another it shows how quickly hate can multiply.

D. THE APPEARANCE AND WORK OF THE SAVIOUR (3:4–7)

4. Against this dark background shines God's love in the gospel, which is described in a two-fold way. The first descriptive word, *kindness* (*chrēstos*), is an exclusively Pauline word in the New Testament, and is often used of the benignity of God, although it is also used of man (2 Cor. 6:6). The second word *love* (*philanthrōpia*) was normally used of love towards individuals in distress, but when predicated of God it denotes love to mankind at large. In Acts 28:2 it is used of human kindness. It has been suggested that the special application of the word to the ransoming of captives may be implied here (*cf.* Lock).

Some see here a borrowing of language from the emperor cult and consider that the linking of *God* and *our Saviour* may be used in direct contrast to the false claims of the Roman emperors. But the application of the same title to Jesus Christ in verse 6 suggests that the ascription springs directly out of the Christian's experience of salvation. *Cf.* 2:11 for the use of the same verb, *epiphainō* (*appear*).

5. The apostle next seems to quote from a Christian hymn as is suggested by the opening formula in verse 8. Jeremias thinks it may have formed part of a baptismal hymn, and this is not improbable in view of the reference to *the washing of rebirth*. The negative statement *not because of righteous things we had done* is intended to bring out by way of contrast the absolute character of the divine *mercy* in the next phrase. RSV is a slightly better rendering of the Greek: 'not because of deeds done by us in righteousness'. The word for *righteousness* (*dikaiosynē*) here denotes observance of the Mosaic Law, in complete agreement with Paul's general usage. The apostle was deeply conscious of the impossibility of attaining salvation by means of human effort. It is God himself who has brought it about *because of his mercy*. This is a theme of which the apostle never tires.

The phrase *through the washing of rebirth* has been considerably

discussed by commentators. The word *loutron* has been translated in the sense of 'washing' by AV, RV, RSV, NIV, but the RV
mg. has 'laver'. In the LXX the word, which occurs three times
only (Song 4:2; 6:5 and Ecclus. 31:25), on each occasion seems to
represent not the receptacle but the washing itself. This is also
the sense in the only other New Testament occurrence,
Ephesians 5:26, 'the washing with water through the word'.
Most commentators take this washing to refer to baptism and
connect *palingenesias* (here translated *rebirth*) with John 3:5. This
Greek word was current in Stoicism for periodic restorations of
the natural world, a sense approximated in the only other use of
the word in the New Testament (Mt. 19:28) where it is used
eschatologically of the new birth of the whole creation. But here
it takes on a new meaning in view of the Christian new birth,
which is applied, not cosmically, but personally. It accords with
the idea of the new creation (2 Cor. 5:17), each believer being
conceived of as a possessor of powers previously unknown.

The *renewal by the Holy Spirit* specifies the resultant renovation
accompanying the *rebirth*. The one points to the act of entering,
while the other marks the quality of the new life. *Renewal* points
to the whole process of 'making new' and does not suggest the
restoration of former powers. Through the work of the Spirit the
believer lives on a higher plane than before (*cf*. Rom. 12:2 for the
same idea of spiritual renewal). There is an instructive parallel to
the present statement in 1 Corinthians 6:11, although some
scholars have drawn a distinction between Paul's conception of
baptism as a seal on the act of faith and the writer of the
Pastorals' view of it as efficacious by itself. Those who hold this
view detect here a step towards sacramental religion in which
the church has a magical estimate of baptism (*cf*. Scott). Yet such
a view is open to dispute on the grounds that the whole passage
is designed to exhibit the grandeur of the grace of God and
many details, such as faith-appropriation, are omitted to serve
that end. In the 1 Corinthians passage there is also no mention
of faith, but Paul has certainly not there substituted baptism for
faith, because of the contrary teaching of Romans 6:2–4. There
seems no more reason, therefore, for supposing that the present
reference to *washing* has no relation to faith.

There are two possible ways of construing this second half of the verse. The *rebirth* and the *renewal* may be regarded as distinct operations, or both may be dependent on *washing* and therefore would describe different aspects of one operation. But since regeneration must always precede the process of renewal and since renewal is never described elsewhere as a washing, the former interpretation is to be preferred. It should be noted that 'washing' in this context is a symbol but not the means of the washing away of sin.

6. The outpouring of the Holy Spirit is directly reminiscent of the historic occasion at Pentecost (Acts 2:33) since the same verb *poured out* (*ekcheō*) is used in each case. The aorist tense of the verb also points back to this historic event, but it clearly refers more directly to Paul and his associates' experience of the Holy Spirit, as the words *on us* indicate. When the apostle stresses that God poured out his Spirit *generously* he uses a word (*plousiōs*) which literally means 'richly' (as translated in RSV, *cf*. Col. 3:16 and 1 Tim. 6:17), to show that God's gift of the Spirit is never niggardly. The mediator of this precious gift is *Jesus Christ our Saviour*, in conformity with the primitive Christian belief (Acts 2:33). There is in these verses a clear Trinitarian statement (*cf*. Spicq), although some scholars dispute this (*cf*. Hanson, Holtz).

7. There is no denying the characteristic Pauline flavour of the next words – *having been justified by his grace* (*cf*. Rom. 3:24). Nevertheless some scholars have disputed that either *justified* or *grace* are here used in a Pauline sense, on the grounds that justification in this context is the fruit of baptism, while 'grace' is supposed to mean 'power'. Yet in so concise a statement of the gospel as is found here, it is gratuitous to suppose that the writer meant to say that justification followed baptism, for this is bringing the allusion to washing into unwarranted prominence. It is much more intelligible to suppose that *having been justified* is an amplification of the previous statement *he saved us* (v. 5), on which the clause introduced by *hina* (in order that *we might become heirs*) must depend. The point of this reference to justification is that no-one who is not justified can hope for an inheritance, and there is no doubt Paul would have consented to such a statement (*cf.* Gal. 3, which begins with justification, 3:11, and ends with inheritance, 3:29).

The *heirs* are not yet possessors in the fullest sense, as the words *having the hope of eternal life* shows. The Greek has the preposition *kata* ('according to the hope'). The whole phrase conveys the idea of solid assurance (*cf.* the comment on 2:13), on the basis of which the justified believer may look forward towards the full appropriation of his inheritance. The words do not exclude any present possession of *life*, but rather anticipate its complete realization (*cf.* the note on the similar phrase in 1:2). The genitive *of eternal life* may be taken with either *hope* or *heirs*. In the former case it gives the content of the hope, and in the latter describes the inheritance. The former seems to agree better with the context.

VI. CLOSING ADMONITIONS (3:8–11)

A. ABOUT GOOD WORKS (3:8)

8. The *trustworthy saying* must relate to the previous theological statement (vv. 4–7), which may be regarded as an epitome of Pauline theology. As Simpson well puts it, 'not a programme of "work and win", but of "take and have" constitutes its very keystone'. *These things* which Titus is *to stress*, are not baptism and its consecration, but all that has been included in the previous part of the letter. The advice that believers should *devote themselves to doing what is good* supports this judgment. The verb translated *stress* (*diabebaioomai*) is used of the false teachers with whom Timothy had to deal (1 Tim. 1:7). They were affirming what they did not understand, but the same is not to be true of Titus or any minister of the gospel.

These affirmations are particularly to be directed towards *those who have trusted in God*, for a true belief is an indispensable basis for the right ordering of conduct. Their specific purpose is to encourage believers to be *careful, i.e.* have a thoughtful approach to the maintenance of good works. The word translated *devote* (*proistamai*) usually has the meaning 'to put before', which in the middle voice as here means 'to be forward in'. It could possibly bear the sense 'profess honest occupations' (as RV mg.). This alternative, however, requires a different meaning for good works (*doing what is good*) than elsewhere in the Pastorals and is therefore less probable (*cf*. Lock).

B. ABOUT FALSE TEACHERS (3:9–11)

9. Since the apostle has already dealt with the Cretan false teachers in 1:10–16, his return to the theme may indicate his particular concern over this aspect of Cretan Christianity. He does the same in 1 Timothy (*cf*. 1:4ff. and 6:4). The Jewish character of the Cretan heresy is brought out as clearly here as in the earlier reference. In spite of this some scholars have supposed the teaching to be gnostic in character, but this is based on the assumption that the 'genealogies' must be understood in a gnostic sense (but see note on 1 Tim. 1:4).

The combination of *controversies* with *genealogies*, found also in 1 Timothy 1:4, shows that there was a marked similarity between the Cretan and Ephesian situations. The adjective *foolish*, also attached to 'stupid arguments' in 2 Timothy 2:23, again emphasizes the stupidity prevalent among these so-called teachers. Two other words which occur here are common to both situations; *arguments* (*ereis*) as in 1 Timothy 6:4, and *quarrels* (*machas*) as in 2 Timothy 2:23, where it is shown to be the product of the questionings. The subject matter of these *quarrels* is the law, which must refer to the Mosaic Law.

These things Titus is to *avoid*, the word *peristamai* literally meaning to turn oneself about so as to face the other way (*cf*. 2 Tim. 2:16 where it is used in a similar manner). The basic reason given for such avoidance is the essential unprofitableness and uselessness of the false teaching. This consideration might well be borne in mind by all who undertake the pastoral office.

10. The Greek word *hairetikos* translated *a divisive person* is to be distinguished in meaning from the English word 'heretic' derived from it. It was only in later times that it acquired a more technical meaning of 'one who holds false doctrine'. Here it refers to one who promotes division by his views. A different verb *paraiteomai* (*have nothing to do with*) is now used for avoidance. It is a vague term (*cf.* 1 Tim. 4:7) which does not convey the idea of excommunication, but means merely 'to leave out of account'. The first approach to these false teachers is to be by means of warning (*nouthesia*, a word used only by Paul in the New Testament, *cf.* 1 Cor. 10:11 and Eph. 6:4). The lenience advocated is striking, for it is only on the third occasion of warning that the more serious action of avoidance is to be taken.

11. If this action, however, should seem rather harsh, Titus must recognize that the stubbornness of the man is evidence of a perverted mind. The sinning referred to must be understood in the light of the previous verse, *i.e.* the desire to promote dissensions. It is useless to contend with men of twisted minds, and there is no need to condemn them for they are self-condemned. The reference, however, seems to be not so much to a deliberate act of condemning oneself, which is admittedly rare, but to the fact that perverted and sinful action in the end automatically condemns the doer.

VII. PERSONALIA AND CONCLUSION (3:12–15)

As so often in his letters, the apostle ends with personal allusions. In fact it is so much in the style of Paul that advocates of some form of fragment theory generally include this section in the genuine parts.[1]

12. Evidently *Artemas* or *Tychicus* was to replace Titus in Crete during the latter's absence. We know nothing of Artemas, but Tychicus appears to have been a close associate of the apostle, and according to 2 Timothy 4:12 the apostle sent him to Ephesus to relieve Timothy (*cf.* the note on 2 Tim. 4:12).

There were several cities named *Nicopolis* (city of victory) established in commemoration of some conquest. It is not certain which *Nicopolis* is intended here, but it is generally assumed

[1]See Introduction, p. 30.

it was the city of that name in Epirus, although no other evidence exists that Paul went to Epirus. Both here and in 2 Timothy 4:21 there is a reference to Paul's plan for the winter and in each case he urges his close associates to do their best to come.

13. *Zenas the lawyer* is unknown apart from this reference, but we meet with *Apollos* in several situations (both in Acts and 1 Corinthians). The word *lawyer* (*nomikos*) may be used of an expert in either Hebrew or Roman law. The Gospels would seem to support the former (*i.e.* the Mosaic Law), but since Zenas has a Greek name, a reference to Roman law is more probable.

Titus is *to help* these two *on their way*. There is no necessity to suppose that Zenas and Apollos were both in Crete, although that would be the most natural assumption. Titus might be expected to meet them on his way to Nicopolis. But since he is to see *that they have everything they need*, this suggests that he was in a position to provide material assistance, in which case it is better to assume that both men are paying a visit to Crete and that the apostle is anxious to secure adequate hospitality for them.

14. After these specific instructions to Titus, a general exhortation is added directed to *our people*. Clearly the Cretan Christians generally are intended, for these people are to *devote themselves to doing what is good*. This is an underlining of what has been said already in verse 8.

The practical side of Christianity is here brought into vivid focus. The words *for daily necessities* can be understood to refer either to necessitous cases or to wants. The more probable interpretation is the former which is followed by the RSV, 'so as to help cases of urgent need'. All who engage in such works of mercy need never fear that they will be *unproductive*.

15. There is no means of identifying the *pantes* (*everyone*) who send greetings. But this linking of fellow-workers with him in the conclusion is thoroughly Pauline, although the exact form of words is not found elsewhere.

The description *those who love us in the faith* brings out a most intimate touch into the otherwise rather vague greetings. The absence of the article before faith may mean that *en pistei* should not be understood as a reference to the Christian faith, but perhaps may be more generally understood as 'faithfully'.

The final benediction is identical with those of 1 and 2 Timothy, except for the insertion of *all*, which is parallel to the same word in the beginning of the verse.

APPENDIX

AN EXAMINATION OF THE LINGUISTIC ARGUMENT AGAINST THE AUTHENTICITY OF THE PASTORALS

The following essay will be mainly concerned with the particular arguments of P. N. Harrison in his book on *The Problem of the Pastorals*. The linguistic discussion consists of four different aspects. 1. The problem of the Hapaxes. 2. The problem of the other non-Pauline words shared with other New Testament writings. 3. The problem of Pauline words or groups of words missing from the Pastorals. 4. The problem of grammatical and stylistic differences.

Before examining the mass of evidence which Harrison ably collated under these heads, a brief indication of his conclusions will be given. By first making a comparison between the linguistic phenomena in the Pastorals with the other ten Pauline Epistles, he considered that the differences are so great as to exclude the possibility that they proceeded from one mind. He then compared the Pastorals with second-century literature drawing mainly on the Apostolic Fathers and Apologists, but also including available secular writers, and concluded that the evidence proves a second-century vintage for the Pastorals. The criticism is, therefore, two-pronged, and any adequate assessment of it must deal with both lines of attack.

I. THE PROBLEM OF THE HAPAXES

This much discussed problem has been fittingly described as the

'Battle of the Hapaxes', and however much a commentator may desire to say as little as possible about them he cannot by-pass the problem in view of the great emphasis that has been placed upon it. It is merely a matter of mathematics to show that the number of Hapaxes per page in the Pastorals is considerably greater than in any other Pauline Epistle. All the other ten Paulines range between 3.3 and 6.2 per page, whereas the Pastorals range from 12.9 to 16.1. Harrison claimed on the one hand that such an unexpected increase is inconceivable for one mind, and on the other that the Pastorals' figures can be paralleled in the Apostolic Fathers and that the Epistles must therefore belong to the second-century period. But there are grounds for criticizing both the deduction and the method of procedure.

a. The words per page method

This was first used in the Pastorals' discussion by Workman,[1] who made a comparison with Shakespeare's plays. These show a Hapax variation of from 3.4 to 10.4 words per page, but Harrison used the data to prove that Shakespeare's plays, when arranged in sequence of ascending Hapaxes, form a general progression parallel in shape to that of the 'accepted' Paulines. But he does not point out that the lowest and the highest extremes occur in plays which, according to Dowden's dating (which Harrison cited), were separated by only one year. Evidently Shakespeare's vocabulary could show considerable variation in a very short space of time. It should be further observed that allowance must be made for the considerably greater number of Shakespeare's extant works (thirty-seven plays), which makes 10.4 per page occurrences of Hapaxes in Hamlet rank considerably higher in proportion than the figures quoted above for the Paulines and the Pastorals. For the greater the number of extant writings with which comparison is made, the greater is the probability that unusual words will be duplicated.

Other literary analogies could also be quoted to show the

---

[1] 'The *Hapax Legomena* of St. Paul', *ExpT* 7 (1896), pp. 418–419.

fallacy of any deductions from such a method. Cicero's Hapaxes, for instance, have been shown to possess remarkable
variation in the different types of his extant works, ranging from
four per page in his oratorical works to twenty-five in his philo-
sophical. In this case[1] subject-matter clearly affects range of
vocabulary and no prediction could possibly be made from one
group of writings to show the vocabulary variation which might
be expected in the others. In short, literary art cannot be
reduced to a mathematical equation.[2]

b. Second-century parallels

Attention must now be given to Harrison's contention that the
writer of the Pastorals not only differs from Paul's vocabulary,
but speaks the language of the second century. If this point is
proved, authenticity is clearly impossible. Now the presupposi-
tion with which he commenced his study,[3] is that all non-
Pauline and non-New Testament words used in the Pastorals
and found also in the Apostolic Fathers and Apologists show
that the writer is lapsing into the language of his own time, i.e.
the second century. But this involves an extraordinary assumption. It assumes that the Pastoral Hapaxes cannot have been
current in the first century because no other New Testament
writer happens to use them. While it is true that some of these
words were used by the Apostolic Fathers, Harrison gave
insufficient attention to the possibility that the Pastorals
influenced the vocabulary of these later writers even where
there is no indication from the context that they are citing the
Pastorals.

To offset this possibility Harrison took refuge in the number
of words and Pastoral Hapaxes common to second-century
secular writers like Epictetus, Appian, Galen and Marcus Aurelius, and argued that these latter cannot have enriched their
vocabulary from the former.[4] But the two cases are clearly not

---

[1]These figures are the result of Dr Purser's calculations cited by Montgomery Hitchcock
(JTS 30, 1929, p. 278).
[2]Dibelius-Conzelmann admit that the statistical method for determining authenticity has
been largely discounted, op. cit., p. 3.
[3]Op. cit., pp. 67–68.   [4]Op cit., p. 82.

analogous for there is a presumption in favour of the Pastorals influencing second-century ecclesiastical writers, but none whatever in the case of the secular writers. It is not a matter of enriching vocabulary so much as using words in common ecclesiastical usage for similar purposes.

Out of the total of 175 Hapaxes, sixty are found in the Apostolic Fathers, and this forms the basis of Harrison's argument that the Paulinist author belonged to this period. Yet several considerations reduce the weightiness of this evidence. 1. There is a high percentage of these Hapaxes which are absent from the Apostolic Fathers (1 Timothy 74 per cent, 2 Timothy 58 per cent and Titus 60 per cent).[1] This hardly supports the idea that the author lapsed into current second-century speech when departing from his Pauline model. 2. Of the sixty shared with the Apostolic Fathers, twenty-eight occur in the latter writings once only and cannot therefore constitute evidence of common language.[2] 3. Only seventeen of the Hapaxes occur in more than one writer of the Apostolic Fathers, which shows the extent of their frequency during this period.

When the evidence from the Apologists is combined with that from the Apostolic Fathers it is found that a further thirty-two may be added to the list of common Hapaxes, although as many as half of these occur once only. During the period AD 95–170, there happen to be no more than forty-five of the Pastoral Hapaxes which occur in more than one author. The great majority of the Hapaxes, therefore, are either absent from or else very rare in the entire range of second-century church writers. Harrison, however, in further support of his claims stated, 'We find more than a few of the Pastoral Hapax Legomena recurring again and again in one writer after another'.[3] The seventeen words he then cites are the only words (with one exception) which occur in three writers or more in the second-century period under review (i.e. AD 95–170). He omitted to point out that all but one of these words occur in the LXX.

The validity of Harrison's deductions is also affected by the total known vocabulary in the two periods he is comparing. He

---

[1]Calculated from Harrison's lists, op. cit., pp. 137ff.   [2]Cf. Harrison, op. cit., p. 73.
[3]Ibid., p. 69.

gives the vocabulary of the Apostolic Fathers as 4,020 words, while the Pauline figure is only 2,177.[1] There are, therefore, almost twice as many words to form a quarry from which to dig out parallels. Before such parallels can prove common vintage, it is necessary to show that the words in question could not have been used in the first century. But Montgomery Hitchcock[2] showed that all but twenty-eight of the non-Pauline words were known before AD 50, while Harrison himself admits that the number unknown before AD 90 is less than a score.[3] Such a small group of words is hardly enough to prove second-century vintage, since their non-appearance in first-century literature may be due to the small amount of such literature still extant.

In addition to the search for parallels among ecclesiastical writers, Harrison brought in a wide range of non-Christian second-century writers. Of the eighty-two Hapaxes not found in the ecclesiastical writings, fifty-seven are paralleled in the non-Christian writings from Josephus to Marcus Aurelius.[4] Some of these occur with great frequency.[5] But this does not mean that they were not current in the first century. Harrison worked on the assumption that the Paulinist writer, when lapsing from his master's vocabulary, reverted partially to the current ecclesiastical vocabulary (using many rare words), partially to the secular literary vocabulary and partially to a vocabulary all his own. In the latter case, Harrison appealed to cognates and analogies with words used in the secular group in justification for these unique words, although such a procedure was rejected for proving a first-century vintage.[6]

c. Parallels in the LXX

No New Testament word-study is complete without examination of LXX influences. In the case of the Pastorals, there are about eighty of the Hapaxes which are paralleled in the LXX.[7] Indeed,

---

[1]*Ibid.*, p. 68.   [2]*JTS* 30 (1929), p. 278.

[3]*ExpT* 67 (1955), p. 79; *cf.* also the discussion in Falconer, *The Pastoral Epistles* (1937), pp. 5–11 and Badcock, *The Pauline Epistles and the Epistle to the Hebrews in their Historical Setting* (1937), pp. 115–133.

[4]*Op. cit.*, pp. 82f.   [5]*Cf.* Harrison, *ExpT* 67 (1955), p. 79, for details.

[6]*Op. cit.*, pp. 65, 83, 84.

[7]See my monograph *The Pastoral Epistles and the Mind of Paul*, pp. 39–40.

no less than forty-two of the sixty shared with the Apostolic Fathers are LXX words, and a further eighteen of those shared with the Apologists. There are in fact, twenty-two LXX words among those not found at all in the second-century ecclesiastical writers. Harrison summarily dismissed this LXX evidence[1] on the grounds that the words in question cannot be shown to be in vogue. But as many of the words which he claimed as proof that the writer belonged to the second-century ecclesiastical group are found in the LXX, it is a much more reasonable assumption that these words were as current in the first as in the second century. Another factor not considered by Harrison is the influence of the LXX on the Apostolic Fathers and Apologists, which clearly affects the value of his linguistic deductions. The writings of the apostle Paul show so rich an acquaintance with the Greek Scriptures, on which it would seem his mind had been nourished since childhood, that parallels with the LXX must carry far greater weight in discussions on the authenticity of the Pastorals than any accidental parallels with second-century secular writers.

d. New Testament cognates and analogies

It is impossible to discuss at any length in our present compass the fascinating subject of the apostle's word-building propensities. But no just appraisal of the Pastoral Hapaxes can be arrived at without some attention to this. If many of the Hapaxes are cognates of Pauline words and many of the new compounds have analogies in Paul's other Epistles, there is a strong presumption in favour of Paul's use of them.[2] Cognates cannot, of course, prove that the Hapaxes in question were current in the time of the apostles, but they can contribute to the contention that the absence of such words from other New Testament writers is no proof that they could not have been known.

Word formation on the basis of analogy is one of the most

---

[1]*Cf. op. cit.*, pp. 65–66 and *ExpT* 67 (1955), p. 78.

[2]Paul, for instance, uses *opheleō* and *opheleia*, and it is difficult to see why he should not have used *ophelimos* in the Pastorals, especially as all but one of the other New Testament words with a similar ending are used by him. Such an example could be multiplied many times.

fruitful sources of language development and the Pastorals show many new forms which may be paralleled in Paul's other writings. Consider, for instance, such a form as *kenophōnia* (not found in the Apostolic Fathers or Apologists), which has only two analogous New Testament forms, *kenodoxos* and *kenodoxia*, and since both of these are Pauline Hapaxes, this prefix appears to have made a strong appeal to the apostle. He clearly had a great love of compound expressions, and this may provide a reasonable explanation for some, at least, of the Pastoral Hapaxes.

Harrison countered this approach by maintaining that cognates and analogies are a greater assistance to his theory than to Pauline authorship, reducing 'almost to the vanishing point those elements in the vocabulary of the Pastorals which cannot be shown to belong to the current phraseology of the period to which our criticism assigns them'.[1] But a radical weakness vitiates Harrison's contention, for he assumed an exact parallel exists between the attempt to show that Paul was acquainted with these words, and the attempt to prove that a second-century Paulinist could have known them. No-one disputes that a postulated Paulinist could have used the words in question, but this does not prove that he wrote the Epistles. On the basis of Harrison's argument from cognates it would be possible to assign the Pastorals to any period.

e. Comparison with Pauline Hapaxes

As Harrison's argument was based on the number of Pastoral Hapaxes in the Apostolic Fathers and Apologists, a corresponding investigation is necessary for the Hapaxes in the other Paulines. If the number of these Hapaxes which occur also in the second-century writers is expressed as a percentage of the total number of Hapaxes in each Epistle, the results are as follows: Romans 25.2 per cent, 1 Corinthians 34.7 per cent, 2 Corinthians 21.7 per cent, Galatians 34.4 per cent, Ephesians 25 per cent, Philippians 37.8 per cent, Colossians 24.2 per cent, 1 Thessalonians 30 per cent, 2 Thessalonians 50 per cent and Philemon 60

[1] *Op. cit.*, p. 65.

per cent. When these figures are compared with the 34.9 per cent for the Pastorals, the fallacy of Harrison's linguistic argument is immediately apparent. Moreover, of the 137 Hapaxes in the ten Paulines which are shared by the Apostolic Fathers, forty-three occur in more than one of these latter writings, a higher percentage than for the Pastorals.

Such mathematical calculations can never prove linguistic affinity, yet this was the basis of much of Harrison's evidence. When the ten Paulines are compared with the second-century ecclesiastical language, it is found that they have 46.8 per cent of Hapaxes in common as compared with the Pastorals 53.1 per cent. It is instructive to notice that 1 Corinthians (55.1 per cent) has a higher percentage than 1 Timothy (50.6 per cent) or Titus (50 per cent). Since it is inadmissible to assign 1 Corinthians to a second-century date, the only alternative is to suppose that this Epistle had a greater influence on second-century writers than others of Paul's Epistles,[1] but the same explanation would be valid for the Pastorals.

Since Harrison claimed that the Pastoral Hapaxes occur with increasing frequency in the second-century writers,[2] it is significant to compare the frequency with which the Pauline Hapaxes were used. There are 899 occurrences, including repetitions, of the 220 Pauline Hapaxes in the second-century writings, an average of 4.1 times per word, but the ninety-two Pastoral Hapaxes have only 319 occurrences, an average 3.5 times per word. Again, the comparison is not favourable to Harrison's theory.

Hitchcock[3] has further shown that there is a greater concentration of Hapaxes in the ethical sections in Paul's Epistles than in the doctrinal, suggesting some correlation between these practical sections and the need for new words. Parry[4] showed that in the case of the Pastorals new subject matter is responsible for a great majority of the new words, and since their purpose is essentially practical this is no more than we should expect.

---

[1]*Cf.* Hitchcock's argument in *JTS* 30 (1929), p. 279.   [2]*Cf. op. cit.,* pp. 69–70.
[3]*JTS* 30 (1929), p. 279.
[4]*The Pastoral Epistles* (1920), pp. cxi–cxxvi.

f. Conclusion

The preceding examination of Hapaxes has provided various grounds for criticizing Harrison's claim to have established the date of the Pastorals on the basis of the occurrence of some of these in second-century writings. The major fallacies in his argument may be summed up as follows: 1. It is based on an arbitrary opinion on the length of time during which words may be current. 2. It proceeds on the basis of heterogeneous evidence, using a wide variety of second-century Christian writings and an even more heterogeneous selection of secular writers.[1] 3. It is capable of different applications, for it is difficult to determine in cases of linguistic affinity which of two sets of writings has been influenced by the other.

None of the evidence from the Hapaxes compels the conclusion that the writer reflects second-century working vocabulary, and there is no reason on this basis for denying that the Pastorals belong to the mid-first century, or for asserting that it is impossible to attribute them to Paul.

II. OTHER NON-PAULINE WORDS

Another linguistic problem is the 130 words shared by the Pastorals and other New Testament writers, but missing from the ten Paulines. Of these 117 occur in the second-century groups of ecclesiastical writings, most of them in both groups. The words in question were not, therefore, confined to any particular era, and are no more characteristic of the second than the first century. Their absence from the ten Paulines is problematic only if these ten Epistles are regarded as representing the apostle's total working vocabulary.

That the prevalence of these words in the second-century writings cannot indicate the date of the writing is evident when similar tests are applied to the ten Paulines. Each of these Epistles has a number of words not found elsewhere in Paul,

---

[1]It is noteworthy that a greater number of Hapaxes is shared by Justin than by any other, but Harrison did not assign the Pastorals to his period.

although paralleled in other New Testament writers, and in the majority of instances the words in question are found in the Apostolic Fathers and Apologists. Romans, for instance, has 148 such words, of which all but eight are in the second century, while 2 Corinthians has 100 with only eight missing from the later writers. The other Epistles show similar percentages of words common to the second century. This investigation suggests that similar results would be obtained from any group of writings we might submit to the test, and any deductions based on such evidence must, therefore, be pronounced valueless.

If further demonstration is necessary, attention is drawn to the fact that whereas 78.3 per cent of the Pastorals' vocabulary is found in the Apostolic Fathers, two at least of the ten Paulines (Colossians 85.6 per cent and Ephesians 86.2 per cent) show a considerably higher percentage.[1] If the Apologists are included, the percentages for the separate Paulines range from 87.6 per cent to 96.2 per cent, and for the Pastorals 86.7 per cent.[2] No other conclusion is possible but that the major part of the Pauline and Pastoral language is current language in both first and second centuries.

III. PAULINE WORDS MISSING FROM THE PASTORALS

Another strong criticism of Pauline authorship is the absence of many characteristically Pauline expressions. To Harrison this fact involved 'a change of perspective, a shifting of horizons, a profound modification of the whole mental and spiritual outlook'.[3] The difficulties may be analysed briefly under the following headings.

a. Characteristic Pauline words

Harrison[4] cited a list of eighty words, in five or more Pauline Epistles, which are absent from the Pastorals, and claimed that Paul could not have written letters without using some of these

[1] See my *The Pastoral Epistles and the Mind of Paul*, p. 11, for further details.
[2] See *ibid.*, Appendix D, for details.
[3] *Op. cit.*, p. 34.   [4] *Ibid.*, pp. 31–32.

words. But all of the words occur elsewhere in the New Testament, all but seventeen are, in fact, in Luke–Acts, and all but three in the Apostolic Fathers. They appear to be equally characteristic of both first and second centuries, and of various writers within the New Testament period. The number of times these words occur both in the other New Testament writers and in the Apostolic Fathers exceeds that of the Pauline writings, which weakens the contention that they are specially characteristic of Paul. Difference of subject matter would again seem to offer the most reasonable solution of the problem of these terms.

It should be noted that Harrison's own theory is not without difficulty here, for the Paulinist, who set out to imitate Paul, not only missed so many characteristic expressions, which would have suggested a Pauline imprimatur, but also avoided expressions characteristic of his own age. Of the eighty words under review, fifty-six occur in 1 Clement and fifty-three in Hermas.

b. Characteristic groups of words

An even stronger emphasis was placed by Harrison on groups of cognate words which occur in five or more Paulines but are absent from the Pastorals. He cites twenty-seven such groups.[1] It may certainly seem strange that Paul has not used them in the Pastorals and due weight must be given to this fact. But it is not immediately apparent that Paul must have used them. The use of groups of words cannot be mechanically determined in this manner, for expressions are called to mind more by the nature of the subject in hand and the indefinable reaction of the human mind towards a given situation, than by previous usage. Yet even if Harrison's line of argument possessed validity some difficulties would confront the fragment theory, for the Paulinist would again have omitted groups of words so characteristically Pauline, and at the same time occurring with great frequency among his ecclesiastical contemporaries. All but five of the twenty-seven groups are used with as great or greater frequency among the Apostolic Fathers than in the ten Paulines. Moreover, if the Paulinist, purporting to give his writings a 'Pauline'

---

[1] *Ibid.*, p. 33.

appearance, could omit so many, there is more reason for Paul himself, with no such necessity, to have done so.

c. Similar words with different meanings

There are a number of Pauline words in the Pastorals which are not used in the same sense as in the ten Paulines. Harrison cited several examples of this,[1] *e.g. analambanō, anterchomai, grammata.* In many of the cases mentioned the antithesis between the Pauline and Pastoral uses is rather forced (*cf.* the use of *morphōsis*, 'form', in Rom. 2:20 and 2 Tim. 3:5), but in any case Harrison admitted not only that no writer can be expected to use every word in exactly the same sense but also that Paul uses words in different senses.[2] It is difficult to see, therefore, what importance can be attached to this evidence. A significant feature of Harrison's list is that, in almost every case, the usage found in the Apostolic Fathers agrees with the Pauline and not the Pastoral meaning.

d. Different expressions for similar thoughts

Where the same ideas are expressed in different ways in the ten Paulines and the Pastoral Epistles, there may appear some justification for regarding the latter with suspicion. But again full allowance must be made for unconscious changes in expression which are not only psychologically possible but even desirable if monotony is to be avoided. Harrison cites twelve instances, of which two examples will be given to illustrate his type of argument. In 1 Corinthians 16:11, *exoutheneō* (despise) is used with reference to Timothy, whereas in 1 Timothy 4:12 the verb used is *kataphroneō*. But since Paul used the latter word elsewhere, the objection is clearly invalid. Harrison pointed out that Paul describes the second advent as *parousia*, whereas the Pastorals (1 Tim. 6:14; 2 Tim. 1:10; 4:1, 8 and Tit. 2:13) use *epiphaneia* (appearing). But this objection is considerably weakened not only by Paul's use of the latter word in 2 Thessalonians 2:8, but its double occurrence in one of Harrison's 'genuine fragments'

[1]*Ibid.*, pp. 27ff.   [2]*Ibid.*, p. 28.

(*i.e.* 2 Tim. 4:1, 8). Most of the other variations are of a similar character, although the use in the Pastorals of such expressions as *charin echō* for *eucharisteō* (I thank), *di' hen aiten* for *dio* (wherefore), and *despotai* for *kyrioi* (masters) is admittedly unexpected.

IV. GRAMMATICAL AND STYLISTIC PROBLEMS

Most scholars agree that stylistic considerations form a more formidable obstacle to Pauline authorship than vocabulary,[1] and these must therefore be carefully examined.

a. The particles, pronouns, prepositions, etc.

According to Harrison's list,[2] there are 112 of these occurring in Paul's ten letters but missing from the Pastorals. These, he maintained, make it most improbable that Paul wrote the Pastorals, since the writer has not used 'a single word in all that list – one or other of which has hitherto appeared on the average nine times to every page that Paul ever wrote'.[3] But Harrison's statement is misleading on two counts. He assumed that all that Paul ever wrote must be restricted to the ten Paulines, and he suggested that these particles, pronouns, *etc.*, are spread with some regularity over these Epistles.

Of the 112 particles, *etc.*, fifty-eight occur in only one or two Epistles and cannot therefore be considered a major obstacle. Of the rest, twenty-four occur in five or more Epistles and thirty in three or four, and these two groups might reasonably be claimed as characteristic of the apostle's style. Yet from Harrison's own figures it will be seen that considerable variation exists among the ten Paulines, for whereas Romans, 1 and 2 Corinthians have more than fifty, Colossians, 2 Thessalonians and Philemon have less than twenty. An interesting feature about the list is that nearly all occur in other New Testament writings, while all but twenty-one are used by the Apostolic

[1] See A. M. Hunter's cautious statement, *Interpreting the New Testament* (1951), p. 64.
[2] *Op. cit,.* pp. 36–37.
[3] *Ibid.*, p. 35.

Fathers. The absence of these twenty-one suggested to Harrison a corresponding tendency 'to dispense with the same series of Pauline particles, *etc.*'.[1] Now all but four of these words occur in only one or two Pauline Epistles and are, therefore, not the most characteristic of Paul. Moreover, it might as logically be claimed that there is a tendency to dispense with these particular words within the Paulines themselves, since the four captivity Epistles contain only seven between them.[2] The same Epistles, furthermore, lack between them no less than fifty-nine of the 112 particles, *etc.*

An even more obvious weakness about Harrison's list is the exclusion of all those which occur in the Pastorals. A parallel list can be compiled showing some ninety-three additional particles, pronouns and prepositional forms, of which all but one are found in the Pastorals and all but eight in the other Pauline group.[3] Romans has seventy-three, 1 Corinthians seventy, 2 Corinthians sixty, Galatians sixty-four, Ephesians fifty-four, Philippians fifty-seven, Colossians forty-six, 1 Thessalonians forty-six, 2 Thessalonians forty-five and Philemon thirty-two. When these are added to Harrison's figures for the separate Paulines, it is found that the Pastorals compare favourably with the captivity and Thessalonian Epistles.[4] It seems a reasonable deduction that 'connective tissue' cannot be mathematically computed in this way, and cannot be cited as conclusive proof against Pauline authenticity. No allowance can be made in such word counts for fluctuations of mood or purpose, and no-one would expect a similar style in a theological treatise as in a private letter or general circular.

If Harrison further appealed to the frequency with which these particles, *etc.*, occur in Pauline writings as indicative of a predominant characteristic,[5] it is strange that he excluded from

---

[1]*Ibid.*, p. 75. Harrison cited twenty-two words missing, but *tou'nantion* occurs in the *Martyrdom of Polycarp.*

[2]*Cf.* Newport White, *The Pastoral Epistles*, p. 71, for twenty-four characteristic particles mostly absent from the captivity Epistles.

[3]The list is given in my monograph, *The Pastoral Epistles and the Mind of Paul*, Appendix E, pp. 41–44.

[4]*Cf. ibid.*, pp. 12–15.

[5]*Op.cit.*, p. 35. It is noticeable that A. Kenny, in his recent stylometric study, considers the Pauline Corpus as a whole before considering the individual Epistles, and this provides a better basis than Harrison's method (*A Stylometric Study of the New Testament*, 1986).

his list the words that do appear in the Pastorals on the grounds that they occur too often to remain significant. But if some words occur frequently in all Paul's Epistles, including the Pastorals, it is surely arbitrary to exclude these from a list of characteristic words, and yet include thirty-five words occurring in one only of Paul's Epistles.

b. Different uses of the article

In addition to the lists already discussed, Harrison appealed to the absence of many characteristic uses of the article, and this objection deserves careful study.

1. The articular infinitive. This is used 106 times by Paul in all his writings except Colossians and Philemon. The exceptions weaken the force of the contention, but in any case the Paulinist theory is in difficulties here since this usage occurs 208 times in the Apostolic Fathers and is used by all the writers.

2. The article with the nominative in place of the vocative. Although occurring twenty-five times, this usage is found in only four Pauline Epistles and is obviously dictated by the subject matter.

3. The article with the numeral. In all the eleven instances (in six Epistles) cited by Harrison the context demands the article, but in the three instances of numerals in the Pastorals (1 Tim. 2:5; 5:9 and 5:19) the article would have been entirely inappropriate. Moreover Paul's more frequent usage is the anarthrous form.

4. The article with an adverb. Harrison cites twenty-three instances for the ten Pauline Epistles, but 1 Timothy 3:7 contains a similar construction. The anarthrous adverbial form *loipon* (henceforth) is used in 2 Timothy 4:8, one of Harrison's genuine fragments, although Paul often uses the same form with the neuter article. The fourfold adjectival use of *ontōs* with the article in the Pastorals (*e.g.* 1 Tim. 5:3) admittedly cannot be paralleled in Paul's other Epistles, but the adjectival use of *exō* and *anō* in 2 Corinthians 4:16 and Philippians 3:14 furnish close analogies.

5. The article with whole sentences. Of the seven instances of this mentioned by Harrison, four introduce citations though this is clearly not Paul's normal way of introducing literary allusions.

The sole objection possible among those mentioned is the supposed contrast between 1 Thessalonians 4:1 where *to pōs diē* is used and 1 Timothy 3:15 where the article is dropped, but even this falls to the ground in view of the anarthrous use of the same words in Colossians 4:6.

c. *The use of* hōs

There are three Pauline but non-Pastoral uses of *hōs*, eleven instances with a particle, five with an adverb and six with *an*. The absence of the first may be paralleled by its absence from Galatians, Ephesians, Philippians, 2 Thessalonians and Philemon. The latter two are absent from six of the ten Paulines, which means they are practically valueless as support for non-Pauline authorship. This, in fact, only corroborates what has already been amply demonstrated, that Paul's style was much more flexible than many scholars allow.

In summing up the stylistic position, the two main criticisms of Harrison's mass of statistics may be stated in the following way. It has been shown in the first place that the same arguments could equally well prove the non-Pauline character of undisputed Pauline Epistles, and secondly that these statistics take no account of mood and purpose. Even where two Epistles such as Romans and Galatians deal with allied themes they share only twenty-five of Harrison's 112 particles, *etc.*, whereas the closely connected Colossians and Ephesians have only six in common.[1] The apostle clearly allowed himself, consciously or unconsciously, a considerable amount of variation in this 'connective tissue'. Lock's[2] opinion that the Pastoral style is closer to Paul than to any other New Testament writer would seem to be amply justified.

---

[1] It should, of course, be noted that Harrison's inclusion of both these Epistles among the genuine Paulines would be challenged by many scholars who have since challenged the Pauline authorship of the Pastorals. Similarly some of the weaknesses of Harrison's argumentation are because of his adherence to a fragment theory, which many scholars now reject in favour of a purely fiction theory.

[2] *Op. cit.*, pp. xxvii, xxviii.

V. CONCLUSION

It has been shown in the preceding discussion that nothing in the linguistic evidence demands the abandonment of Pauline authenticity, and it remains now only to summarize the variety of suggested solutions to the phenomena of linguistic differences from the earlier Paulines.

1. Dissimilarity of subject matter undoubtedly accounts for many new words.[1] Themes not previously dealt with unavoidably produce a crop of new expressions.

2. Variations due to advancing age must be given due weight, since style and vocabulary are often affected in this way.[2]

3. Enlargement of vocabulary due to change of environment may account for an increased use of classical words.[3]

4. The difference in the recipients as compared with the earlier Epistles addressed to churches would account for certain differences in style in the same way that private and public correspondence inevitably differs.

[1] *Cf.* Parry, *op. cit.*, pp. cxi–cxxvi. *Cf.* also W. E. Bowen, *The Dates of the Pastoral Epistles* (1900).

[2] *Cf.* Spicq, *op. cit.*, p. xci, and Simpson, *op. cit.*, pp. 15–16.

[3] *Cf.* Montgomery Hitchcock, 'Latinity in the Pastorals', *ExpT* 39 (1927–28), pp. 347–352, and Simpson, *op. cit.*, pp. 20–21.